NORMANDIE

Queen of the Seas

Bruno Foucart • Charles Offrey

François Robichon • Claude Villers

RESEARCH AND CO-ORDINATION

François Robichon

THE VENDOME PRESS

NEW YORK   PARIS   LAUSANNE

First published in the United States by
The Vendome Press
515 Madison Avenue, New York, NY 10022

© 1985 Éditions Herscher

English translation © 1985 The Vendome Press

Distributed in the United States by
Rizzoli International Publications
597 Fifth Avenue, New York, NY 10017

Distributed in Canada by
Methuen Publications

Library of Congress Cataloging-in-Publication Data
Main entry under title:
Normandie: queen of the seas.

  Translated from the French.
  1. Normandie (Steamship)   I. Offrey, Charles.
VM383.N6N67 1985 387.2'43 85–11173

ISBN 0-86565-057-8

Printed and bound in Italy

PREFACE

There simply is no end to the rhapsodic encomia that *Normandie* has trailed in her slender, elegant wake since 1935. "Standard-bearer of French Quality," "Floating Exhibition," and "Monster of Steel" are typical of the adjectives invented to extol *Normandie* as a "national" symbol, a monument to art, and a triumph of technology.

Floating city or floating factory? Of these two images, which seized the imagination more effectively?

In 1935, certain "modernists" devoted to forms derived from function wanted to make the liner a masterpiece of the aesthetic so passionately advocated by Le Corbusier. More numerous, however, were those who loved the richly versatile language of French classicism. And if the resulting design proved, here and there, to be a bit of a hodgepodge, *Normandie* nonetheless emerged as the masterwork of her generation. Bringing *Normandie* back to life, out of the realm of myth—where a tragic and lamentable end consigned the ship and denied her a distinguished old age—has required the efforts of several authors. Their very number, quite apart from the special knowledge possessed by each, seemed the best possible way to achieve an "impartial" portrait of the "Giant of the Seas."

Charles Offrey took charge of recapitulating the history of the vessel during the period of her construction, her commercial service in the years 1935–39, and, finally, the time of her internment in New York, which ended in the fire of 1942. In describing this fatal event, M. Offrey has also tried to clarify the circumstances that produced it and the plethora of fanciful, even preposterous, hypotheses to which it gave rise. Bruno Foucart has reconstructed the liner's fitting out and interior décor, while Claude Villers transformed the legendary *Normandie* into breathing reality by recounting the daily existence of her passengers and crew. And last, as a tide of nostalgia rises toward the ship's fiftieth anniversary, François Robichon examines the fetishistic devotion that has nimbed *Normandie* in glory since her maiden voyage in 1935.

All have been mindful, however, that no homage would be worthy of this "New Wonder of the World" which was not brave or sincere enough to maintain a certain critical distance.

CONTENTS

THE CREATION OF NORMANDIE

CHARLES OFFREY

The Creation of *Normandie*

Conceived in 1928, ordered on October 29, 1930, by the French Line (La Compagnie Générale Transatlantique, the Transat, or the CGT) from the Société des Chantiers et Ateliers de Saint-Nazaire-Penhoët, laid down on the stocks the 26th of January 1931, and launched on October 29, 1932, *Normandie* began servicing the Le Havre–New York traffic on May 29, 1935. It had taken seven years for the great passenger ship to be brought from initial idea to that historic maiden voyage across the Atlantic.

Once under way, *Normandie*'s career would last somewhat less than seven years, since the ship burned and capsized on February 9, 1942, while docked in New York. Meanwhile, due to the outbreak of war, she had had only four and a half years of active navigational and commercial life. For *Normandie*, however, these were years of triumphant success.

The ephemerality of so much splendor and glory, all brought to such a premature and tragic end, has endowed the *Normandie* story — and drama — with an aureole of legend, making the vessel a virtual cult object more than fifty years after her auspicious but doomed launching.

In 1928, the year *Normandie* went onto the drawing boards, the CGT reached the zenith of its prosperity. Since 1920 the company had been under the direction of John Dal Piaz, a man of many parts, dynamic, imaginative, daring, in love with modernism and grandeur, art and beautiful things. By making prestige a matter of policy, Dal Piaz was absolutely at one with the economic expansiveness of the time. Under his presidency, the French Line would grow remarkably in whatever direction it took. Thanks, in considerable part, to the genius of Dal Piaz, a great friend and admirer of Marshal Lyautey, North Africa was opened to international tourism with the creation of the Société des Voyages et Hôtels Nord-Africains.

For sheer glamor, however, nothing in the realm of travel could compare with the North Atlantic. Simultaneously as the great waves of immigration — the source of most westbound traffic across the Atlantic — began to subside, a more "up-scale" travel market emerged, largely as a consequence of the prodigious growth in the American economy and the fantastic new wealth this placed in the hands of private individuals. Alert to the opportunities presented by such a development, the French Line prepared to offer accommodations suitable for a new middleclass clientele. This brought into being the so-called "tourist class," which replaced the old "second class," and also a new "third class," designed to serve the needs of more modest travelers, those replacing the emigrants who had traveled in steerage.

Still, it was the first-class market that remained the most courted and the most lucrative. To conquer it, steamship companies of every nationality competed with one another for dominance in tonnage, speed, luxury, and comfort. As the pride of its Le Havre–New York line, for instance, the CGT deployed two internationally famous vessels: the *France* and the *Paris*. Both were enormously successful. At a time when American "high society" went "abroad" every year, complete with massive luggage, several servants, and even guns, places on the *France* were auctioned to the highest bidders.

In 1927, the French Line enhanced its transatlantic fleet with the *Île de France*, a luxury liner Dal Piaz had ordered in 1924 from the Chantiers et Ateliers de Saint-Nazaire–Penhoët. This magnificent boat measured 791 feet long and 92 feet wide, and she weighed in at 43,450 gross tons. With 64,000 horsepower, the ship could ply the waves at a speed of 23 knots.

In fitting out the *Île de France,* the CGT brought its own tradition of luxury and comfort to a new high. In public areas and staterooms alike, everything was of an unprecedented refinement, with furnishings and decorations overseen personally by Dal Piaz and executed by the greatest names of the period. Stylistically, the project had its inspiration in the Exposition des Arts Décoratifs — the origin of the famous "streamlined" Art Deco mode — that had just been held in Paris in 1925. As a result, interiors and vistas possessed an elegance and a harmony that approached perfection itself.

With accommodations for 1,644 passengers, 478 of them in first class, the *Île de France*, like her sister ships the *France* and the *Paris*, became all the rage. The whole International Who's Who of politics, aristocracy, business, theater, arts, letters, and sport boarded the ship at one time or another. Captain Joseph Blancart and his chief purser, Henri Villar, actually achieved worldwide celebrity in their own right.

With the contribution made by this splendid vessel, the French Line ended the year 1928 with record earnings. For the first time its receipts exceeded a billion francs, and half of this derived from the New York service, which had transported 90,000 passengers. The dividend paid to stockholders came to the maximum allowable amount of 20 francs a share.

Except for the *Île de France,* however, the French transatlantic fleet was, on average, too old to remain successful much longer in its fight to hold the French flag high on the seas. The *France* had been launched in 1912, and while the *Paris* entered service only in 1921, the ship had been planned in 1913 and its construction subsequently delayed by the war. The *De Grasse,* the actual flagship of the CGT's New

France (1912)

Paris (1921)

Île de France (1927)

maiden voyage the *Bremen* broke the record for a transatlantic crossing, doing it with an average outbound speed of 27.33 knots and an average inbound speed of 27.92 knots. Right off, the German ship won the mythical Blue Ribbon (or Blue Riband) that until then had been held by Cunard's *Mauretania*.

The English, meanwhile, made no mystery of the fact that they intended to modernize their fleet, in which the principal vessels active on the New York run – the *Mauretania*, the *Olympic*, and the *Aquitania* – dated, respectively, from 1902, 1912, and 1914. What the British planned was a consolidation of their service under the single standard of the Cunard–White Star Line, with weekly transit guaranteed by a single pair of gigantic liners. The first, actually ordered in December 1930 from John Brown at Clydebank in Scotland, would be the *Queen Mary*, the future direct competitor of *Normandie*.

All this made such an impression on John Dal Piaz that by the time the *Île de France* made her maiden voyage in 1927 the directors of the CGT had already begun planning the new vessel. Furthermore, they were spurred on by a clause added in 1923 to the postal convention of 1912 stipulating that, in exchange for government use of the Compagnie Générale Transatlantique, the line would be required to place a new vessel into service no later than 1932, and "in designing the ship to take account of its competition and to take advantage of all important new developments."

Meanwhile, passenger traffic continued to grow throughout 1927 and 1928, in tandem with the ever-expanding economy and prosperity of the United States, a situation that enabled the CGT to realize exceptionally good earnings in 1928.

Given this combination of favorable factors, plus the eagerness of President Dal Piaz, the company decided to undertake a vast program of construction, involving not only the fleet of passenger liners, whose average age – all routes considered – was more than thirteen years, but also cargo ships. Altogether, three passenger vessels and eleven cargoes had already been ordered when the decision was made to build a huge high-speed liner designed to supplement the *Île de France* on the New York route.

Then in June 1928, with the planning and technical studies scarcely under way, John Dal Piaz suddenly died, which threw the CGT into a crisis of managerial succession. The problem resolved itself, however, with the appointment of the financier Octave Homberg as president of the CGT. Thus, it was during Homberg's regime that the project for a super-*Île de France* would evolve and that, under the discreet, anonymous rubric "T6," the plans for the future *Normandie* would be elaborated.

York service, dated from 1924, but it was a vessel of medium tonnage – 18,000 in all – and had only one class and an inadequate speed of 17 knots.

Moreover, there could be no denying that the *Île de France*, whatever her qualities and success, remained a "six-day" ship. This was simply not good enough, given the fact that foreign lines on the North Atlantic route were becoming much more competitive in matters of speed.

Germany, resurgent less than ten years after the Treaty of Versailles, was preparing to put into service, under the aegis of North German Lloyd, two new vessels that seemed likely to surpass everything then afloat. Thus, in 1929 came the famous *Bremen* and *Europa*, each measuring 938 by 102 feet, weighing 51,825 tons, and propelled by 135,000 horsepower, producing a cruising speed of 27 knots. Even on her

René Fould

Paul Romano

From T6 to *Normandie*

Studies began in earnest at the outset of 1929, undertaken simultaneously by the French Line and Penhoët at Saint-Nazaire, the only shipbuilders in France capable of carrying out such a project. They were supervised, on the owner's side, by President Octave Homberg and his general manager, Maurice Tillier, assisted by Chief Engineer Paul Romano, and engineers Mérot du Barré and Thomain, and, for the builder, by René Fould, president of the Société des Ateliers et Chantiers de Penhoët, who also happened to be a vice-president of the Compagnie Générale Transatlantique, and his general manager, André Lévy, assisted at Saint-Nazaire by Fernand Coqueret, head of the shipyards, his deputy Conard, and Chief Engineers Sée (hull division), Caldaguès (machinery division), and Lavallée (electrical division).

The particular problems that had to be solved were already well known. The *Île de France*, with its 140- to 160-hour crossings, was out of the race. Thus, the target speed had to be at least up to that of the *Bremen* and the *Europa* if the new French entry was not to be obsolete even before she entered service. Moreover, the accelerated speed had to be such that it would not require passengers to embark or disembark at inconvenient hours of the day or night. All this added up to the absolute necessity of a "5-day" ship, a vessel that would leave Le Havre on day J at 2 P.M. and, after a stopover in England, reach New York early in the morning of day J + 5 — that is, after only four days at sea.

From these *données* the principal characteristics of the new boat would flow quite naturally. Given the 3,200 miles that had to be covered, a minimum speed of 28 knots was imperative, whatever the weather conditions, which meant a 30-knot capacity to allow the necessary margin for maneuver. The ship should also be able to accommodate a sufficient number of passengers to assure a biweekly departure from Le Havre, a schedule that until then could be maintained only with two boats.

The first drawings produced a length of approximately 984 feet, a breadth of about 115 feet, a draft of 34 to 36 feet, and a displacement of some 60,000 tons.

Working in close collaboration, the engineers for the French Line and Penhoët, supported by a whole team of technicians and designers, would energetically proceed with their studies leading to final plans for the ship.

Managerial Vicissitudes

The management of the French Line would soon be presented with unforeseen complications of the gravest sort.

The first problem they had to overcome was the harbor work needed at both Saint-Nazaire and Le Havre in order to accommodate a ship whose proposed dimensions exceeded the capacity of the existing facilities. The very scale of this work proved extremely difficult to finance and thus caused major delays.

Another, even more onerous trouble developed when, just as the final plans were being drawn and work commenced in the shipyards, the American stock market began to collapse, setting off a world-wide economic and monetary crisis. So severe were the consequences of this disaster for the operations of the Compagnie Générale Transatlantique that it would threaten the very existence of the corporation and, simultaneously, that of the future luxury liner.

The keel under construction

Part of the stern

At the Penhoët shipyards in Saint-Nazaire, the largest stocks — on which the *Île de France* had been built — measured only 902 feet long. After first considering the possibility of lengthening it, the directors decided to have a new one built. This work began in February 1929. Then, after its launch, the great ship would have to go into wet dock for fitting out. In 1928, the only passage leading through the Loire to inland wet docks was by way of a lock measuring 692 feet in usable length and 98 feet in breadth. Work was therefore undertaken in 1929 to install a new twin lock. This water chamber would be the 1,148 by 164 foot Joubert Lock, which could also serve as a dry dock when necessary. Finally, to prepare for the ship's exit once the fitting out had been completed, it became necessary to dredge and widen the channel that cut through the Charpentiers Bar and gave access to the sea.

Le Havre presented similar problems. The port's access channel had to be excavated to a depth of some 33 feet, as did the outer harbor and the tidal basin. In addition, the entrance to the port needed widening, which required moving the outer harbor's jetty in order to enlarge the passage from 574 to 984 feet of usable width. It also became necessary to rebuild the tidal basin's quays so as to extend the Johannès-Couvert Quay by 1,640 feet and thus make it ready to receive four large ships at once. Finally, it was decided to erect a huge two-story Gare Maritime, or station, with the ground floor reserved for the handling of goods and the upper story for the processing of passengers.

The hull under construction

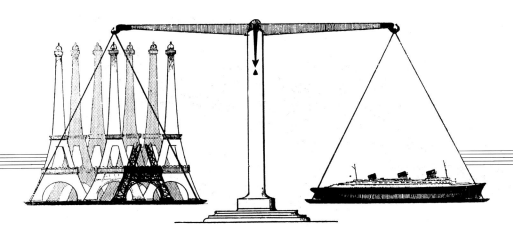

View of the Promenade Deck

Skeleton of the shell enclosing the foredeck

While that work was progressing at Saint-Nazaire, on the other side of the Atlantic, in New York, the stock market crashed on October 24, 1929. This was Wall Street's infamous "Black Thursday." With it came the first symptoms of the Great Depression, which would soon have repercussions in Europe. The crisis hit the CGT just when it was particularly vulnerable, committed as the corporation was to the vast new construction program set in motion by President Dal Piaz.

During the second half of 1929, operations began to show signs of weakness and recession. Receipts were dropping. With the beginning of 1930 the problem grew apace, and it became still worse in the second half of the year.

Nevertheless, a firm order for the T6 was given to the Société des Chantiers et Ateliers de Saint-Nazaire-Penhoët on October 29, 1930, with costs, subject to revision, estimated at 700 million francs. In the shipyards the official start of work was on January 26, 1931, the day the first steel plate was laid down.

A Problematic Future for the French Line and the T6

The directors of the French Line had already informed the government that it would be impossible to meet the deadline — summer 1932 — cited in the convention for placing the new ship in service, even though the delay was due to the rebuilding at Saint-Nazaire and the requirement that the latest, most advanced competition be studied. The date for ful-

filling the contract was thus extended, first, to March 1933 and then to the beginning of 1934.

Furthermore, under the pressure of circumstances and the mounting economic crisis, the CGT had arranged, after long and difficult negotiations with the Ministry of the Merchant Marine, for a codicil to be added to the convention providing for an increase in the postal subsidy and thus also for financing the new construction by means of loans guaranteed by the state, which would take responsibility for paying all interest charges in excess of 3 percent. When signing the new codicil, the President of the French Line took care to make the following statement: "Only by the means that you have been willing to grant us has it been possible to begin work on the new passenger ship, and it is therefore all the more evident that if the said codicil should not be approved, and if, for whatever reason, the advances fail to be made, or if the interest rate of 3 percent should not be supported, we shall find it necessary to stop construction...."

The worsening crisis throughout the next months soon rendered these arrangements null and void. This was because the company simply could not adapt quickly to the altered circumstances. Moreover, there was no way to stop a long-planned construction program continuing on its inexorable way, with payments to the shipyards having to occur on the contractual dates. To meet these obligations, after the operations for 1930 ended with a heavy loss of 65 million, the CGT had no other recourse but to borrow and to request advances from the French Treasury.

At the beginning of 1931 the financial situation became

14

Henri Cangardel

Pierre Laure

Shell of the "whaleback" designed to conceal foredeck machinery

Building the superstructure

quite distressing. In order to honor its obligations, the company had once again to approach the government for credit, which brought new and endless discussions, constant shuttling between one ministry and another, and much waste of time. Meanwhile, the shipyards grew restive, threatening a work stoppage in the event conditions were not met on schedule — and the workers not paid. Thus, the construction of the great ship proceeded in a climate of excruciating uncertainty.

In June 1931, when some of the financial assistance it had counted on failed to materialize, the Compagnie Générale Transatlantique appeared to be on the verge of bankruptcy. Acknowledging that national interests were at stake, the government decided to step in and take official responsibility for guaranteeing a new loan of 160 million, which would permit the corporation to meet its obligations for 1931. In exchange, however, the state would take control of the business, which meant that the board of directors had to resign so that they could be replaced by a new team of the government's own selection.

On July 3, 1931, the Chamber of Deputies voted to authorize the loan of 160 million. A commission was then named to prepare an accounting of the entire situation and to draw up a plan for placing the operation on a more solid footing.

The new board, which met for the first time on August 3, 1931, was composed of seven members, among whom were two vice-presidents — the president to be named later — in the persons of Raoul Dautry, general manager of the Chemins de Fer de l'État, and René Fould, president of the So-

ciété des Chantiers et Ateliers de Saint-Nazaire–Penhoët, the sole holdover from the old regime. The chief operating officer designate was Henri Cangardel, general manager of the Société des Armateurs Français.

Presiding over the study commission, meanwhile, was Germain-Martin, former minister and member of the Institut de France, assisted by two inspectors from the Finance Ministry, Jean Le Bec and Pierre Laure.

Henri Cangardel would emerge as the man of the hour, the chief architect of the plan to refloat the French Line and save the ship. The intelligence, directness, and energy he brought to every task showed forth in the steady gaze that illuminated the whole of his otherwise sober visage. Even though arriving from outside the company — at the Armateurs Français he had already caught the eye of President Dal Piaz — Cangardel lost no time in espousing both the cause and its past, spirit, and tradition. He identified himself with it and gave the staff new confidence by struggling to head off the dangers that threatened them all. His name, coupled with that of Pierre Laure, crops up throughout the history of Normandie.

For the moment, however, new managers were still dealing with the T6, and in the Saint-Nazaire shipyards the project provided employment for some 2,500 laborers, their ranks swelled by the employees of all the subcontractors: Als-Thom in Belfort, Schneider at Creusot in Lyons, and still others in Marseilles, Grenoble, Nancy, etc. The ship had become a nation-wide enterprise.

Could all this be stopped for reasons of economy and

efficiency? In his writings, Henri Cangardel would recall that it was just such questions of conscience that confronted him: "Did one have the right? Any decision entailed risks. Those who had ordered the boat had acted in good faith. For our part, we too believed in the future, albeit with less élan and optimism. We slowed down the construction of the boat, the delivery date for which had already been set back. In numerous ways, we completed and rectified the plan in its initial form...."

Despite the new measures, the problems had not all been solved. Only on July 20, 1933, did the Deputies enact two laws, one of which established the lines along which the ultimate financial reorganization of the Compagnie Générale Transatlantique should take place and the status of the company as a corporation of mixed public and private ownership, while the other law established the new postal convention and the formula for calculating the subsidy it would provide. However, the documents had nothing to say about the new liner or the financial effect its entry into service would have on the operations of the company. It was only in March 1935 that a codicil to the 1933 convention would be approved by Parliament and thus finally resolve the issue, by establishing a system of accounting for the ship's cost within the books kept by the CGT. The cost (amortization, interest, and taxes) of the loans taken out, with the state's guarantee, for construction purposes would be absorbed by the state, while the company would pay the cost of operations and general overhead.

During this long waiting period, the new management of the French Line had to clear endless financial hurdles, engage in ceaseless negotiations with the shipyards, under the most unfavorable conditions, in order to make the payments due, and do constant battle in the ministries, the Chamber of Deputies, the Senate, in stubborn hope of preserving the house they had inherited, a house in which the T6, still under construction, was the very keystone.

Despite all these vicissitudes, the studies carried out over the months made it possible to define the characteristics of the liner and establish the specifications for the contract ordering the boat from the Penhoët shipyards. They called for a type of vessel that, from every point of view, could be considered truly revolutionary.

The Launch

Several weeks after the first plate had been laid, the keel was put in place. Gradually the hull took form, then the inner hull, the ballast bridge, and finally the main deck. By January 1932 the hull had been almost completed. During April the upper deck of the superstructure was finished. Now the ship's silhouette rose high above the huge Penhoët slip, dominating the surrounding countryside.

The time for launching the vessel was near. The first discussions of it occurred in the early months of 1932. After consultation with the shipyards, the directors of the French Line held a board meeting on July 13, 1932, and scheduled the launch for October 29 at 2:30 P.M.

Naming the ship, however, was quite another matter, and a delicate one at that. Actually, several names had already been proposed and certain premature initiatives taken that fell somewhat short of universal appeal. In Saint-Nazaire, the labor organizations had the name *President Aristide*

Normandie a few days before her launch

Briand, the "apostle of peace," put forward. Others suggested *La Belle France*. In Paris, one minister was moved to sound out the widow of Paul Doumer and suggest that she offer his name for the boat, in memory of the French President who had been assassinated a few months earlier. The name, however noble the inspiration behind it, promised to be a rather unfortunate choice in purely linguistic terms. When pronounced in English, Doumer came out altogether too close to "doomed." For the very reason of this coincidence, the proposal seems, with hindsight, to have been an ill omen. Moreover, it was hardly a happy notion to christen a liner meant to symbolize pleasure and success with the name of an assassinated man, great and worthy as he may have been. However, this did not prevent the name *Paul Doumer* from being given, after some delicate bargaining, to a ship built for service in the Far East, where the late leader had played a prominent role as Governor General of Indochina.

Finally, acting on a recommendation made by Henri Cangardel, the French Line's board of directors agreed at its meeting on October 18, 1932, to call the ship *Normandie*. The name offered the triple advantage of honoring the maritime province where the vessel would have its home port, of evoking the memory of the ship that in 1881 had made

the reputation of the Compagnie Générale Transatlantique on the New York route, and of being easy to pronounce for an Anglo-Saxon clientele.

At the meeting on July 13, 1932, the board took formal note of the acceptance by President of the Republic Albert Lebrun to attend the launching ceremony, with Mme Lebrun serving as godmother. The board also formalized, at last, the installation of a president – a post left vacant since July 1931 – who had just been appointed by the government. He was Marcel Olivier, former governor general of Madagascar, who had distinguished himself at the side of Marshal Lyautey in organizing the great Colonial Exhibition. In Olivier the French Line and *Normandie* had found an ardent and steadfast champion, a man imbued with the rightness of their cause. With the help of Cangardel, he would deploy all the refined weaponry and subtle authority of the practiced diplomat to wage an unremitting battle to overcome the last obstacles leading to the completion of the work under way. Never, therefore, would he forget to emphasize the national character of the enterprise.

Now, in Penhoët's huge building berth at Saint-Nazaire, *Normandie* was ready for launch. She loomed up as the largest commercial ship ever put on water anywhere in the world, and for the Penhoët shipyards, of course, she represented the most important launch ever prepared. This was because of her size and, even more, her weight. With her cradle, *Normandie* weighed, in fact, 28,100 tons, or approximately twice as much as the hull of the *Île de France* at the time of that vessel's launch. This statistic alone suggests the importance of the operation and the risks borne by those responsible, foremost among them the director of the Saint-Nazaire shipyards, Fernand Coqueret, and his two deputies, the engineers Conard and Sée.

All kinds of scientific and complex calculations, minute measurements, and extraordinary precautions were taken in preparation for the crucial moment. For example, the lower part of the launching ship was greased with a quarter-inch layer of paraffin mixed with tallow. In addition, this part of the slipway received an application, some 3/8 inch thick, of another mixture consisting of paraffin and Castile soap, the whole greased anew with 5/8 inch of malleable paraffin and an application of lard and oleonapht oil. In all, some 52 tons of lubricants had been used to facilitate a smooth passage down the slipway. Further preparation came in the form of the most elaborate devices installed to guy or brake the vessel as it glided along the slip: "dogshores," "salt blocks," and hydraulic triggers. Finally, to keep the craft from lurching out of control once it was in the water, 100-ton bundles of chains, on either side of the slipway,

would be drawn out by the hull for a maximum distance of 99 feet, where they could then stop the vessel.

These abundant precautions had to be understood not only in relation to the exceptional nature of the vessel about to be launched, but also in the light of the possibilities of foul play or bad luck that tantalized a good many interested parties. Alarmed and pessimistic rumors began circulating among the public, to the effect that the slipway might collapse under the weight of such an enormous mass once it began to move, a rock could have been left in place despite all the dredging of the Loire bed, or a strike would be called at the fateful hour just to sabotage the operation. Fernand Coqueret and his team were only too aware of how much was at stake.

On the morning of October 29, 1932, Saint-Nazaire prepared to live through one of the most momentous days in its history. From every point in Brittany, the Vendée, Brière, and all the adjacent regions, the curious set out at dawn, on foot and, more often, on bicycle. They jammed into the city and moved forward slowly, in long corteges, like so many tributaries flowing and converging toward the river's estuary – toward the famous berth – above which *Normandie* revealed a silhouette that seemed both crushing and soaring. It was witnessed by a crowd estimated to number at least 100,000 spectators.

The President of the Republic, M. Albert Lebrun – accompanied by the godmother, Mme Lebrun, and several ministers: Léon Meyer, Minister of the Merchant Marine; George Leygues, the Naval Minister; Germain Martin, Finance Minister; Julien Durand, Commerce Minister; all preceded by the Chief of Protocol, M. de Fouquières – was received on his arrival by President Fould and Governor General Olivier surrounded by their principal collaborators.

At the banquet before the launch, René Fould delivered a speech extolling the technical advances made in *Normandie*. Another speaker was President Olivier of the Compagnie Générale Transatlantique, who paid tribute to the shipyards for their work on a project "that exceeds the bounds of private interests to become a national enterprise." He went on: "You know that this undertaking has not been without its critics, and the economic and financial depression now raging in France, as everywhere else, is not something to mollify them. Our company has been accused of imprudence and foolhardiness. But every time I am confronted by one of those unforgiving censors and merciless fault-finders, I remind myself of this definition given by one of our finest European economists: 'Shipping is the art of speculating on profits from risk overcome!' " In his conclusion, Olivier emphasized the incomparable role of a liner as a

Governor General Olivier,   president of the French Line

Official guests arriving at the Penhoët shipyards.
Center: President of the Republic, Albert Lebrun. On his left, François Blancho, mayor of Saint-Nazaire, and Fernand Coqueret, director of the shipyards. On his right, in the background, President René Fould, and, in the foreground, André de Fouquières, chief of protocol

Christening the ship

Below: On the platform, Mme Lebrun, the ship's godmother, throwing the bottle of champagne, assisted by René Fould, Governor General Olivier, and Admiral Le Bigot

Normandie's *launch*

means of communication: "Every one of our liners constitutes an international salon, where in a French environment, under a French standard, the elite of the whole world hold a permanent peace conference. Thus, we serve our country in a manner and along lines most in keeping with her genius and her traditions."

In his remarks closing the ceremony, the President of France saluted the naval construction industry, "which has given tangible proof of its value and possibilities, and demonstrated decisively that France has reserves of constructive energy ready to be developed when it can be tapped by leaders worthy of the name." Then he expressed every wish that "in the great international movement of travelers joining Europe to North America [the new liner] would win the place she deserves by virtue of her outstanding qualities."

At the end of the banquet the officials took their places in the grandstand at the foot of the slipway. At 2:30 P.M. the liner was set free of all restraints except the last guys. In a brief religious ceremony the vessel received the traditional blessing from priests of the local clergy.

The moment of truth had arrived! At the sound of a bugle, the hydraulic triggers fell out of their slots and the salt blocks melted away under flushing torrents of hosed water. With a brisk and authoritative gesture, Mme Lebrun cut the tricolored ribbon holding the bottle of champagne, which immediately exploded on the bow. *Normandie* shuddered, slowly and majestically, as *La Marseillaise* rang out, the tugs and other ships in the harbor blew their sirens, and the crowd erupted in wild cheering.

The heaviest mass that had ever been set afloat slid smoothly and made contact with her natural element, water, thereupon setting off an enormous wave. Rolling with tidal force, it caught a number of imprudent spectators who had broken through the barriers and sent them tumbling into the water. They were more or less fished out, having suffered little but an unsolicited bath.

Now tugs took charge of *Normandie* and towed her to Penhoët's fitting-out berth to be completed. And so the curtain fell on the first act, which had opened on October 29, 1930, with the order given to the shipyards. Lasting two years to the day, it had been fraught with incident!

The second act promised to be no less suspenseful and hectic.

"Vessel of Light"

Journalists and writers of the period all but smothered *Normandie* under a heavy blanket of adjectives, from the most ordinary to the most lyric: "King of the Oceans," "Giant of the Seas," "Wonder of the Seas," "Greyhound of the Seas," "Adonis of the Seas," "Marvel of Nautical Art," "Flagship of French Quality," "Cathedral of the French Merchant Marine," "Floating Versailles," "Ambassador of French Genius," "Messenger of Peace," "Vessel of Light," to cite only a few.

True enough, light — as we shall see — would be one of the ship's chief characteristics. Used lavishly, it would flood every part, emphasizing the beauty of the architecture and bringing out all the decorative details. It was also true that *Normandie* became a convergence point for everything in the period that represented enlightenment: science, the arts, communication. The best there was, in learned and inventive minds, in common and skilled labor, in talent of every sort, took part in the realization of this liner and contributed to her success. An impressive assemblage of iron and steel would take on life and color, and *Normandie*, as the fitting out of the interior progressed, would become truly a "Vessel of Light."

For these fittings, both *noblesse* and *tradition obligent*! When it came to decorating passenger ships, the history of the French Line was too rich in quality productions — the *Île de France* being the most recent — for the company to stumble and go slack in finishing *Normandie*. This ship exceeded the tonnage of everything that had ever sailed. All the more reason, therefore, that she had an obligation to be also the most beautiful ship of all time.

The men responsible for *Normandie*'s construction were fully conscious of this. They had begun deliberating the issue early and, wisely enough, had decided to seek the advice and counsel of the art world. On October 6, 1931, two months

The wash set off by the launch

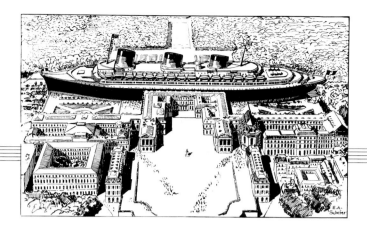

after its installation, the CGT's new board of directors decided to appoint a committee of architects to study the program of decoration and assure its execution by the most select designers then at work in France. As chairman of the committee, they named Chief Engineer Paul Romano, the better to ensure good liaison with the overall management. The services of the Merchant Marine would be represented by Maritime Engineering's chief engineer, Jean Marie. The four architects appointed to the committee were among the most notable of the period: Bouwens de Boijen, Expert, Patou, and Pacon.

The committee got down to work straightaway. They drew up plans for the whole, defined the spaces and volumes of the large public areas, and established the general style of their décor. "For the first time," wrote J. Baschet in the June 1935 issue of L'Illustration, "nothing has been spared in the service of a beautiful idea. For the first time, engineers, architects, decorators, painters, and sculptors have joined together in an enterprise that borders on the irrational but stirs all those who dream of victory in the realm of beauty."

By the beginning of 1933, after the management of the French Line and their advisors had studied and made their choice among the various maquettes, the creative people and the workers, from tapestry weavers, cabinetmakers, electricians, and painters to plasterers, were hard at work. The result? It would soon be known, when the finished liner was finally delivered to its owners and, following trials at sea, docked at Le Havre for the first time, to a din of sirens and the clamor of an enthusiastic throng.

Attacks and Delaying Tactics

All the while that at Saint-Nazaire talent and imagination were being lavished on Normandie's decorative program, in Paris factions of every sort were working overtime to complicate the task of the CGT's management, who found themselves obliged to fight on two fronts at once. On the one hand, they had to proceed with rehabilitating the company, to secure its future and that of the liner by persuading Parliament, finally, to settle the terms of the state's aid, in legislation that would not come up for a vote until June 1935. On the other hand, the company also had to deal with a violent campaign of denigration, orchestrated by parties whose interests had been more or less directly injured at the time of the French Line's insolvency and the government's intervention.

In the Chamber of Deputies a vigorous opposition emerged, mainly in the Foreign Affairs Committee, which noted the disproportion between the credits expected by the CGT and the ridiculously small subvention earmarked for

the encouragement of French influence abroad: "When one must and when one wishes, one finds a great deal of money. An example: the hundreds of millions for a public relations ocean liner.... The unintelligent parsimony with which we treat French information and works abroad proves to be as ridiculous as it is scandalous in the light of a kind of budgetary largesse that simply boggles the impartial mind.... A superliner, good propaganda...but at what price?... The idea behind Normandie had to do, primarily, with propaganda, advertising.... Such a huge and overwhelming effort on behalf of propaganda and prestige on a single ocean, for the United States alone.... It was abnormal and illogical in and of itself, but it also runs the risk of soon being neutralized or even overcome by Germany and England!"

Complaints could also be heard from the public sector. Some of these arose from the CGT stockholders who, of course, had more or less lost the whole of their investment at the time of the government-imposed reorganization. Others derived from businessmen in the steamship industry who hoped to divide up spoils from the French Line — that is, take over the best routes in the event a bankrupt CGT had to abandon them — and who had nothing to gain by a refloating of the rival company.

Both factions directed their appeals to the politicians and the economic and financial journalists, who stirred up public opinion and made life difficult for Marcel Olivier, Henri Cangardel, and the representatives of the Merchant Marine. "In matters of boats," wrote one newspaper at the time, "Normandie is the biggest ever charged to the French taxpayer!" A pamphlet entitled An Assault on the Public Treasury violently attacked the new board of directors' management. The publication had wide circulation — some 30,000 copies — and it was distributed even along the halls of Parliament. The calumnious character of the piece prompted the company to bring a libel suit, at the same time that the board issued an official account confirming the accuracy of their figures and thus effectively answering the accusations made against them. To justify his policy and air the problem of Normandie, Henri Cangardel, backed up by Jean Marie, decided to man the battlements himself.

When the liner was ordered in 1930, Jean Marie, the chief engineer in France's Maritime Engineering Department, was the deputy in charge of Naval Materiel at the Merchant Marine Ministry. By virtue of this position, he knew all the details of the original conception as well as all the complications involved in putting the ship into production. He played an important part in the elaboration of the plans, especially as these touched on security. In July 1933, Marie was among the government representatives who were appointed to ad-

A REVOLUTIONARY HULL

The first tests of the models began in April 1929 and continued through March 1931, initially in the test tanks of the French navy and then in the tanks at Hamburg, Germany.

The first model hulls conformed to a classic type. But in early 1930, Vladimir Yourkevitch, a Russian émigré engineer living in France since 1917, proposed a new form whose distinctive characteristic consisted of hollowed out water lines in an area between the stem and a point of inflexion mathematically calculated according to a patented formula.

The hydrodynamic qualities of the hull might be explained as follows: At or above the water line, the sides of the ship, beginning at the stem, form two concave planes extending to a point that, instead of following a rectilinear or convex line, varies relative to the length of the ship and the speed to be attained. The advantage of this ingenious solution is that the satellite waves generated by the moving vessel are carried beyond that part of the hull where they cause serious drag, while the angle formed by the waves is closed in such a way that the runnels of water do not break up and thus are able to flow around the forms of the ship without producing vibrations. To compensate for this lost displacement, some volume can be recovered by expanding or flaring the ship's forefoot — that is, by giving this part of the hull a bulbous shape. Providing it is carefully calculated in relation to the hollowed water lines, the bulb helps diminish the drag by facilitating the flow of water drawn by the ship's forepart, therefore significantly reducing the height of the stem or bow wave. The use of these principles in the conception of *Normandie*'s hull proved to be a long and difficult process. A great many models were tried and the dimensions modified several times until the following characteristics were attained:

Overall length	313.75m	(1,029')
Length between perpendiculars	293.20m	(962')
Width or beam, to the outside of frames	35.90m	(118')
Width of the overhanging Promenade Deck	36.40m	(119')
Depth from the keel to the beam line of the Promenade Deck	28.50m	(94')
Distance from the top of the first funnel to the bottom of the keel	56.00m	(184')
Distance from the truck of the highest mast to the bottom of the keel	73.00m	(240')
Average loaded draft	11.16m	(37')
Corresponding displacement		c.68,500 tons
Displacement, light		c.54,600 tons
Approximate gross registered tonnage		79,500
Approximate net registered tonnage		38,000
Number of decks		12

Called, from top to bottom: Upper Sun Deck, Sun Deck, Embarkation Deck, Promenade Deck, Main Deck, Decks A, B, C, D, E, F, and G

It has often been said, especially in the United States, that the underlying conception of *Normandie* had come from Vladimir Yourkevitch. Without diminishing the eminent role played by that great naval architect, it is only proper for it to be known that in reality the gigantic task represented by the ship was, and could only have been, carried out by a whole team. In fact, it involved the staff of the Penhoët shipyards, under the direction of Fernand Coqueret, and that of the Compagnie Générale Transatlantique, under the direction of Paul Romano, which determined the form of the "working parts" (the submerged portion of the ship) in the mid and after sections of the hull,

The hull's form fore and aft

The first-class Dining Room under construction

which comes with riding over, rather than through, the wave crests. On the other hand, parting the waves can cause serious damage, since even a high open deck may occasionally be swept by great masses of heavy water. To remedy this problem, the engineers of the Penhoët shipyards and those of the French Line developed a whole range of devices as innovative as they were effective.

From the bow to approximately one-third the way along the ship's forward section, the sides were steeply sloped, in keeping with Yourkevitch's recommendations, in a way that the waves would be cast away on either side of the hull and thus unable, except in extreme instances, to roll over the deck. But the heavy seas churned up by the rough weather so often prevalent on the North Atlantic prompted the engineers to carry the concept still further. They gave the stem an almost clipper-ship profile — that is, arched forward, rather than straight and almost perpendicular to the water line as in all previous modern passenger ships. This form made it possible for the ship to part the waves more efficiently, as well as for an anchor to be installed in the stem, which gave Normandie three forward anchors. To provide for unusually high seas, the foredeck was covered with a monumental shell or "whaleback," beveled or chamfered along the sides, which ended in an upsweeping breakwater and rested on a specially reinforced frame.

All the deck or mooring machinery (capstans, winches, chains, etc.) were concealed under the whaleback, there sheltered from high waves. Thus, the ship could maintain near-normal speed even in the worst weather without fear of damage. Aft, the hull terminated in a spoonshaped, overhanging yacht stern.

The Superstructure

The flaring sides of the foresection and the swelling form of the stern resulted in a midbody (the main central section of the vessel where the sides are almost parallel) of extraordinary length at the level of the Promenade Deck. This in turn allowed Normandie's designers to create a superstructure that stretched to 734 feet, or 71.5 percent of the ship's overall length!

The superstructure began only 171 feet from the bow and ended just 123 feet short of the stern. The brief distance between the forepart of the superstructure and the bow gave Normandie a rather bluffheaded look from certain angles, a look nicely balanced by the broad, rounded configuration of the forecastle pierced by the vast bay windows of the Winter Garden and the elegant sweep of the bridge wings. Aft, this curving line would reappear, this time divided into the steppedback tiers of broad, beautifully open, uncluttered terraces. The upper decks (Sun Deck and Upper Sun Deck) were equally free of air intakes and ventilators to become immense open-air esplanades. The purpose here was to give passengers the maximum space possible while also reducing the aerodynamic drag of the superstructure to an absolute minimum.

The same concern for the least resistance to thrust into the air dictated the form of the funnels. Instead of being cylindrical or elliptical in section they were swept back into a tear-shape. These three smokestacks all had the same diameter but diminished in height from fore to aft, at the same time that they inclined at a 10-degree angle. The fake third funnel was added not only for aesthetic reasons, but also as a counterbalance to the first two, so that the effect of wind striking the ship would be equalized throughout her length. The dummy funnel housed the kennel, the main exhaust from the airconditioning system, and the uptake for evacuating fumes from the kitchen. Behind the third funnel stood the mizzenmast, placed there, rather than in the traditional position before the bridge, so as not to block the helmsman's view.

in such a way as to compensate totally for the metacentric radius resulting from the narrowing of the forward water lines, while at the same time providing for good stability. And it was the same team that calculated the appendages (the bosses encasing the propeller shafts and their connecting struts and the bilge keels projecting along either side of the hull for a length of 63 meters [207 feet]). Thanks to these daring experiments, it was possible to limit to 9 percent the increase in drag caused by these appendages. Altogether, the tests made it possible to reduce the ship's displacement by 4,000 tons and achieve a 2 percent economy in the developed power needed to realize an average in-service speed of 28 knots, while also making it possible to count on a maximum speed of more than 1 knot better than that which would have been possible with a more traditional hull.

This remarkable result translated into an exceptionally thin, fine wake. Even when going all out, Normandie did not generate the big satellite waves produced by other ships, and fishermen, once they knew this, ceased to stay wide of her path, since she posed no problem for their boats. "She skims over the water like a seagull," they said.

The Forms of the Fixed Parts

The "fixed parts" (those above water) also had an entirely new configuration, quite different from that of older ships. To one degree or another, it has served ever since as the point of departure for virtually all naval architects.

The Yourkevitch form, owing to the loss of displacement, considerably reduced the buoyancy of the ship's extreme forepart. This resulted from a net diminution of the period and amplitude of tonnage. In other words, ships with a hull of this shape tend to cut through waves rather than ride over their crests. For passengers, this offers a clear advantage, since the rolling it entails is less unpleasant than pitching,

Joining the uptakes for one of the smokestacks

Aerodynamic form of the funnels or smokestacks

C.195.

The prelaunch hull showing the hydrodynamic form of the struts for the propeller shafts

The chain for one of the bow anchors

Workmen leaving the Penhoët shipyards

Jean Marie

minister the Compagnie Générale Transatlantique, and he became a member of the board's committee. Thus, he too played a decisive role in safeguarding the future of the liner, whose cause he faithfully championed and defended furiously in government circles.

Henri Cangardel and Jean Marie therefore initiated a series of conferences designed to inform opinion by airing the *Normandie* problem in the most objective way possible. By means of memoranda to the Naval Academy, lectures at the Sorbonne, the Michodière Theater, etc., Cangardel was able to stress all that the ship would bring to France in the way of prestige, tourist trade, commerce, and inspiration for the young. In conclusion, he declared:

Building *Normandie* was a daring enterprise, the act of a nation eager, in the aftermath of military success, to confirm its readiness to engage in peaceful competition in the realm of maritime commerce.

Dare we present our youth nothing but signs of discouragement and pessimism? Is it good form to believe that nothing exists but old rules, to insist that everything dwindles away, to stand quaking in the presence of financial loss or ineluctable changes in the lives of individuals and nations? Our young folk fail to find in these sorrows what they seek: a reason to live and to act, a well opened to their thirst for knowledge and self-affirmation.

Our young people are vigorous, healthy, and rich in hope. For them I should like us to exalt our maritime enterprise as well as our finest industrial achievements.

Given the right example, our youth will applaud with us, like a victory over pessimism, the proud arrival in America, under our standard, of the world's grandest and most beautiful liner.

In the shipyards at Saint-Nazaire the construction of the liner was nearing completion. And while the decoration of the ship may have absorbed the best of every available talent, the mounting of the driving apparatus required nothing less than the boldest and most advanced technique, for the delivery of the vessel was set for April 20 at the latest.

Just then, however, new clouds began to gather on the horizon! Seeing the ship's next departure as a unique opportunity, labor became restive. The unions were perfectly aware of the pawn *Normandie* gave them in bargaining for extra benefits. They threatened to prevent the vessel from leaving on schedule for her first trials. Picket lines appeared in the hope of stopping all overtime work. On May 3 the strikers barricaded access to the quay. In response, the shipyard management filed a complaint against the interference with the right to work. The pot was boiling over!

Now Jean Marie arrived at Saint-Nazaire to try negotiating an end to a dispute whose continuation would surely compromise the whole program for putting the ship into service. Following long and intensive bargaining, a decision was made to pay the shipyard workers a one-time bonus on condition that they resume normal work and that the liner be ready and permitted to leave on May 5.

With peace restored, it was actually on May 4 that *Normandie* entered the huge lock that had been built for her use — and size — and left Saint-Nazaire on May 5 to go through the acceptance trials.

In Paris, finally, the schedule of operations was established once the Élysée Palace confirmed that the President of the Republic would attend the inauguration ceremonies on May 23 and that Mme Lebrun, the godmother, would take part in the maiden voyage, whose departure was set for May 29, 1935.

View of the ship during construction

Normandie seen from the shipyard

Normandie *leaving the Penhoët fitting-out berth by way of the Joubert Lock, built in 1929–32 for Normandie and named for the President of the Saint-Nazaire Chamber of Commerce*

The Trials

On May 5, *Normandie* finally sailed out of Saint-Nazaire, escorted by two destroyers, *Adroit* and *Foudroyant*, and, without a hitch, passed through the channel that had been dug for her. She had on board, apart from a full complement of managers from the CGT and the shipyards, the Minister of the Merchant Marine in the person of William Bertrand and a veritable army of painters, electricians, upholsterers, decorators, etc., who would be working night and day, throughout the trials, to get the interior finished on time. Also present, to assure media coverage of the event, were several leading maritime reporters and historians, among them Raymond Lestonnat and Hervé Lauwick.

The sole master on board, after God, was Captain René Pugnet, assisted by a second commanding officer: Pierre Thoreux. In charge of the engine room were Chief Engineer Jean Hazard and his deputy, Kerdoncuff. All had been involved with the liner throughout her construction, and thus knew the vessel inside and out.

To witness the departure, the Nazairiens thronged onto every quay and inch of high ground. They arrived en masse to say farewell to a ship they had watched grow up from birth, a liner whose fate they had shared for four and a half years and that on occasion had brought them a good measure of anxiety. Now that she was leaving, *Normandie* seemed all the more their very own. And no one felt this more than the Penhoët workers. For all those chaps from Brière — half-laborers, half-peasants, uncouth, tough, quick-tempered, but bursting with pride in their work — it was a moment of high emotion. And when *Normandie* passed majestically in front of them, slowly slipped out of the lock, as

if reluctant to leave, and set sail for the open sea, they could scarcely hold back their tears.

The acceptance trials rolled on from the 5th through the 11th of May, with miscellaneous exercises taking place on the 6th and 7th and preliminaries on the 8th, when, in the evening, *Normandie* dropped anchor in the Brest channel and allowed Minister William Bertrand to disembark. Then came the equipment trials on May 9 and 10, followed by speed trials on the Glénans course. Finally, the ship went through a new round of equipment trials on the 11th.

Normandie passed every test with flying colors. During the speed trials, which lasted 8 hours, the ship attained a maximum rate of 32.125 knots, making a horsepower of just under 170,000 and a propeller speed of 228.38 rotations per minute.

Every aspect of the technology functioned to perfection, and the ship turned out to be remarkably maneuverable, thanks to the shape of the hull and backing power made possible by turbo-electric propulsion. Proof of this came after the first trials off Penmarch when Captain Pugnet decided, along with the pilot, to return to Brest, across the Sein current, a deep but narrow, twisting passage that *Normandie* cleared at 30 knots without a problem. If only to show the sensitivity of her capacity to respond, the helm was turned full circle, whereupon the liner heeled obediently — and threw the kitchen into total chaos! "At the expense of a good many plates, *Normandie* was anointed as the easiest of all liners to maneuver," said Henri Cangardel.

Another illustration of the highly evolved qualities of *Normandie* was the fact that while traveling at a speed of 31 knots, the ship could be stopped dead within 5,577 feet.

The only shadow in the bright picture were vibrations that

Captain Pugnet

Commander Thoreux

Chief Engineer Hazard

could be felt in the rear third of the ship, even at cruising speed. The causes seemed beyond immediate explanation, which left no possibility of remedying the situation before the ship sailed on her maiden voyage the 29th of May.

Right on schedule, *Normandie* appeared in Le Havre channel on May 11 at 7 P.M. Her reception was triumphal. From Sainte-Adresse to the semaphore, the quays, the breakwaters, the balconies of the Hôtel Frascati, and the waterfront roadway were black with people. The moment the liner cleared the breakwater, at the entrance to the great tidal basin, the horns and sirens of all the port craft rang out, echoed by the roar of the crowd. In this ear-splitting din, the ship, helped by tugs, made an impeccable maneuver and swung round. At her first try, *Normandie* came alongside the Johannès-Couvert Quay, doing so with remarkable ease and precision.

The technical trials *Normandie* had just passed with such brio would now be followed by "social" trials. She confronted them in the course of a heavy program of festivities, which went on from the 23rd to the 29th of May, the date of her first departure for New York.

Before that could happen, however, the directors of the French Line would have to endure a new set of crises. For several months, negotiations had been under way for the purpose of establishing a set of rules for the company's sea-going personnel and of settling the issue of their permanent employment. The opposite positions taken by the unions and the CGT created a standoff which had yet to be resolved.

Summoned to arbitrate the differences, Minister Bertrand of the Merchant Marine had made it known that he would render a decision on May 15. On the eve of this date, the representatives of the local unions sent Bertrand a veritable ultimatum, demanding that permanent status be granted to four-fifths of the employees and that a response be given the following day, the 15th of May at 9 A.M., failing which "they renounced all responsibility for future events."

On the morning of May 15, in the absence of news, the unions made good on their threat. The staff of the liner *Champlain* struck just as their ship was about to leave for New York. They were then followed in their walkout by the staff of the *Lafayette* and the personnel already aboard *Normandie*. Refusing to be blackmailed, Bertrand announced that he would not render a decision until all employees had resumed their duties.

Léon Meyer, deputy mayor of Le Havre, and Léon Jouhaux, president of the General Federation of Labor, began mediation. Finally, on May 19, in a vote cast by secret ballot, the majority opted for a return to work. With this Bertrand gave his decision on the 20th, which held that, in principle,

permanence should be granted to 50 percent of the seagoing personnel.

Peace had been restored, but only after a nerve-wracking alarm. Within three days the official inauguration would come.

The Inauguration Festivities

Throughout these last vicissitudes, hard work had been going on behind the scenes to make sure that everything would be in place by the time the curtain went up.

Young Edward Lanier, an attaché of the CGT management (at the end of a very brilliant career, he would become the French Line's next-to-last president), was in charge of organizing the ceremonies. In his memoirs Lanier would recall the horror with which he discovered, upon arriving on board the morning of May 23, that a great many beds had not yet been installed in cabins where guests invited from Paris for dinner and a soirée were to be accommodated. Moreover, the luxurious apartments reserved for the most important of the expected personages remained almost empty!

Once again, a miracle happened. By midnight everything was more or less in order, other than a number of toilets and bathtubs which, because still unconnected, had to be filled with jugs of hot water delivered by cabin boys working in relays!

Finally, the great day arrived. *Normandie* received the Republic personified by President Lebrun and a cohort of ministers and high officials. Among these were Mssrs. François Pietri, Louis Rollin, Henry Roy, William Bertrand, respectively Ministers of the Navy, Commerce, Public Works, and the Merchant Marine; cabinet members from the Élysée: Secretary of Defense General Braconnier, Interior Secretary M. André Magre, Chief of Protocol Pierre de Fouquières; Rear Admiral Le Bigot, aide-de-camp, etc.

The morning in Le Havre was devoted to "on-land" visits, to the memorial monument to the dead, the general hospital, and the city hall, followed by a banquet and speeches. In the afternoon, before boarding *Normandie*, guests were taken to see the port in operation and the new work that had just been completed: the southern jetty, the tidal basin, the oil tanks, and the south station of the industrial and maritime company.

At the gangway Governor General Olivier, Henri Cangardel, Captain Pugnet, and their general staff received the long line of top hats, morning coats, bicornes, and bemedaled chests — for this was a period that took its protocol quite seriously.

The President of France was accompanied to his apartment — the ultra-luxurious Caen Suite — which he soon va-

Ladders used by Normandie's engineers

The Turbo-electric Propulsion

In order to move *Normandie*'s enormous mass at a speed of 30 knots, it was known that the ship would require drive equal to 160,000 horsepower. And it was essential that a 30-knot speed be attained in order to guarantee an average cruising speed of 28 knots, for in the event the vessel should have to slow down, she could thus make up for the delay by substantially increasing her velocity. Only a system of steam turbines offered the possibility of achieving so much power.

The Choice of Steam Equipment

The boilers, developed by the Penhoët shipyards, were of the water-tube variety (in which combustion gas and hot air circulated around tubes containing the water to be vaporized) and furnished steam heated to 350–360 degrees centigrade, as well as 28 kilograms of pressure per square centimeter. Each boiler had a 3,280-square-foot heating surface, weighed 100.5 tons empty, and was oil-fired.

The 1930s had the technology necessary to build boilers producing steam at a much higher pressure and temperature, but it was only prudent to remain at relatively modest levels, levels that had been respected in Germany for the *Bremen* and the *Europa*, in Italy for the *Rex* and the *Conte di Savoia*, and in England for the *Queen Mary*. Moreover, the steam equipment on all the units was, like that on *Normandie*, of more than respectable dimensions, with a weight and a bulk that today would seem truly excessive. On *Normandie* there were 29 main boilers of the type just described and 4 cylindrical auxiliary steam-tube boilers tested at 10 kilograms per square meter, installed in 4 watertight compartments stretching to a total length of around 312 feet.

The Choice of Propulsion Equipment

Ever since the Englishman Charles Parsons invented the steam turbine, the system had continually posed a problem. In order for a turbine to be truly efficient, either it had to turn rapidly or the circumferential speed

of the staged blades be high – that is, steam had to encounter as it traveled the maximum number of blades. The propellers, on the other hand, had to turn as slowly as possible because, beyond a certain speed, there formed around the propeller blades a pocket of air mixed with steam that considerably reduced efficiency and provoked a rapid deterioration in the propeller itself. This phenomenon was known as "cavitation."

In the period of *Normandie*'s conception, there were three solutions to the problem:
1 Shafting the propellers directly to the turbines, which required that the turbines have an enormous diameter in order for the circumferential speed to be sufficient.
2 A reduction of speed between the turbines and the propellers by means of a series of gears.
3 An electrical reduction obtained by utilizing, on one side, a set of alternators shafted directly to the turbines and, on the other side, propulsion motors linked to the propeller shafts. The alternators being equipped with fewer poles than the motors to which they supplied power, the reduction between the alternators and the motors increased proportionately as the difference in the number of poles between the two groups of machinery became greater.

The first solution, which had been adopted for all the big French transatlantic liners, including the *Île de France* (1927), was immediately eliminated as unworkable for *Normandie*, since the power required (40,000 horsepower on each of the 4 shafts) could have been generated only by turbines that were impossibly large and cumbersome.

The second solution, that of reduction by gears, was apparently the simplest and had been adopted on the largest and the most recent of the foreign vessels, mainly the German liners *Bremen* and *Europa* and their Italian counterparts, the *Rex* and the *Conte di Savoia*. The gear system offered the advantage of increased efficiency (between 97 and 98 percent energy transmitted between turbine and propeller), but it was afflicted with certain flaws. Since, by definition, turbines always turn in the same direction, they had to be backed up with less powerful turbines to effect travel in reverse. Moreover, geared reduction, in its mid-1930s technology, still produced the unwelcome side effects of noise and vibration.

This left the third solution, that of turbo-electric propulsion. Its efficiency was a bit less (about 96 percent), and it also had the drawback of more rapid propellers since reduction was limited by the motors

Main Penhoët-type water-tube boilers

The Als-Thom turbo-alternator room

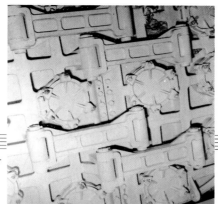

The relief surface of a condenser

whose size could not exceed certain norms. On the other hand, the presence of two air gaps between the turbines and the propellers gave the machines an extraordinary flexibility and thus allowed sharp changes of direction without risk of damage. But most of all, it provided as much power in reverse as in forward motion simply by switching the direction from which the motors received power. If the mechanical-reduction turbine was slightly more fuel efficient in forward motion, turbo-electric propulsion offered the possibility of sharply reduced fuel consumption by supplying the 4 propulsion motors with only 2 alternators. Thus, during certain months of the year, when the ship would be expected to function well below her maximum speed, the conditions of use would become quite advantageous, for given the fact that propulsive power increases in approximate ratio to the cube of the ship's speed, a reduction by one-half of the propusive power, according to the process described above, would correspond to a reduction of only 20 percent of speed.

Finally, if turbo-electric propulsion was a bit heavier and bulkier than the mechanical-reduction turbines, it produced neither noise nor vibration. This was why it was adopted for *Normandie* despite its complexity. The decision was exceptionally daring in that this type of propulsion had never been adopted for vessels requiring more than 160,000 horsepower. The system was built by Als-Thom.

The 4 alternators each had a theoretical maximum of 33,400 kilowatts (making 45,411 horsepower) generated by 2,430 rotations per minute. They produced a three-phrase current with an 81-period capacity at maximum speed, under 5,500–6,000 volts. They included 4 poles.

The four propulsion motors each had a theoretical maximum of 40,000 horsepower and included 40 poles. Since the machines were synchronous, except when the ship was casting off, stopping, or changing directions, the reduction obtained through the difference in the number of poles between alternators and motors was therefore 10 to 1. As a result, the maximum speed of the motors shafted to the propellers was 243 rotations per minute. The speed of travel was controlled by a release of more or less steam into the turbines shafted to the alternators.

Here it should be noted that this driving apparatus had been considerably overscaled so as to be able to deliver 160,000 horsepower with a propeller speed sharply lower than the maximum rate of 243 rotations per minute, thus with a more resistant torque. On the other hand, the driving apparatus could generate at its maximum 25 percent more

than the designed 160,000 horsepower. In other words, the motors were capable of developing about 50,000 horsepower per shaft line, making a total of 200,000 torquemetric horsepower in superoverload (160,000 horsepower being considered as permanent overload and 130,000 horsepower as economical running). Given this purpose, and the 2 percent loss in the motors, the alternators were designed to develop each at least 37,600 kilowatts (51,122 horsepower). This possibility of running in super-overload was kept from the public, since it had been decided not to use it during the first year of commercial activity.

Auxiliary Generation of Electricity

To light and heat the ship, provide for ventilation, and operate a very great deal of ancillary equipment, it was necessary to have an additional supply of power other than that of the alternators reserved exclusively for propulsion. This power or current came from 6 turbodynamos fed by one of the 29 main boilers. Each of these turbodynamos had a normal generating capacity of 2,200 kilowatts, making a combined total of 13,200 kilowatts. In overload, this equipment could generate 25 percent more power, making 16,500 kilowatts. The direct current this produced was 220 volts. The magnitude of these generators can be appreciated only in relation to the electric power of the *Conte di Savoia* – the most thoroughly electrified of the passenger liners prior to *Normandie* – which did not exceed 5,100 kilowatts, and that of the *Queen Mary*, which entered service the year after *Normandie* did and had a 9,100-kilowatt capacity in normal operation. Quite apart from propulsion, *Normandie* therefore was far and away the most totally electrified ship of her time. The turbo-dynamo sets were supplemented by 2 stand-by diesel generators each capable of developing 150 kilowatts in normal running and 187 kilowatts in overload.

Altogether, under normal operating conditions, the power of the turbo-electric propulsion system and that of the generators, with all in normal operation, add up to a total power of 146,800 kilowatts. With all systems in overload, including the back-up generators, the power could go as high as 167,274 kilowatts. The whole metropolitan network of Paris did not utilize more than 120,000 kilowatts at the time *Normandie* entered service. Moreover, this massive electrical power made *Normandie* the fourth largest thermal power station in Europe in 1935, and the only one not on land. The power generated on the ship could have supplied enough electricity for one-quarter of France.

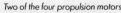

Two of the four propulsion motors

The main propulsion control panel

cated to make a rapid tour of the liner under the guidance of Commander Thoreux, Chief Purser Villar, and Security Officer Le Huédé. He went through the principal facilities on the upper decks whose dimensions, elegance, and decoration left him visibly impressed. Some 700 persons had already surged into these spaces, conveyed from Paris that afternoon on two special trains.

At 8:00 P.M., following a short rest in his stateroom, where he joined Mme Lebrun, the President, this time in full evening dress, complete with the great ribbon of the Legion of Honor, made his way toward the first-class Dining Room for the gala dinner.

It was a spectacular scene: an immense hall measuring 282 feet long, 46 feet wide, and 28 feet high — larger than the Hall of Mirrors at Versailles — a sumptuous environment of onyx, gold, and crystal, shimmering showers of light refracted by a ceiling of gilded coffers, by walls clad in panels of molded, engraved, and etched glass, by Lalique's sconces and "fire pot" light towers, by the splendid table settings and brilliant flowers. Round the tables men in formal attire ablaze with medals and multicolored decorations and women in evening dress bearing the labels of the greatest couturiers stood to applaud the entrance of the President of the Republic, whom the stentorian voice of maître d'hôtel Olivier Naffrechoux had just announced.

At the head table, dominated by Dejean's monumental gilded figure of Peace holding an olive branch, gathered the Head of State and Mme Lebrun, members of the cabinet and diplomatic corps, the president of the Compagnie Générale Transatlantique, and other such luminaries. In addition to the 650 guests gracing the Dining Room were another 350 who could not be fitted in and thus took their dinner in the adjacent tourist-class dining room.

In the kitchen, meanwhile, it was indeed a baptism by fire! The reputation of the ship hung in the balance. At the head of his brigade of 210 men, Chef Magrin stood watch over the storm and succeeded in serving a thousand meals with a menu equal to the best and the most noble traditions of French gastronomy — and the transatlantic service.

It was, therefore, in a state of total euphoria that the one thousand guests of the French Line composed themselves to sit through a series of speeches. That of Governor General Olivier stressed the consideration given to comfort and harmony, a concern that had embraced the whole of the boat's facilities, even those in third class, as well as those designed for petty officers and staff: "It is not solely for a few super-rich guests that the world's most beautiful transatlantic liner, a product of egalitarian France, has been created." He also emphasized the necessity of harmonious competition on the North Atlantic: "Our aim is not to diminish the foreign lines. It is to expand world shipping in the spirit of progress." And, in reference to Cunard's announcement of the approaching entrance into service of the *Queen Mary*, Olivier concluded: "This is why we rejoice that England joins us with her splendid *Queen Mary* in the domain of five-day crossings and bimonthly departures."

The speech of the Merchant Marine Minister lauded the achievement just carried off: "By her name, which glorifies one of the most beautiful provinces in France, by her technical features, which bear admirable witness to the quality of our science and industry, by her beauty, which honors French art, by her mission, which is to bring us more closely together with our great friends, the Americans, *Normandie* is worthy to become the flagship of France on the high seas of the world."

Thereafter the President of the Republic delivered a spirited homage "to all those — engineers, workers, craftsmen, and artists — whose efforts and care have produced such a masterpiece of comfort, art, and beauty." He underlined the national character of the endeavor, declaring: "Because — and this we should bear foremost in our minds — *Normandie* is a realization of an essentially national order. There is not a province, a big city, a major industry, an outstanding art that did not participate. Under the *tricolore*, it is her true face, in all its seductiveness and variety, that France will tomorrow send sailing across the seas."

President Lebrun also justified the prestigious nature of the enterprise when he added: "Should we regret having aimed too high, when only too often we have been reproached for doing the opposite? There have been quite enough occasions when our notions could be blamed for an excess of caution and pusillanimity. This time, at least, let us be proud of our daring and our work. Is it impermissible to hope for a future more favorable than the depressing time in which we live, and must optimism be considered a subversive doctrine? On the contrary, let us admire those who, acknowledging neither discouragement nor regret, have not been afraid to see the adventure all the way through. They have had the faith that alone makes great things possible."

The President then concluded by giving his best wishes for successful sailing: "Go — with all the joyous élan of your propellers ploughing the sea with long furrows of silver, after a passing salute to and a brief stop among our friends in Great Britain — toward our sister Republic who, as a young people with a passion for the new, prepares to celebrate you for the grandeur of the effort and the magnificence of the achievement you represent!"

Now, on to the entertainment! It would unfold simultaneously in both the Theater and the Grand Lounge. The Theater's auditorium could seat only 375, whereas 2,000 guests had come aboard, thanks to two other special trains that arrived after dinner, swelling the flood of Parisians invited for the soirée.

The performance given in the Theater was a premier in every sense of the word. It had been prepared by Robert Trébor, who would thereafter serve as director of the *Normandie* Theater. Manager of the Madeleine Theater in Paris and president of the Association of Paris Theater Directors, Trébor was as charming as he was effective. With friends galore, he could, "out of his sleeve," pull every great star of the period, French or international.

For the premier Trébor offered a program tailored to *Normandie*'s prestigious setting. For example, the master of ceremonies was that wittiest of all Parisians, Saint Granier. *Le Billet de loterie*, a play written for the occasion — a true à-propos or *pièce d'occasion* — was by Francis de Croisset, one of the era's most talented playwrights. The distinguished audience saw it performed by none other than Gaby Morlay and Victor Boucher, two of the Paris boulevards' greatest comedians. In a cantata dedicated to the liner, a work by composer René Dorin and lyricist Henri Casadesus, opera singers Georges Thill and Fanny Heldy ennobled the soirée with their resplendent voices.

In the Grand Lounge the program held its own quite successfully with the one given in the Theater. Here, the popular singer Jean Marsac introduced the corps de ballet from the

The Queen Mary

Paris Opéra led by Aveline, Mireille in her latest creations, and other numbers, which included mimes, acrobats, and cabaret artists.

Following the prepared entertainment, President Lebrun mingled with guests in the jam-packed lounges, opened the ball, and then prudently retired, while the night owls continued celebrating a while longer before returning to their cabins. The crowd was so large that 500 of the guests had to be lodged on board the *Paris*, moored just behind *Normandie* at post no. 2 of the new Gare Maritime.

On its debut night, *Normandie* had had a *succès fou*.

In succeeding days still further ceremonies and social events marked the birth of *Normandie*. At 8 o'clock in the morning after the debut, President Lebrun met the entire general staff of the liner and, on the Promenade Deck, received a delegation of 150 men from the ship's crew. A graduate of the École Polytechnique, Lebrun then inspected the engines under the guidance of Chief Engineer Hazard, before disembarking. Shortly thereafter another special train left, returning the celebrants to their homes in Paris.

The cleaning crews scarcely had time to tidy up from the night before when a new wave of visitors rolled in during the late morning, set afloat by two more special trains from Paris, this time filled with 750 steamship agents and members of the press. Yet another gastronomic lunch and a further tour of the liner. By the end of the afternoon all had returned to the capital.

Now the decks were cleared for the arrival of the local Havrais and Norman gentry, who had their turn at the sparkling new liner. Dressed for the occasion in evening clothes, they attended another gala, this one staged in the Grand Lounge with a program of numbers organized by Robert Trébor.

The festivities of the 25th would even surpass the brilliance and elegance of everything that had gone before. In the wake of the official world and the business world, it was the world of society which came aboard *Normandie* that evening. The new arrivals were paying guests who had responded to an invitation from Mme Pierre Étienne Flandin, the wife of the Premier, to attend a *fête* in benefit of the Seamen's Fund and the unemployed. The program — soon to become a tradition — included a special round-trip Le Havre–Paris train, a dinner, and then entertainment in the Theater and Grand Lounge, followed by a ball. Premier Flandin would have made a personal appearance, but for the injuries he had suffered in an automobile accident several days earlier. The Groupement des Saisons de Paris had marshaled *le Tout-Paris* — that is, all the best-known names from the aristocracy, the *haute bourgeoisie*, business, the arts, etc. – whose own luxury and elegance easily rivaled those already seen in the sumptuous setting of the Dining Room, Grand Lounge, and Theater.

For this soirée, Robert Trébor exceeded himself in gaining the cooperation of the most prestigious artists of the day. In the Theater the leader of the revels was André de Fouquières. The Comédie Française appeared in the person of Catherine Fonteney, while Villabella of the Opéra and Fanely Revoil of the Porte-Saint-Martin sang *bel canto*. Alice Field and Jean Debucourt played a scene written by Louis Verneuil. Reynaldo Hahn conducted his *Divertissement pour une fête de nuit*, and André Brulé did a conjuring act. In the Grand Lounge, Jean Marsac's variety show provided an entertainment of fully equal quality. From the 2,000 visitors *Normandie* had just received in the name of charity, she created 2,000 new devotees who would go away singing her praises and spreading her fame.

Three days to go before the great departure! Meanwhile, however, the program of inaugural ceremonies called for another pair of events: the consecration of the Chapel and a reception for travel agents. On the 27th, therefore, the temporal gave way to the spiritual. At 11 o'clock a cortege of prelates filed in, led by Monsignor Dubois de la Villerabel, Archbishop of Rouen, Canon Alléaume and the Archpriest of Le Havre, and the Very Rev. Father Dom Pierdait, Abbot of Saint-Wandrille received His Eminence Cardinal Verdier, Archbishop of Paris, who had come specially to preside at the ceremony. Henri Cangardel represented the Compagnie Générale Transatlantique.

Following the benediction, attended by a delegation from the liner's general staff and crew, along with a variety of local personalities, a luncheon was served on board. Cangardel, in a short but eloquent address, made this statement: "Today, Your Eminence, it is a great liner that we ask you to bless. Those who built this fast and luxurious ship have not committed a sin of pride. They have simply desired that France engage in international competition with a vessel worthy of her. *Normandie* provides a true image of what our country can produce."

On the morning of May 29 one final wave of guests swept on to *Normandie*. It was composed of travel agents from France and neighboring countries, the importance of whose tour of the ship could hardly be exaggerated. In terms of the tourist market, the luncheon served these guests was no less significant for the boat's reputation than those that had gone before.

Scarcely had the travel agents left the boat when the first passengers booked for the inaugural crossing began to arrive. Among these were godmother Mme Albert Lebrun, Minister William Bertrand, and their suites.

At the last moment a technical problem caused Henri Cangardel, also on board for the trip, and the liner's general staff, especially Chief Engineer Hazard, one final anxiety attack. Shortly before noon, just five hours prior to the scheduled departure, *Normandie* lost all electrical power. The lights went out, elevators and freight lifts suddenly stuck, winches for loading luggage ceased to turn, kitchen ovens went cold. Last-minute sabotage! It looked as if the departure had been compromised. After a worried hour, the lights came back on, and order was restored. The total shut-down of the generators had been caused by an extremely sensitive automatic protective device designed to activate the second it detected a functional anomaly, which had been the case when the turbo-dynamos were cut off.

The last operations went forward normally and, at 6:25 P.M., *Normandie* pulled away from her pier and got under way for New York via Southampton. The big moment had arrived for the ship to undergo the most serious and decisive of her tests: the ocean and the transatlantic clientele. Upon the results hinged the whole of her future!

The Maiden Voyage across the Atlantic

A few minutes later, aided by the tugs *Minatoure*, *Titan*, and *Ursus* flying the CGT colors, *Normandie* cleared Le Havre's jetties. They were loaded with people. The whole of the port city had returned to salute the ship's first departure. People were there from all over France and adjacent countries. Every hotel room had been booked weeks earlier in anticipation of the event. With a great commotion of *vivats*, flailing arms, and waving handkerchiefs, the crowd wished *Normandie* a safe and jolly voyage.

As a tribute to that immense gathering, as well as to the tugs and host of escort craft, *Normandie* sounded three long, deep-throated notes on her powerful horn. The semaphore flag then came down three times. The great liner slipped into the Channel after having disembarked the pilot.

At 7:28 P.M. the engines were set in a cruising mode, while on board life began to get itself organized. The multiple wheels of this formidable floating machine would now be broken in on the ocean itself. All operatives were at their posts, ready to carry out orders from Captain Pugnet, who, from the bridge, commanded the voyage and, alone, assumed full responsibility for it.

How many operatives were there? And who were they? Under the command of Captain René Pugnet, assisted by Commander Pierre Thoreux, the general staff comprised: bridge service: 16 officers, 6 of them radio operators; passenger service: 6 pursers and 3 doctors; engine service: 21 officer engineers and 20 assistants.

Head Chef Magrin

The crew consisted of:
120 petty officers and sailors;
184 mechanics;
972 passenger service.

The total, not counting the Captain and his deputy, came to 63 officers and 1,276 crew. On the maiden crossing, they were at the service of 1,261 passengers, 830 of them in first class, 308 in tourist class, and 123 in third class.

The General Staff

Captain René Pugnet, chosen as commander of the CGT flagship, had entered the company's service in 1907, following the sailor's tough apprenticeship. Second Captain in

Normandie departing Le Havre

1914 and mobilized, he was drafted into naval aviation and made commander of a hydroplane base in Ajaccio. He distinguished himself in several brilliant actions, mainly in the defense of the airbase on Corfu. Named Captain on January 1, 1918, Pugnet assumed command of various cargo ships before being put in charge of the *Jacques Cartier*, the period's training vessel on which future captains were formed during long cruises. He then commanded the liner *Espagne*, which served the Saint-Nazaire–Havana–Vera Cruz route. In November 1928, Pugnet became replacement Captain on the New York route, and two years later he took command of the liner *Paris* before being selected for *Normandie*.

René Pugnet was not only a seaman of vast experience and a peerless handler of ships; he was also very much a man of the world, as well as something of an artist. Great nephew of the sculptor Bartholdi, whose *Liberty* still lights up the world at the entrance to New York Harbor, he displayed no small amount of talent in painting and portraiture. Intellectually curious and avid for everything new, he had carried out quite important research and experimentation in color photography. Then, too, he was a discriminating music-lover who played both violin and piano and amused himself making his own instruments. As if this were not enough, he had also become an accomplished aviator and a fine sportsman, a first-class fencer, and occasionally a boxer. A good man in every sense of the word! On the moral plane, Pugnet had character, while physically, he was a force of nature.

As his assistant, the French Line appointed another officer of exceptional qualities: Commander Pierre Thoreux. A Breton, the son and grandson of sailors, he too had been trained on Cape Horn sailing ships. *Tradition oblige!* From the four-masted bark *Valparaiso* of the Bordes Company, which "did" Chili, the twenty-year-old Thoreux transferred to the battleship *Brennus*, a training vessel for Merchant Marine officers. After joining the CGT with the rank of Lieutenant, he was mobilized in 1914 and assigned to the cruiser *Kléber* for action in the Dardanelles campaign. When his ship struck a mine in 1917, he was one of the few to survive. By the end of the war he had become commander of the second division of hunter-killer submarines based on the Algerian port of Bône. At demobilization, Thoreux rejoined the French Line, where he was posted as officer of the watch on the New York liners.

Thoreux assumed his first command in 1931 on the *Rochambeau*, then went on to command the *Cuba*, the *De Grasse* in 1932, the *France* in 1933, and the *Île de France* in 1934. He was finally made Commander, or Second Captain, on *Normandie*, whose full command he assumed at Pugnet's retirement in 1936.

Thoreux was a calm man. Precise and methodical, he kept an eye on everything and took charge by virtue of his natural authority and strong character, the products of a profound maritime and scientific culture. And like Pugnet, he was also an accomplished man of the world. A handsome presence, Thoreux was much sought-after by the passengers, who valued his courteous reception and the sureness of his command.

The Pugnet-Thoreux tandem, whose fame spread day by day on both sides of the Atlantic, commanded a hand-picked general staff of officers.

In the engine room, Chief Engineer Jean Hazard had been

Chief Purser Villar

Purser Henry

Purser Mallet

Purser de Nieuwenhove

The complete crew of Normandie

General staff, deck

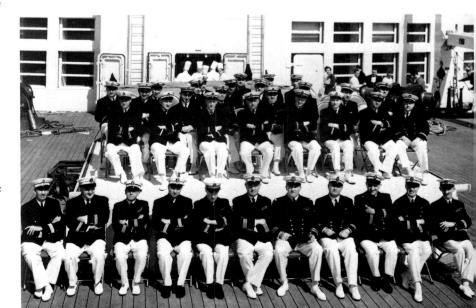

Chief Engineer Cusset

Chief Engineer Maurice Coquin in 1938

Dr. Bohec

General staff, engines

appointed on the basis of his technical mastery and intellectual astuteness. A man of immense culture and experience, he had witnessed the evolution of modern technology from coal-firing to oil-firing. He was also a leader of men. But in addition to these assets, he possessed an even greater quality in his great modesty. For him, the satisfaction to be gained from work well done and duty fulfilled meant far more than any other award he could possibly receive. And he had it in full measure aboard *Normandie* on May 25, 1935, during a quiet moment away from the noise and dazzle of the inaugural festivities. That day, in a discreet ceremony, he was made an officer of the Legion of Honor, bestowed by Henri Cangardel in the presence of Governor General Olivier, president of the CGT.

The civil or passenger service came under the authority of Chief Purser Henri Villar, who was, without a doubt, the most popular man in the whole of the transatlantic tribe. He too had come up through the ranks on the principal ships of the French Line, the *France* and the *Paris*. But it was on the *Île de France*, at the side of the famous Captain Blancart, that he had won his great fame. To legendary courtesy (he treated every passenger as his own personal guest) Villar brought a great natural distinction, technical sureness, an infallible memory, and the incomparable talents of a diplomat. He would in fact set a style, not only for the French Line but also on competing foreign ships, and would endow the role of purser with an unprecedented cachet, importance, and prestige. Villar became one of the primary ingredients of *Normandie*'s success.

As Villar's second, Purser Jean Henry had his own success in winning unanimous favor among the passengers, doing so by his unfailing amiability, efficiency, and quick wit. The charm of the welcome he extended was further enhanced by a touch of originality, which came in the form of his on-board collection of elephants. It delighted the visitors to his suite and long remained famous in the annals of the North Atlantic service.

This remarkable pleiad of officers unleashed the full array of their talents during the maiden voyage, when the reputation of *Normandie* was held in the balance by a particularly demanding and difficult clientele.

The Call at Southampton

The passengers barely had time to settle into their cabins, meet their stewards and chambermaids, see the maître d'hôtel about places at table, reserve deck chairs, or locate the public rooms, such as the Winter Garden, the Chapel, or the Swimming Pool, before *Normandie* came into view of the Isle of Wight. At 11:15 P.M. she met the pilot boat from Southampton.

The English awaited the great French liner with considerable curiosity and a certain amount of concern. After all, she was designed to be the rival of their forthcoming *Queen Mary*. Still, they gave the liner a warm and vociferous reception. On the ferries *Colshot* and *Greetings*, loaded with passengers from London, as well as municipal authorities, bands played *La Marseillaise*. *Normandie* responded with a rousing rendition of "God Save the King" broadcast over her loudspeakers. On this day, at least, it was *l'entente cordiale*!

Numerous other port craft also came alongside, marine Lilliputians swarming about the Gulliver of the seas. They carried hundreds of visitors who received a friendly welcome at the gangway. A tour of the liner was organized just for them. And they responded with visibly sincere admiration, which affected the French, especially those responsible for *Normandie*, as a kind of reward and tribute that could be appreciated all the more for having come from connoisseurs.

But there was a schedule to keep, and so the demonstrations had to be cut short; otherwise, the call would have lasted until dawn. At 3:07 A.M. *Normandie* weighed anchor and got under way. The Atlantic spread wide before her.

At 10 o'clock on the morning of May 30, the liner came up by the Scilly Islands and the famous Bishop's Rock lighthouse, the point of departure for calculating the speed used to establish the record for the mythical Blue Ribbon. The "top" was sighted from the bridge, and the race was on.

All the while that on the bridge and in the lounges and theater, social events and attractions succeeded one another at such a pace that the buffeted passengers hardly knew which way to turn, or when they would ever have time to view the sea, those in charge of the engines had to deal with problems of a totally different sort. First of all, there were the worrisome vibrations, the cause and full effect of which no one had yet had either the time or the opportunity to discover.

Now the trouble could be looked into. The unsteadiness affected a full third of the aft section and thus mainly the public lounges in third class, a fact that, of course, could not escape the critical scrutiny of the journalists, one of whom would write: "It quivers a bit. Very little, that is, in the first-class dining room. There it's really nothing. Just the sensation of a passing bus. Altogether tolerable. Which it isn't, however, in tourist class. The cabin I've just visited, that of our photographer, dances a convulsive jig like a roaring storm fit for opera!" The engineers and mechanics were on edge, because the trembling was also causing problems in the

Wheel preserved at the South Street Seaport Museum in New York City

The bridge on Normandie

electrical system meant to circulate sweet and salt water.

Several other technical troubles plagued the voyage, particularly during the day of May 31. The rupture of a condenser tube allowed sea water into the central starboard alternating turbo, which required that the equipment be shut down for more than 24 hours, the time necessary to empty the connecting boilers, rinse and then refill them with distilled water. But thanks to her turbo-electric propulsion, Normandie suffered only a 25 percent loss of power, and thus could maintain a speed of 28.72 knots. The rest of the crossing went off to perfection, with Normandie "gobbling up" miles at a rate that accelerated as she traveled.

The speed data for the maiden voyage, as recorded at noon each day, are the following:

May 30: 228 miles at 26.33 knots
May 31: 744 miles at 29.08 knots
June 1: 718 miles at 28.07 knots
June 2: 748 miles at 29.92 knots
June 3: 754 miles at 31.04 knots

Beginning at noon on the 2nd of June, everyone felt certain that victory was at hand and got set to celebrate — under a symbolic Blue Ribbon! In an atmosphere of almost feverish excitement, the passengers contrived to dress entirely in blue, decorate the ship blue, and make an enormous banner of blue muslin, some 98 feet long, which would soon be raised on the high mast.

That evening at dinner, Henri Cangardel extemporized a speech for the occasion: "Tonight Normandie is 'vowed to blue.' The azur dresses and blue scarfs worn on this joyous occasion signal the world record broken by our giant of the seas. Blue Ribbon, Blue Ribbon! The trophy so ardently coveted by world steamshippers in the rapid crossing of the North Atlantic. We have wanted blue to be the order of the day in honor of the long streamer that flies from our high mast to the greater glory of the French Merchant Marine!"

In the wee hours of June 3, Normandie was in sight of the American coastline. At 5:00 in the morning she came up on the Nantucket lightship. At 11:30 she passed Ambrose light and took on the pilot.

On the bridge "a reckoning was then made." The crossing from Bishop's Rock to the Ambrose lightship had been exactly 2,907 miles, and Normandie had taken 4 days, 3 hours, and 2 minutes to cover them, which made an average speed of 29.98 knots. For the whole of the distance from Le Havre to New York, which was 3,266 miles, the average speed

The Blue Ribbon on arrival in New York

The Hales Trophy

came to 29.6 knots. The record set by the *Rex* at 28.92 knots had therefore been officially broken, and the Blue Ribbon won!

The news simply carried the pervasive enthusiasm to a still higher and almost hysterical pitch. At the Captain's order the great flag was raised as a companion to the long blue pennant that still streamed in the wind.

In the midst of the general commotion and rejoicing, Antonio Cosulich, president of the Italian Line, and Henri Cangardel gave one another a fraternal embrace, while a telegram was read congratulating Captain Pugnet on behalf of the captain of the *Rex*, who declared that his ship ceded the Blue Ribbon "with a smile"!

From that moment on people all but rioted as the noise and tumult swelled minute by minute. The passengers threw themselves into a veritable frenzy, which reached a state of paroxysm when *Normandie*, following her stately glide up the Hudson against the backdrop of Manhattan's skyscrapers, turned into Pier 88.

The Triumphant Arrival in New York

Writers and journalists pulled out all the stops in describing the scene. *Normandie* had a clutch of scribblers on board, including some of the era's most famous. Indeed, they were the most celebrated of all the celebrities. Prudence, therefore, dictates that they be cited in alphabetical order: Jacques Baschet, Gérard Bauer, Pierre Brisson, Blaise Cendrars,

André Chevrillon, Colette accompanied by her husband Maurice Goudeket, Claude Farrère, Bertrand de Jouvenel, Raymond Lestonnat, Lugné-Poë, Odette Pannetier, Jean-Michel Pagès, Olivier Quéant, Jean de Rovera, Philippe Soupault, François de Tessan, and Pierre Wolff.

After a berthing maneuver that confirmed the extraordinary flexibility of her turbo-electric propulsion, *Normandie* came smoothly alongside a Pier 88 completely beribboned in tricolor and chockablock with spectators. Behind them the French national anthem rang out once again, now from a municipal band perched on a balcony.

A few minutes before, as the liner was entering the Hudson, motorboats had put on board a group of high-ranking officials come to reconnoiter and welcome *Normandie* along with Mme Albert Lebrun and her suite. In the greeting party were the Chief of Protocol from the State Department, the Honorable Richard Southgate; His Excellency, the Ambassador of France and Mme de Laboulaye; de Fontenelle, the French Consul General in New York; Morin de Linclays, principal representative of the Compagnie Générale Transatlantique; Joseph Baldwin, president of the reception committee; and Mrs. Fiorello La Guardia, wife of the Mayor of New York City, who presented Mme Lebrun with a huge sheaf of flowers in the form of a key to the City of New York.

That evening a brilliant dinner was given in the banquet hall of the Waldorf-Astoria — decorated in the French national colors — by Mayor and Mrs. La Guardia in honor of

Reception in the Grand Lounge with Commander Thoreux at the center and, on his right, H. Keates Hales, the trophy's donor

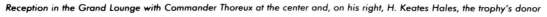

The arrival in New York

The Statue of Liberty greeting Normandie

Mme Lebrun and William Bertrand, the representative of the French government. The occasion brought warm and gracious speeches from the Mayor, Senator Baldwin, and Lieutenant Governor Bray.

Meanwhile, *Normandie* was staging another soirée, with Americans pouring on board to inspect the facilities and marvel at the scale and beauty of the décor.

The next day, June 4, life began early on board, at 7:45, with a Mass in the Chapel followed by a ceremony that brought together a hundred nuns from the French Hospital and some 150 members of the local Catholic clergy.

At 10:30 Mme Lebrun and the members of the French delegation left for Washington at the invitation of President and Mrs. Franklin D. Roosevelt. There they were greeted by Secretary of State and Mrs. Cordell Hull.

A small, private reception followed at the White House, where Mrs. Roosevelt gave a tea for the Dames de France, while the President held a meeting with Minister William Bertrand and his party.

From 5:00 to 7:00 P.M. M. and Mme Laboulaye were hosts during a reception at the French Embassy. The day ended with a grand dinner given by the Roosevelts at the White House.

In New York, *Normandie* was the scene of a second soirée and then a ball, this too attended by hundreds of invited guests.

On June 5, while Mme Lebrun was taken by her American hosts to visit Mount Vernon, *Normandie* continued to be the setting of various events, beginning with a Protestant service

for some 200 local clergymen and continuing with wave upon wave of visitors.

That evening it was France's turn to receive. The ship's great Dining Room and lounges were ablaze with light for a formal dinner attended by the whole of American high society, along with officials and representatives of the diplomatic corps.

The French Ambassador, the Minister of the Merchant Marine, and the President of the Compagnie Générale Transatlantique took turns proclaiming Franco-American friendship, which *Normandie*'s entry into service promised to make closer and more cordial than ever.

A sumptuous soirée extended the dinner and concluded with a *fête* given, for the benefit of the Seamen's Church Institute, in the Starlight Roof on the 19th floor of the Waldorf-Astoria, which Mme Lebrun honored with her presence. The occasion was also brightened with a show of French *haute couture* put on by Parisian models brought to New York on board *Normandie*.

The 6th of June brought further organized tours of the liner, new receptions, dinners, and entertainment, all in keeping with a ritual that now was almost commonplace for the Americans.

June 7 was the scheduled date of departure. That morning Mme Lebrun and the official French delegation visited the French hospital in New York and then were officially received at City Hall by the Mayor of New York City. This brought a new round of mutually complimentary speeches and gifts, all in a climate that the close ties developed during

Morin de Linclays, the French Line's representative in New York

The crowd at Battery Park on the tip of Manhattan Island overlooking New York Harbor

Coming alongside at Pier 88 in New York

the previous days and the enthusiastic atmosphere generated by *Normandie*'s visit had rendered more than friendly — really affectionate!

However, even the best of things must come to an end, and at 12:30 *Normandie* pulled away — regretfully — from Pier 88 and set sail for Le Havre, applauded by a multitude of Americans who came to cheer what for several days had been the talk of not only New York City but also the entire United States.

Normandie arrived at Le Havre on June 12, having completed the crossing at an average speed of 30.35 knots. The voyage recorded for purposes of the Blue Ribbon, from Ambrose light to Bishop's Rock, a distance of 3,015 miles, was done in 4 days, 3 hours, and 28 minutes — that is, at an average speed of 30.31 knots, with 32.30 knots attained at one point. Thus, *Normandie* had broken her own record!

A sizable crowd — the Havrais population supplemented by thousands of curious souls brought from everywhere on special trains organized for the occasion by travel agents — had surged onto the jetties and the waterfront drive, all the way from Sainte-Adresse, whose summit was bristling with serried ranks of spectators. The city, the port, and everything afloat were decked out in flags in honor of the victorious liner, which brought back the trophy and with it paid homage to its home port. The hydroplane *Lieutenant de vaisseau Paris*, another star performer of the 1930s, took to the air specially to salute *Normandie* and escorted her by flying over the access channel.

The other voyages made by *Normandie* in the year 1935 went off with equal success, despite the vibrations that unfortunately continued to affect the ship. In the course of the 18 crossings made during her first year of service, the liner transported 17,872 passengers, making an average of 992 per voyage.

To resolve the stubborn problem of the unsteadiness, which could no longer be tolerated, a decision was made to stop *Normandie* and to lay her up in Le Havre. She would remain there, in dry dock and berthed, from October 28, 1935, to April 28, 1936.

Normandie resumed normal service in May 1936, just as the Cunard Line entered the scene with its *Queen Mary*, which the King and Queen of England had inaugurated to great pomp. The two giants were now in direct competition on that artery, so vital to steamship companies, known as the North Atlantic Route.

With characteristics quite close to those of *Normandie* — 1,019 feet long, 80.773 gross registered tonnage — the new British liner, with its 200,000 horsepower, possessed a distinctively more powerful driving apparatus. Even so, it took the *Queen Mary* three months to win the Blue Ribbon from *Normandie* by making, in August 1936, a crossing at an average speed of 30.14 knots on the way out and 30.63 knots on the way back. *Normandie* bowed sportingly before this achievement, but the directors and engineers of the French Line were not ready to give up, mindful of the extra margin their contender still had in reserve.

Commercially, the year 1936 saw *Normandie* transport 27,292 passengers on 30 voyages, making an average load of 909 per crossing.

The technical rest taken during the winter of 1936–37 was used to make improvements in the boilers allowing travel with an extra charge of power. The ship was also equipped with new propellers designed, like the first ones, by the engineer Brard, but this time appropriating characteristics of Mérot du Barré's four-bladed propellers and aiming for more efficient propulsion.

New Feats by *Normandie*

In Paris the 1937 World's Fair was in full swing, an event favorable to passenger traffic, a good share of which the French Line claimed, thanks to its sensational flagship. Moreover, one of the most popular pavilions at the fair was called *Aboard the Normandie,* a deluxe restaurant managed by Purser Jean Henry on special assignment from the liner. It drew a large international clientele.

At Le Havre, on October 12, 1937, Governor General Olivier and Henri Cangardel organized a pre-sail visit to

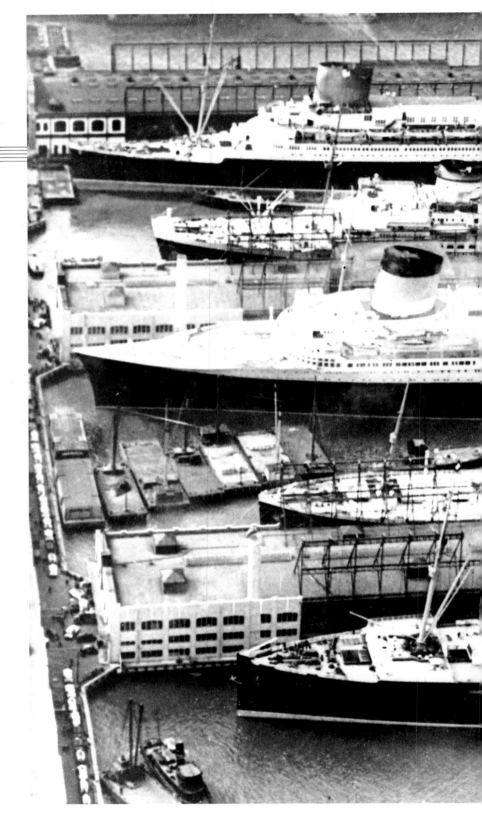

the ship during the morning for the benefit of the managers of the fair's foreign pavilions, led by M. Edmond Labbé, general manager of the fair. Thereafter the group gathered for lunch at the Hôtel Frascati. From that vantage point, over dessert, they watched through the glazed bays overlooking the port as the liner made her departure. The majestic ship cleared the channels and glided slowly before their eyes. The spectacle so impressed them that as a single body they rose and sang *La Marseillaise!* One more tribute, and one of international significance, paid by way of *Normandie* to the creative genius of France.

In the technical sphere, the improved efficiency and power

Side by side, on March 25, 1937, in the Port of New York: Berengaria, George, Normandie, Rex, and Europa

of the ship at sea could be clearly noted since the last modifications. And the results were soon in coming. During the return trip from New York, from the 18th to the 23rd of May 1937, the 2,978-mile distance from Ambrose light to Bishop's Rock was covered in 4 days and 6 minutes at an average speed of 30.99 knots. This represented an average developed horsepower of about 180,000.

The record set by the *Queen Mary* had been broken! But *Normandie* did not stop there, and on her thirty-third voyage the liner, while returning from New York, would perform in ways that were then without parallel. Departing New York on August 4, *Normandie* passed Ambrose light at 5:36 P.M.

She was abreast of Bishop's Rock on August 8 at 7:43 P.M., having covered 2,936 miles in 3 days, 22 hours, and 7 minutes, making an average speed of 31.20 knots, which easily surpassed her own preceding record. Another technical feat came on the final day of this crossing when at one point the liner achieved developed horsepower of 195,850, making a speed of 32.70 knots!

These figures constituted a pinnacle that would not be capped until August 1938, when the more powerful *Queen Mary* won out at 31.69 knots, a record that remained unbroken until the liner *United States* entered the competition, after World War II, and smashed through at an average

Vibrations and Propellers

The engineers were on the whole agreed that the vibrations did not originate in the machines. On the other hand, they had observed that the period of vibration was precisely equal to the time it took for a propeller blade to replace, in relation to the ship's hull, the immediately preceding one. The original propellers comprised three blades, and the vibration period corresponded to the number of the propellers' rotations per minute multiplied by three.

But since no one knew whether the propellers were alone responsible for the vibrations, the engineers decided, additionally, to reinforce the struts supporting the propeller shafts and to change their shape. Moreover, a great deal of stiffening was added to the after third of the ship, so as to reinforce the structural frame. Some of this stiffening would have come anyway so as to prepare the Embarkation Deck, where the terrace outside the first-class Café-Grill originally lay, for a new lounge and bar serving passengers in tourist class.

The addition of this "deck house" would somewhat alter the ship's silhouette, which had seemed so perfect. At the same time, the original bridge wings, with their streamlined curvature, would be replaced with straight wings, which, albeit less elegant, made it easier to carry out berthing manoeuvers. On either side of the dome over the first-class Grand Lounge, were added a series of cabins for the radio-telegraph operators. The resulting enlargement of the upper Sun Deck made it possible to install a standard-size tennis court between the second and third funnels. Meanwhile, the Sun Deck between the second and third funnels got a row of covered, windbreaker benches aligned with the ship's longitudinal axis.

All these changes were made at Le Havre, from the end of November 1935 to the end of April 1936. They had the effect of making the ship

Three-bladed propellers and their connecting struts

Mérot du Barré

noticeably heavier, so that her draft went from 36'7" to 37' and her displacement from 68,836 tons to 70,171 tons. In May 1935 a provisional certificate of tonnage was issued for *Normandie* citing a gross registered tonnage of 79,280. Thereafter the construction of the new tourist-class lounge and various other enlargements would carry this weight to 82,779 tons, then, with the completion of the expansion work, to 83,423 tons, the final figure.

The old three-bladed propellers, with their 15'7" diameter, their 17'5" pitch, and their 23.20 ton weight, were replaced with new propellers designed by a CGT engineer, Arthur Mérot du Barré. The new four-bladed propellers — 16'5" in diameter, 24' pitch, and 27 tons — were meant to reduce the vibrations and prevent cavitation by means of a slower rate of rotation.

Thus transformed, *Normandie* pulled away on April 28, 1936, to run through a new series of sea trials. The improvements recorded were spectacular. At 30 knots the vibrations were less than 20 percent of what they had been, and they could be felt only in a few places.

cluded, were put in place. This third type was characterized by four blades, a diameter of 15'9", a pitch of 17'6", and a weight of 22,500 gross registered tons. Beginning with the very first voyage made by *Normandie* from the 11th to the 15th of March 1937, the remarkable efficiency of these screws was clearly evident, both in terms of propulsion and in those of stability, all of which were considerably improved over the preceding year.

Mounting the four-bladed propellers on April 22, 1936

Partial view of the four-bladed propellers, 1937

But to what should these welcome results be attributed? The new propellers? The new struts? The internal stiffening?

An unexpected event would soon enlighten the engineers. After returning to Le Havre, on April 30, a diver was sent down to inspect the redesigned screws. Resurfacing a half-hour later, he declared them to be in excellent condition — all *three* of them! The center port propeller had come loose and disappeared. Unable to believe his ears, Paul Romano and Captain Thoreux dispatched a second diver, who confirmed the information given by the first — to the utter consternation of everyone, since the liner was scheduled to leave for New York the following day. And there were no stand-by screws. Very quickly, *Normandie* was put into dry dock where the original tri-bladed pieces had remained. One of these propellers was mounted on the center port shaft, and, to prevent disequilibrium, one of the new screws was removed from the center starboard shaft and replaced with a three-bladed model, leaving the lateral shafts still fitted with the new propellers. In this way, *Normandie* was able to make her announced departure. Crossing the Channel at a reduced speed, she seemed to be none the worse for the last-minute half-measures taken at Le Havre. Alas, once the ship entered the Atlantic and resumed her cruising speed, the vibrations returned, almost as bad as in the preceding year.

Thus, the new form of the struts, the purpose of which was to make the water flow evenly toward the propellers, had little effect, other than perhaps increasing drag rather markedly.

As for the internal stiffening, so deleterious in its effect on the ship's appearance, it seemed only to displace the center of the vibrations more forward without reducing them very much. But it did prove that the problem lay solely with the propellers. Furthermore, by the time *Normandie* returned to Le Havre, two new screws had been delivered, allowing all four shafts to be fitted with four-bladed pieces and the vibrations to disappear forever.

But the new propellers themselves brought a pair of problems. Being too wide and too sharply pitched, they could not rotate faster than 190–195 turns per minute, owing to an increase in the resistant torque, and they also made it impossible to exceed 160,000 horsepower without risk of significant thermal fatigue in motors designed to generate that power by means of rotation in excess of 200 turns per minute. On the other hand, and quite unexpectedly, the new screws produced fairly significant cavitation at speeds above 25 knots, despite their slower rotation. Thus, they limited the ship's speed to a maximum of 30 knots.

Yet another set of propellers, designed like the first set by engineer Brard but with some of Mérot du Barré's anti-vibration features in-speed of more than 35 knots, with, true enough, an "acknowledged" horsepower of 243,000. Actually, the maximum power of this ship remains a secret to this day, her plans having been drawn up in cooperation with the United States Navy, which regarded the vessel as a cruiser as much as a passenger liner.

In 1937, Normandie demolished another record, this time for the number of passengers transported: 37,542 on 36 crossings, making an average of 1,042 per voyage. This figure would not be surpassed in the life remaining to Normandie. In 1938 the total came to 31,075 passengers on 34 crossings, for an average of 913, and in 1939, 18,727 on 21 crossings, averaging 891 per voyage.

In July 1938, Normandie celebrated her one-hundredth Atlantic crossing. By then she had covered 330,000 miles — the equivalent of more than 15 times around the world — at an average speed of 28.28 knots, without ever slowing down even for the worst winter storms, and had transported more than 100,000 passengers.

Cruises to the Antilles and Rio de Janeiro

In 1937 the French Line began studying the possibility of using Normandie as a cruise ship to provide a service out of New York for an American clientele with the habit of wintering in the Caribbean sun. The program and itinerary of the cruise were prepared in cooperation with Robert Whitcomb, one of the most respected travel agencies in the United States.

The cruise went forward from the 5th to the 27th of February 1938, making stops at Nassau in the Bahamas on February 7, at Trinidad on the 9th, at Rio from the 15th through the 19th, and at Fort-de-France on the 24th. Almost 1,000 passengers were aboard, among them M. d'Ormesson, the French Ambassador, who was returning to his post in Brazil.

The cruise was an enormous success. No better evidence of it could be found than in a pair of radio messages, one French and the other Brazilian, the laconicism of which tells more than any amount of description could. The first came from Morin de Linclays, general representative of the French Line in the United States, who was aboard, and went to Henri Cangardel in Paris. The second originated with the Brazilian Foreign Minister, His Excellency Mgr. Mario Depumental Brandos.

Radio Normandie:

Liner's Rio arrival ended up sensational. Stop. Largest and most beautiful ship created considerable interest and curiosity. Stop. Several thousand visitors every day and several tens of thousands

came from surrounding area to see boat from bay. Stop. Official dinner nine ministers present plus government officials and French organizations, military mission, lycée, French veterans. Stop. Great ball thousand persons Brazilian society, government, diplomatic corps. Prince and Princess Orléans Braganza. Magnificent soirée very elegant, drawing North American passengers together with Brazilian society. Stop. Yesterday afternoon garden party given at Petropolis by French Ambassador for five hundred people on occasion our layover. Same guests as aboard. Stop. Government, city, and press give Normandie warm welcome. Stop. Rex arrived almost unnoticed. Stop.

To M. Morin de Linclays:

The visit of your superb boat, which is an admirable creation of the artistic and scientific genius of France, has left us with the most agreeable, the strongest, and most lasting impression. Stop. You and the captain, officers, crew, and shipboard personnel have earned our liveliest admiration of your talent for organization, discipline, and exquisite courtesy worthy of the great people whom you so brilliantly represent and with whom we form the strongest and most solid ties of old friendship, confirmed by unparalleled intellectual and cultural influence. Stop. I am happy to send you the most cordial and sincere good wishes and my very ardent hope to see Normandie and our very distinguished guests soon return to this country, which will always be happy to offer them the most fraternal welcome.

Extraordinary as its success may have been, the cruise was also impressive for the incidents that marked it. For example, the day after the ship's sailing, on February 6, Dr. Bohec, assisted by Dr. Samuel, a New York surgeon among the passengers, removed the appendix of a female passenger and thus did the first operation ever performed aboard Normandie. Then, on February 7, the officers and crew mourned the sudden death of an officer engineer second class. February 11 brought another appendectomy, now complicated by septicaemia. Once again Drs. Bohec and Samuel performed an operation. The patient needed a blood transfusion, which was made possible when a young purser, Michel Couetoux du Tertre, became a donor. The female patient was saved, but just in time.

The call at Rio began badly. The ship arrived in sullen weather — rainy, gray, overcast — which totally spoiled the marvelous view of the bay. Sugarloaf was barely visible through the thick fog, while the upper reaches of Corcovado remained invisible.

Normandie stimulated enormous interest, but the arrangement for visits to the liner proved totally inadequate. Since the ship was moored in the channel, she could be approached only by tender ferries, motorboats, and other such harbor craft. The local agent literally collapsed under the avalanche of requests. Passes of every sort and source had been sold, many on the black market, without the ship's company having any means of determining their validity. The situation produced such an unforeseen flood of visitors that the crowd quickly exceeded the liner's capacity. The officers responsible for keeping order had no choice but to send them back to shore and to prevent the departure of ferries loaded with furiously protesting pass-holders who had paid their admission! A small riot broke out on the gangway. Normandie's own officers got roughed up, some of them even by the Brazilian police. Several, such as the young Lieutenant Robichon and Dr. Bohec, would leave Rio with bitter memories.

On the 24th the call at Fort-de-France took place under excellent conditions and in extremely beautiful weather. The official reception, presided over by the Governor of Martinique, proved most impressive. The entire population converged from every part of the island and prepared for a grand time, with the black and tricolor flags mingling in fraternal goodwill. Organized visits to the ship were ar-

ranged by means of a specially fitted-out tender and motorboats. Everything went off in perfect order. Captain Thoreux weighed anchor at 7:40 P.M. Responding to a request from Gratien Candace, the deputy for Guadeloupe and former minister, the liner sailed close to the Leeward Islands and floodlit her smokestacks to permit the inhabitants of Roseau and Basse-Terre to enjoy a night view of the ship.

Overall, Normandie's first cruise came off as an unqualified success on every count; commercial, financial, political, and promotional. The aftereffects of it, albeit impossible to measure precisely, worked wonders for the prestige of France.

In almost every detail, the cruise planned for 1939, from the 4th of February to the 28th, would be a repetition of the preceding one, the experience from which simply served to make the second voyage more impressive than the first.

Who would have predicted that Normandie had just logged one of the last great moments of her career, or that from the time she returned to her normal transatlantic route in March, her days would be numbered!

ART ON BOARD NORMANDIE

BRUNO FOUCART

Art on board *Normandie*

When it comes to the passenger ship *Normandie*, superlatives seem to flow quite naturally. The fastest and most luxurious liner of her time would also be the most beautiful. The muses decided to make their crossing on this boat and the arts to fly their standard from the same vessel. In the so-called "artistic" journals, enthusiasm knew no bounds: "Proportion, harmony, fantasy, and taste, all the flowers of France — it's your bouquet the liner *Normandie* will offer across the sea to the entire world," wrote Yvanoé Rambosson in *Mobilier et décoration*. For Magdeleine A. Dayot in *L'Art et les artistes*, the ship was "a floating museum of contemporary French art," a "first-class artistic creation, an ensemble unequaled by any other architectural or decorative event of our time." This liner, to use a kind of language now quite familiar but actually invented for *Normandie*, was simultaneously the "harbinger," the "ambassador," and the "showcase" not only of French technology but also of French art.

The so-called "national" character attributed to *Normandie* actually created a rather serious problem. The idea had been to call upon a whole pleiad of artists, vastly increase the amount of art usual in a great liner, and disperse it lavishly in lounges and cabins alike, as well as throughout all classes of accommodation, so that third-class passengers would not feel as if they were traveling in steerage. But would this program yield something representative of the 1930s? And just what was "a French art"? Posterity would respond, a bit prematurely, in the negative, or at least with a good measure of skepticism. The disappearance of *Normandie*, the Second World War, the triumph of abstraction after 1940 — all served to reject the great ship as a lost and unverifiable dream. "It is only too true that, for a century, France has been searching for a style. We are still groping, as the 1925 exhibition proved.... The experience of *Normandie* preceded that of 1937 [the Paris World's Fair]. And it runs into the same difficulties even now," was how Claude Roger-Marx summarized the situation.

Normandie was the product of a loose but all-important cooperation between the Société des Artistes Décorateurs and the Union des Arts Modernes. The SAD, founded in 1901 for the promotion of the decorative arts, had been organizing an annual salon since 1904. It was the SAD that created the décor for the "French Embassy" at the 1925 "Art Deco" exhibition. To be sure, Mallet-Stevens and Chareau were in charge of preparing the entrance hall to the Embassy, but their assignment provoked a certain amount of controversy,

since the "purists" constituted a minority in the SAD. Returning to the theories of Le Corbusier in *L'Esprit nouveau*, begun in 1920, Mallet-Stevens and Chareau would bring about a kind of "secession" by creating the UAM in 1930. Obviously, the teams in charge of *Normandie* called on the big guns in the SAD, and not on the "modernists" of the UAM. Herbst, Mallet-Stevens, Chareau, and Perriand were not approached, whereas Leleu, Süe and Mare, Dominique and Montagnac had been chosen to decorate the large, luxurious lounges, those symbols of effort brought to fruition. It was not the Delaunays, nor would it be Dufy, André Lhote, Lipchitz, or Laurens (the great founding Cubists, who probably would not have accepted even in the unlikely event they had been asked to participate) who took charge of decorating the grand lounges, but rather Dupas and Janniot, among others, those once despised but now cherished exponents of a classicizing modernism. Rather than quarrel with the choices made for *Normandie*, and criticize them as more arrière than avant garde, one would probably be better rewarded by taking a different approach and respecting the decisions as conceivably representative of a certain moment in the history of art. In this way the choices might be seen as part of an ongoing search for a modern, pleasing solution *à la française* to modern problems. To find an answer, we should consider the results or artifacts themselves, such as we can know and appreciate them from examining the period's documents and the evidence, as well as the vision, represented by several "salvaged" works.

Normandie's Immediate Ancestry

It was only after 1914 that decorators responsible for passenger liners had broken away from their long-established historicizing and eclectic traditions. This has often been demonstrated by contrasting the *France*, an "old-fashioned" ship laid on the stocks in 1910 and put into service in 1912, with the *Paris*, on stocks in 1913 and in service by 1921, and even the *Île de France*, ordered from the shipyards in 1926 and sent on her maiden voyage in 1927, the latter pair representative of the new generation of "modern" liners. When the *France* set sail she carried abroad the whole panoply of grand decorative styles that the French had inherited from the successive reigns of Louis XIII, XIV, XV, and XVI. In her dining room, one of the first to be a full three stories high, making a central void encircled by a gallery, it was the 18th century of Louis XV that reigned supreme. The grand staircase giving access to the dining room was supposedly in the manner of Robert de Cotte, especially his Hôtel de Toulouse (now the Banque de France). The conversation lounge, with its fluted Corinthian columns supporting a flattened,

The Grand Lounge of the Île de France

skylit vault, constituted an effort to bring on board the Palace of Versailles itself. Moreover, copies of portraits of Louis XIV and his family and of van der Meulen's battle scenes made it seem as if the passengers were traveling under the very eye of *le grand monarque*. Clearly, this historicizing mode stood at considerable remove from the contemporary development then under way in an art justifiably known as *nouveau*.

The reasons for such a conservative approach to design hardly seem persuasive, at least as given by Georges Philippar, president of the CGT's rival steamship company, the Messageries Maritimes, in a 1927 conference devoted to the decoration of passenger ships. "Until recent years, French lines were mostly decorated in the great styles of the past, Louis XVI and Empire in particular.... One might well fear that the adoption of an exclusively modern style of art would be a mistake, in that we have no way of knowing, at the time artists propose new ideas, which of them will 'survive' and become what is called a 'style.' It is evident that most of the art works ... inspired by the style of the Paris World's Fair of 1900, the style then called *art nouveau*, ceased to be tolerable less than six years later. Thus, had a ship been decorated in a manner suggested by artists of the period, the vessel would have come to look démodé in no time at all."

Given this simplistic excuse, it seems all the more regrettable that a liner was never entrusted to Hector Guimard or one of his disciples. Still, the Belle Époque taste for the 18th century (as in the façades of the Petit and Grand Palais) has its own proper place in the aesthetic history of the early 1900s. As an antidote to Art Nouveau's whiplash lines and febrile, organic forms, the neo-Louis XVI manner is closer than one might suspect to the structural rigors of Cubism. Indeed, it followed a parallel line of development and can be understood as another manifestation of the "return to order" that triumphed after 1914. Therefore, the grand historical schemes found in the pre-World War I liners were not quite so removed from the art of the 1920s as some would claim. More important, by introducing the palatial element — by installing décors that evoked famous historic residences — designers reinforced the sense of a relationship between luxury liners and palaces, a relationship that would become virtually consanguineous. But it was in the *Paris* that a taste for the modern first took hold in passenger ships. John Dal Piaz — the CGT president who had been so astute in grasping the evolutionary character of styles produced during the early 20th century, an evolution the war had merely slowed down — made contact as early as 1916 with the exponents of an art that would become "deco" in the aftermath of the 1925 exhibition. In the grand lounge of the *Paris*,

René Lalique left hardly a trace of Henri Nelson, the author of the historicizing re-creations in the *France*. A comparison of this ship's grand staircase, *à la* Robert de Cotte, with the same feature designed by Bouwens de Boijen for the *Paris* tells the whole story. The architectural solutions may be similar, but a purist aesthetic has taken over in the design of the pillars, tamed the curves of Edgar Brandt's ramp, and imposed a geometric rigor on the dome dominating a hall cinctured by galleries in the manner of the big department stores. The names of the decorators involved here will crop up again and again: Subes, Follot, Prou, Dufet. The *Paris*, therefore, became the proving ground for a new kind of passenger ship suitable to a 20th century that was already well under way.

Begun in 1926 and put into service in 1927, the *Île de France* was the elder sister of and model for *Normandie*, which began to rise at the Saint-Nazaire shipyards at the beginning of 1931 and sailed on her maiden voyage in 1935. The congruence in time between the *Île de France*'s conception and the Exposition des Arts Décoratifs in 1925 was too close for the one not to appear derived from the other. "On June 22, 1927, barely twenty months after the closure of the decorative arts exhibition, the liner *Île de France* weighed anchor, carrying toward New York the flower of the fresh, new art that had enchanted Paris for an entire summer," wrote Henri Clouzot. *Normandie*, in turn, would provide a prelude to the Paris World's Fair of 1937. Furthermore, the design team in charge of *Normandie* had already had their trial run on the *Île de France*. There Bouwens de Boijen created the *grande descente*, "that grandiose staircase which cleaves the ship to a depth of four decks," completely clad in gray Lanel stone and yellow marble. There Raymond Subes designed the metalwork banisters and handrails, using motifs infinitely richer and more dense than those he would create for *Normandie*. And this was symptomatic, for the evolution from the *Île de France* to *Normandie* would be marked by a tendency to greater concision, a more discreet opulence, an almost transparent kind of design, at the same time that the spaces would be more open and the architecture of the interior organized to more formal, sober effect.

The conversation lounge designed by Süe and Mare, who in this instance worked as architect-decorators, almost invites retrospective comparison with the future Grand Lounge that Bouwens and Expert eventually created for *Normandie*. On the *Île de France* the collaborators laid out a space measuring 79 by 59 feet, an immense volume flowing without interruption by either wall or conduit. However, they articulated the walls with deep-red pilasters and columns crowned by gilded capitals in the form of "simply knotted draperies." The overall impression of richness and architectural opulence was such that it reminded Clouzot of the Salon aux Maréchaux in the Tuileries, which had disappeared in 1871. The use of glass or lacquer on the walls of *Normandie's* Grand Lounge, even where they were animated by paintings, engravings, or shallow reliefs, endowed these spaces with a new fluidity. The dark, resonant red of the lacquered panels in the *Île de France* conversation lounge found an echo in *Normandie's* transparent silver and gold. Similarly, the motifs in the fabric Maurice Lauer designed for the *Île de France* furniture was of a much denser character than those he did for the first-class on *Normandie*. Another revealing comparison would be the *Île de France* châteaux images woven into the tapestry covering the canapés of the older ship with Gaudissart's light, exotic bouquets on the chairs in the *Normandie* lounge. "Let us admit," wrote Clouzot, "that in this formal room, an integrated program of modernism which brought forth the noble order of columns . . . [and] all those plastic elements clothing a naval structure like flesh on a skeleton, betrayed an excess of pure reason."

Pacon's smoking room on the *Île de France*, finished in a manner that would be echoed in Patou's Dining Room on *Normandie*, led "to that stripped-down beauty that our period has borrowed directly from the interiors of passenger liners, luxury trains, and automobiles." This permits us to trace modernity to specific locations and, simultaneously, to postulate that on the *Île de France*, as on *Normandie*, the smoking room was avant-garde. In the *Île de France* smoking room, Pacon's vertical wall panels of ash were joined by projecting metal srips, giving the room an armature-like solidity. Meanwhile, Patou's dining room for the same boat — measuring 75 feet long at the center, 144 feet along the lateral galleries, 88 feet wide, and 29 feet high — paralyzed "the impotent pen to capture the effect of that immense room at the heart of the ship." On *Normandie* the Dining Room would be 282 feet long, but the impact of that new space can be explained only by a determination on the part of the designer to do better as well as bigger. Like Pacon, Patou was moved to surpass himself.

Most of the artists who would work on *Normandie* had already been involved in the decoration of the *Île de France*. To be sure, Émile-Jacques Ruhlmann, who died in 1933, could not serve *Normandie* in the same way he had the *Île de France*. But the sculptors Poisson and Pommier, who in the *Île de France* conversation lounge had modeled in high, freestanding relief, first, the *Seine* and the *Aisne* and, then, the *Marne* and the *Oise*, would execute two of the bas-reliefs for the *Normandie* Dining Room. Moreover, Janniot, who in

the *Île de France* tea room had done a group centered on a handsome young poet, would give *Normandie* a beautiful young woman with stag representing the Fontainebleau nymph. Even though the erect, pedestaled statues of Baudry and Dejean stood guard over the vast spaces of her floating gastronomic temple, *Normandie* would be a realm, not of freestanding sculpture, but of bas-reliefs in which stone functioned like a wall hanging. Jaulmes, inexplicably, made no appearance on *Normandie*, although Dupas, who had contributed a personification of Gérard de Nerval's *Sylvie* to the *Île de France* tea room, would animate the glass walls of *Normandie's* Grand Lounge with his decorative fleets of ships. Leleu gave the *Île de France* her reading room and to *Normandie* one of her *grand luxe* suites. Dufet, who on *Normandie* would be responsible for a series of first-class staterooms done in the purest manner, had been assigned the children's playroom on board the *Île de France*. Once again, both ships would claim the services of decorators Marc Simon and René Prou and the painters Voguet and Edy Legrand.

The Conception of the Décor

Veritable teams of well-known, proven artists came together, therefore, and defined a style that would be as much *transat* as *art déco*. Unfortunately, the reasons why these particular artists were chosen cannot be easily sorted out. There was, of course, the determination on the part of President Dal Piaz to make the *Paris* and then the *Île de France* a reflection of the art and, even more, the ambience of contemporary France. "Why, Mesdames, would you, with your short skirts and bobbed hair, want to sit down in Louis XVI bergères?" was his rhetorical question at the time of the *Île de France's* inauguration. President Olivier would continue this youthful tradition, which in fact was said to have become a virtual law. No shipping magnate since has ever conceived the notion of mandating a style that would not be regarded by contemporaries as anything but characteristic of their time. Still, it is difficult to discern what the personal tastes of the CGT presidents may have been. Dal Piaz and Olivier did not have the same relationship to their liners as Louis XIV did to Versailles. No trace of their involvement with the design decisions remains, and their statements were not researched in time. What is known, at least, is the role that Léandre Vaillat played in the formulation of the *Île de France* décor, as this derived from the 1925 Exhibition.

For *Normandie*, the minutes of the CGT board meetings, being of necessity quite brief, give only the results and not the deliberations that led to them. On the 6th of October, 1931, for example, they indicate the "constitution of a committee of architects that will be responsible for studying a program of decoration and for ensuring its execution by decorators." The names cited were on the whole well known: "Messieurs Jean Patou, Pacon, Expert, and Bouwens de Boijen." October 20, 1931, was specified as the date on which work should begin. The minutes for December 21, 1932, state that "the decorative projects proposed by the architects Patou and Pacon are to be presented to the management at the beginning of January." On January 17, 1933, the request was made that the preliminary projects be modified in the light of more thorough research into "the incombustibility of the décor." The minutes for February 16, 1933, disclose a division of the spaces among the Patou-Pacon and Bouwens-Expert "teams." "Messieurs Patou and Pacon have been assigned the dining room and the great hall in first class, the chapel, the swimming pool and its adjacent facilities. Messieurs Bouwens and Expert are to do the large areas above the promenade deck, that is, the theater, hall, lounge, smoking room, grill room, bridge room, and café-terrace, it being understood that the two groups should cooperate in order to produce an harmonious ensemble."

Even though "simplified," the decorative program for *Normandie* would be astonishing in its amplitude. There was, for instance, the almost sublime contrast between the exigencies of surface, on a ship where everything was hemmed in by structure or function, and the apparent monumentality of the décor. By comparison with contemporary construction, at the time of HBM research into what would later be called the *minimum vital*, *Normandie* turned all the norms upside down. "The small dimensions of modern housing have left decorators unaccustomed to working on a large scale. . . . And so here is another benefit realized by *Normandie*. She recaptured the rhythm of grand decorative schemes that express such a keen sense of life, of big, comprehensive ideas or aims. Decorative art, one of the noblest of arts when thought of in terms of the Parthenon, our cathedrals, the Campo Santo of Pisa, was losing some of its true significance. Will the impetus from *Normandie* revive it?" asked Magdeleine A. Dayot. The reference to the Parthenon and the cathedrals raised a few eyebrows. Nonetheless, it would be picked up by other critics and observers, as if the *Normandie* enterprise were so coherent and ambitious that the CGT could assume the status of a sea god high above the plane of ordinary mortals. Within the circumscribed world of a ship everything takes on a certain power, an effect not always possible in contemporary projects on land. Thus, *Normandie* provided a crutch for

those who had only to cite the liner by way of excusing the dryness and poverty of their own creations. *Normandie*, in fact, had little to do with the facile qualities of the so-called *paquebot* style.

It was *Normandie* which proved that the "machine for living" imagined by Le Corbusier could take inspiration from high-speed motors and luxury cars and trains. However, that cathedral-palace served an almighty god and king, who came in the guise of what the French call *dépaysement*, a special freedom of spirit and comfort made possible by an ocean voyage. Henri Clouzot explained, in relation to the *Île de France*, that the demands and expectations of passengers are not those found on land. There, "we may want things that are crisper, more precise and direct, ensembles that reveal themselves at the first glance as if perceived through the window of a moving vehicle. But at sea, the conditions are reversed. It is the house that moves at full speed, where the occupants have the sensation of absolute repose. . . . In the leisure of this sumptuous patio, our appetites have to be fed a more refined fare . . . the pleasure of works of art." The superabundance of décor completed the extraordinary feeling of a miraculous moment of arrest in the rapid glide between two continents, two realms of activity. It was not so much the iconographical program that could captivate eyes and hearts as the warmth of the materials, the variety of handling, the contrast of atmospheres. The theme chosen for *Normandie*, like that for the *Île de France*, permitted agreeable and even light variations on the riches and pleasures of a province. It was not, however, a particularly uplifting subject.

Modern life and its trepidations might have seemed more suitable sources of imagery than the greenness of good old Normandy's pastures, cows, and people. On the CGT ship, even the swift and cruel Vikings did little to trouble the delights of the province. This soothing and largely unproblematic theme reflected an eagerness to allow the liner and her passengers to escape the very contemporary life that *Normandie* so perfectly symbolized, a life in which the passengers otherwise participated very actively. In this basilica of modernism, the dominant religion was that of a Golden Age rediscovered, where indolent beauties and "a mass of lazy, handsome men," as Ingres put it in speaking of his Golden Age fresco at Dampierre, come together — albeit not nude but in dinner jackets and evening gowns — and pretended that nothing else existed. The décor would have been perfect for Atlantis, just as it was for *Normandie*, a floating paradise island where 1,714 passengers who had only themselves to blame if they failed to seize, in the course of a rapid crossing, the bliss of being alive and able to look about.

The Promenade Deck and the Spaces of Bouwens and Expert

The floating palace, the sea-going Versailles called *Normandie* had, as was proper, her grand suites or apartments. This was most apparent on the Promenade Deck, with its unforgettable enfilade of rooms, which, from bow to stern, comprised the Theater, the Hall (the point of departure for everything else on the ship and the point of access to the lower decks), the Grand Lounge, the Smoking Room, and the Grill. All open to one another, they constituted an urban and theatrical perspective as fantastic as the 18th-century creations of the Bibiena. And the rooms were worth going through with guidebook in hand, for the pleasure of identifying and admiring the art works arranged along the way and the special character they gave to each space, while simultaneously easing the progression from one environment to the next. However, this was no approach to the throne, but rather a suite on a floor reserved for first-class democrats, a program designed to nurture the satisfaction of being together and well off, away from it all but with every refinement that could be found in the great capitals of *terra firma*.

Such an organization demanded architects and not just decorators. And the fact that the CGT assigned it to such form-givers was symbolic of the ambitious goal set for *Normandie*. As a result, the spaces and volumes of the great artery would possess true architectural value in their own right. They had their independence and their own necessity, all at the heart of that other and ultimately constraining space, which was the volume of the ship itself. Given the discrepancy between the exterior and interior forms, the feat of laying out such an avenue within the pod of the hull simply magnified the victory of functionalism over strict rationalism, as the modernists themselves would have phrased it. A rationalist might well disapprove of those vastitudes with their autonomous geometries, but the necessary functions of a boat-palace — an enchanted liner — justified all the architects' effort, including its practical consequences.

R.H. Expert to M. Bouchard, the 1st of March 1934

Monsieur,
A special meeting has been held at the CGT headquarters to determine the name [sic] of the artists who should be called upon to collaborate in the work of decorating the passenger ship *Normandie*.

I am not unaware that you were a member of the committee concerned with the ship's aesthetic character. Nevertheless, I have permitted myself to mention your name for the assignment of the four bas-reliefs in the entry gallery-lounge.

The Governor General, the President, and the General Manager, being pleased with this choice, have been of the opinion that there was no incompatibility with your role as a member of the committee....

(Musée Henri Bouchard, Paris, 25 rue de l'Yvette)

The program for *Normandie* included the necessity that *luxe, calme et volupté* — the civilized, even richly spiritual qualities evoked by the poet Baudelaire and the painter Matisse — prevail in those grand, transparent spaces within the most exact, constrained, and cutoff of microcosms. The opportunity was too fine for conquered spaces of this size and quality not to be awarded to architects and artists capable of ennobling them. Richard Bouwens (1863–1939) was well known to the CGT, since he had created the great hall on the *Paris*, inaugurated in 1921. Then for the *Île de France* in 1927 he had done the grand staircase, using a similar formula but reconceiving it a more simplified and distinctly Art Deco manner.

Richard Bouwens was therefore in no way a second-rate architect, a fact borne out by the sense of order and the decorative invention he displayed in his *hôtel particulier*, or town house, at 8 Rue Le Dota in Paris (1890–1900) and in his apartment house at 27 Quai Anatole France (1905–06). He had married Marthe Lazard, daughter of the banker Alexandre Lazard. His father, William Bouwens, was also an architect and had involved him in the work on the Crédit Lyonnais, the elder Bouwens's masterwork. However, Richard Bouwens — architect to bankers (in 1903–04 in Neuilly, for example, he had built a neo-Louis XVI town house around the collections of David-Weill), of banks (in 1914 he had produced the large glazed hall of the Société Centrale des Banques de Provinces in the Rue Cambon), and of passenger liners (where he specialized in *grandes descentes* staircases) — had reached the end of his career. In 1935 he would be 72 years old. Thus, Roger Expert functioned somewhat as a deputy, backed by the patriarch, and ended up making virtually all the decisions. In the Bouwens-Expert duet the lead voice was that of Expert.

Born in 1882 and thus twenty years younger than Richard Bouwens, Roger-Henri Expert was, according to François Loyer, an architect in "the purely classical" mold, a form-giver who had demonstrated his ability to reinvent the Palladian language in the 20th century. This could be seen in four villas at his native Arcachon in 1926–27 and in the French Legation at Belgrade, a work of 1928–33. In the Villa Téthys, built as the Rumanian Embassy in Paris, Expert organized the great salons around a circular plan in the Italian manner, which, from Paris's Hôtel de Salm to Brussels's Pal-

The Upper Hall, looking toward the Theater; grilles by Raymond Subes

ais Stoclet, forms one of the great themes of the classical tradition. Together, these houses evince the architect's sense of order and his mastery of interpenetrating spaces. At the Vincennes Colonial Exhibition in 1931, Expert, along with Granet, had been responsible for the decorative illuminations. Their fountains — "that delight of water, sculpture, color, and light," transformed under a blaze of electric light — still dazzled in the memory. *Totem*, *Cactus*, and *Water Theater*, all of which enjoyed color reproduction in *L'Illustration*, seemed to be the modern equivalents of those vast plays of water and light that had been the glory of Versailles in the 17th century. All the while that he was purifying and internationalizing it, the "antique-modern" Expert did not hesitate to appropriate the classical vocabulary of columns, proportions, and symmetry and, in the 1930s, to subject it to a rigorously reductive process. In the school building on the Rue Kuss in Paris (1931–34), with its cascading terraces and its cubist forms, and in the studio annex for the École des Beaux-Arts on the round corner of the Rue Callot (1931–32), both more or less contemporary with the laying out of the *Normandie* Promenade Deck, Expert proved himself to be a confirmed modernist. Meanwhile, the buildings themselves proved that the virtues of the *style paquebot* had passed through the architecture of Roger-Henri Expert. Altogether, the Bouwens-Expert team, by its experience in the treatment of liners, its mastery of decorative architecture,

and its ongoing grasp of modernity, would seem to have been uniquely suited to the aims of the program set for *Normandie*.

The Upper Hall

First-class passengers entered *Normandie* and circulated to her various interior spaces through the Upper Hall, situated forward just between the first and second funnels. By means of its staircases and elevators, this vertical well gave access to the ship's different levels: D Deck with its Swimming Pool; C and B Decks, where the Dining Room and Chapel were located; A Deck, loaded with the Information Center and the deluxe suites and staterooms; and, finally, the Promenade Deck, offering the big lounges and the Theater.

By analogy to a building, *Normandie* could be said to have had her kitchens and pool in the basement, the dining room on the ground floor, the cabins, lounges, and gardens on the upper floors and even the roof, all in keeping with the classic scheme of a "modern" structure, where the higher reaches are favored and the lower ones abandoned to services. This, indeed, was the Le Corbusier model.

The hall was one of the forms most cherished by steamship architects. It lent itself to those *grandes descentes* that permitted passengers to make "grand entrances" down the stairs into the ship's lower quarters. By means of their play of encircling galleries, the stairs created the possibility of

Four bas-reliefs by Georges Saupique

social encounter and provided an open, free aisle or cell within the podlike world of the ship. Such a solution was one that Bouwens had already tried out first on the *Paris* and then on the *Île de France*.

It was not on *Normandie*, however, that the architects would emphasize horizontal perspectives with vertical flights. The lateral stairs descended between the four elevator shafts, which clearly took precedence and provided the principal services. On *Normandie*, the shafts were enclosed, cagelike, by metal grilles or fretwork designed by Raymond Subes, who used a symbolic décor of gilded seashells giving an immediate accent of coloristic richness. Subes was the great metalworking artist of the period between the two World Wars. He had a major presence in the 1925 Exposition des Arts Décoratifs, just as he would in the 1937 Paris World's Fair. Even after World War II, his career remained tirelessly intact. Having rehabilitated the genre of monumental metal work, Subes would go on to design the entrance grille for the Saint-Germain-des-Prés Church as well as that for the Palais d'Iéna. Indeed, there was hardly an important public place where Raymond Subes did not leave his mark. In the passenger liners, it fell to him to produce the gates leading to the journey and its pleasures.

The flattened dome vault, with its system of indirect lighting inherited from the *Île de France*, created a trompe-l'oeil effect that endowed the Hall with a height and an overall vastness that it did not actually possess.

On the walls, four bas-reliefs by Georges Saupique evoked "legendary maritime Normandie." "One side," read the CGT's brochure, "is devoted to the mythology of the Vikings: Odin on his fiery steed venturing forth ahead of two long ships tossed about on a raging sea. A Walkyrie, with torch in hand, flies above a flotilla of long ships rowing up a river." Opposite Odin and the goddess Frigga two other bas-reliefs represented "the remembrance of the Norman sagas and conquest." Here, the companions of Erik the Red, swathed in animal skins, reached the world of icebergs, beyond a foreground filled with an angry polar bear and a sperm whale. Thus, right from the beginning, so the brochure explained, the ship's iconographic program would offer "the poetry of sea and adventure in a wild and primitive atmosphere."

Halls were the places where people would scarcely linger, and it seems rather unlikely that Saupique's lifesize bas-reliefs made much impression on passengers. However, they did provide quite a good contrast with the smooth forms of the Upper Hall itself, as well as with the richness and curvilinearity of the grilles. The deliberately rough, gradine-carved stone and the highly simplified forms seemed well suited to those unexpectedly heroic reliefs, which invoked an era when navigation went on in direct contact with the elements and not in unsinkable hulls where life unfolded as if in a world apart, in what today might be called a "Hiltonian bubble." Saupique was there, if for no other reason, to give a peril-free crossing a whiff of adventure.

The Theater

A low grille, somewhat like a communion rail in churches — a work by Subes, of course — separated the Upper Hall from the Theater, located forward under the first smokestack. This balustrade was composed of six panels whose meanders duplicated motifs found in the elevator grilles. A pair of gilded masks, inspired by those of antique theater, announced the purpose of the interior beyond, which could be penetrated once the balustrade was swung back. The auditorium, done up "in pale silver tonalities," had a seating capacity of 380. In the words of the brochure, "It has modern equipment, and its acoustics are perfect. The stage is fully mechanized, and in the afternoon a screen is pulled down to permit a continuous run of movies from 14:30 to 19 hours." On inauguration day, the acoustics, despite all the claims made for them, left something to be desired. The auditorium was devoid of décor, other than the contrast between the silver of the walls and the red of the seats, curtains (both stage and entrance), and carpet. The slow, rather apsidal

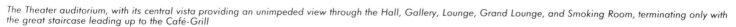

The Theater auditorium, with its central vista providing an unimpeded view through the Hall, Gallery, Lounge, Grand Lounge, and Smoking Room, terminating only with the great staircase leading up to the Café-Grill

The children's playroom, decorated by Marc Simon and Jacqueline Duché

curve of the space found an echo in the responds that extended across the "hanging" vault to join, in continuous, unbroken lines, the lateral walls' baylike divisions, which overhead concealed the Theater's indirect lighting. In this simple hall, the assembled audience and the spectacle on the stage sufficed as embellishment. Understandably, the whole ensemble of lounges constituted the real theater on board *Normandie*, where the play about a society on a transatlantic crossing was performed every day. The entrance Hall functioned as a foyer to this double theater, one in which the works of playwrights were put on and the other where the passengers invented their own dialogue and plot.

The Winter Garden and the Reading and Writing Rooms

Toward the bow of the ship, the garden opened onto a panoramic view of the parting waves. "*Normandie* carried on board a bit of French earth, along with its flowers, its roses, and its lilies." The Vilmorin firm, which designed and maintained the garden, had another mission, which was to give the "world's most elite group of passengers ... a genuine sample of the beautiful horticultural species produced on our soil." This oval area, a fore counterpart of the Grill Room aft, was practically the only space on the ship that was not open and free. Instead, it bristled with terraces, pergolas, and a pair of metal aviaries set upon two bronze basin fountains, deliberately complicated circulation and thus added to the surprise of finding, on the high seas, an escape into virgin forests and classical gardens. Green was dominant, providing the color of chairs furnished with white-leather cushions. A. Ruhlmann, along with Marie Chauvel, had been the author, under the direction of Expert, of this fragment of terrestrial paradise on water.

Behind the Winter Garden came a writing room, on the starboard side, and, on the port side, a library. In the former, paneled in rosewood and sycamore boiseries and furnished with red-leather chairs, hung a painting by Alexandre Iacowleff (1887–1938), a sort of Bathing Nymphs scene that served as a justifiable distraction for passengers afflicted with writer's cramp. The reading room had a pair of paintings, somewhat golden in tonality, by Paul Jouve (1880–1973), the great *animalier* of the 20th century. Composed as pendants, *Normandie*'s royal tigers and black Hué ele-

Expert's project drawing for the Winter Garden (Académie d'Architecture)

The Winter Garden

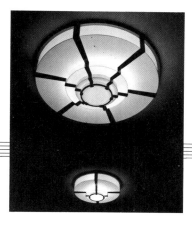

Ceiling light and sconce by Perzel

The Writing Room, with furniture by Nelson

Paul Jouve, Royal Tigers and Sacred Elephants of Hué (private collection)

Henri Bouchard's bas-relief entitled Commerce

phants were vintage Jouve. But they would seem to have been more appropriate for the Far Eastern routes than for a reading room dedicated, oddly enough, to Farrère and Kipling rather than to Morand and Proust.

Two decks higher, on the Sun Deck, the playroom with its puppet theater, Aunt Sally, and carousel, also contained fantasy chairs, characterized by red backs and armrests in the shape of white horses. Humor and fun had alighted on the planet of children. It was as if Saint-Exupéry's Little Prince (from the 1943 book) had made a preliminary call on his young confreres, beginning with the little princes in first class. This seems all the more possible since Mme Duché, of the Marc Simon studios, had created a festive ceiling spangled with lights in the form of moons, stars, and balloons.

The Gallery-Lounge

On the other side of the Theater, a gallery led back toward the Grand Lounge. It was known as the "gallery-lounge," since it had room enough to contain chairs and canapés aligned along the sides. Four stucco colonnettes, supporting alabaster lamp-vases, served to define a kind of central aisle, a rather absurd idea given the miraculous freedom of the space. Lamps, of monumental conception, would often be used to structure space, and those made of alabaster and illuminated from within would project light onto the ceiling, there to be refracted in a subtly indirect luminosity. In these daylightless environments the mystery of the lighting sources was fundamental to *Normandie*'s special ambience. The gallery-lounge, thanks to its simulated semicolumns,

which gave it something of a temple-like nobility, resembled a propylaeum leading to the sanctum sanctorum, the Grand Lounge. What might be called broad pilasters framed Bouchard's reliefs and Ducos de la Haille's paintings, an arrangement that completed the appearance of a strong architectural structure, without in any way wasting space or filling it to no purpose. The Bouchard reliefs, being set under a cornice against slightly sunken panels, like echoes of absent windows and doors, were perfectly integrated with the architecture of a corridor-cum-lounge.

The reliefs commissioned from Henri Bouchard represented Commerce, Fishing, Animal Husbandry, and Art. In keeping with the name of the ship, the iconography, like that in the Hall, drew on Norman themes. In his youth, Henri Bouchard, the Prix de Rome winner for 1901, had been much taken up with a monument to labor, an unfinished work that owed its inspiration to Jules Dalou and Constantin Meunier. "I should like," he said, "my realism to achieve the grandeur of that in the antique statues of Egypt or Hellas, the Charioteer of Delphi, Charles V in the Louvre." What moved him was "the sense of humble and worried humanity in the peasants and fishermen that I sculpt, all the while that I strive to discover large forms, beautiful, carefully distributed accents, and fine planes."

Strong and ambitious as these declarations may have been, the works produced by Bouchard did not gainsay them, for indeed there was a fine archaizing Greek character to those reliefs. This was especially true in *Art*, with its two women seated on the ground near the frontal plane, the one on the

Sketches for two pictures by Ducos de la Haille (private collection)

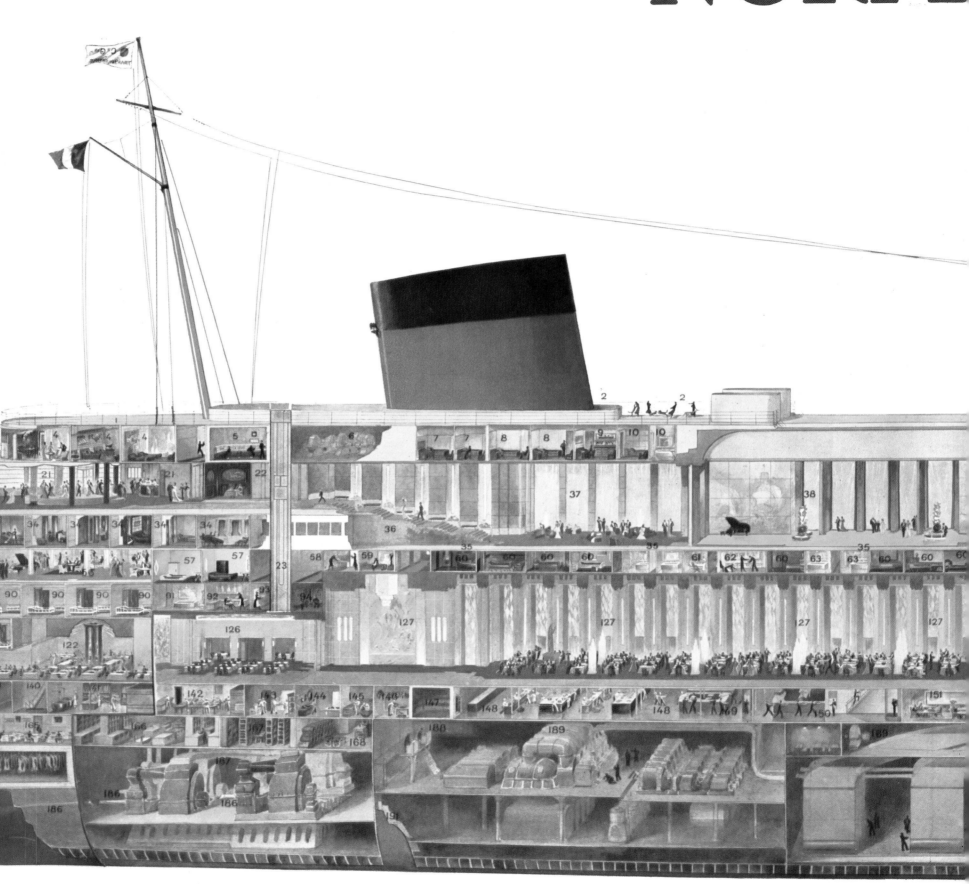

THE VENDOME PRESS

DIFFUSION FLAMMARION

UPPER SUN DECK
1. Open promenade for officers and student engineers
2. Kennel and dog run
SUN DECK
3. Private terrace or veranda attached to a deluxe suite
4. *Grande luxe* suite
5. Main telegraph office
6. Ventilators
7. Chief electricians' room
8. Deputy engineers' room
9. Main office of the chief engineer
10. Chief engineer's suite
11. Deck tennis and other games
12. Children's playroom
13. Flower storage
14. Forward stairs for first-class passengers
15. Captain's suite
16. Bridge telegraph office
17. Game (bridge) room
18. Wheel house or navigation center
19. Bridge
EMBARKATION DECK
20. First-class esplanade or promenade
21. Café-Grill Room with dance floor
22. Café-Grill private dining room
23. First-class elevator
24. Officers' room
25. Officers' wardroom
26. Floodlight
27. Starboard light
28. Small foward esplanade
PROMENADE DECK
29. Open promenade for tourist class
30. Covered promenade for tourist class
31. Tourist-class smoking room
32. Tourist-class elevators and stairway
33. Tourist-class deck service
34. Terrace or veranda cabins
35. Covered Promenade Deck in first class
36. Smoking Room grand staircase
37. First-class Smoking Room
38. First-class Grand Lounge
39. Gallery-lounge
40. Upper Hall and elevators
41. Theater
42. Stage
43. Performers' dressing rooms
44. Projection room
45. Reading room
46. Winter Garden
47. Electric cranes and cargo hatch
48. Crew's ladder
49. "Whaleback"
MAIN DECK
50. Tourist-class swimming pool
51. Covered promenade in tourist class
52. Gymnasium in tourist class
53. Free space
54. Tourist-class cabins
55. Tourist-class reading room
56. Tourist-class lounge
57. First-class cabins
58. Deck service
59. Chambermaids
60. First-class cabins
61. Massage room
62. Supply room
63. First-class baths
64. Main telephone switchboard
65. Radio-telephone office
66. Radio-telephone booth
67. Safes
68. Information Center in first class
69. Lower Hall
70. Florist and retail shops
71. Hairdressing and manicure salon
72. Deluxe suite
73. Fire-fighting equipment
74. Press room
75. Printing shop
76. Head printer
77. Chief hairdresser
78. Fire watchmen and fighters
79. Auxiliary watchmen
80. Petty officers second class
81. Master carpenter's workshop
A DECK
82. Open promenade in third class
83. Covered promenade in third class
84. Third-class smoking room
85. Third-class stairway
86. Bar in third class
87. Purser in third class
88. Tourist-class information center
89. Tourist-class hairdressing salon
90. Tourist-class cabins
91. Baths in first class
92. Floor service
93. Aft stairs in first class
94. Central security
95. Chief purser's room
96. Chief purser's office
97. Doctor's office
98. First-class cabins
99. Forward stairs and elevators in first class
100. Service stairs
101. Musicians' wardroom
102. Chief musician
103. Pages' quarters
104. Pages' lavatories
105. Deck machinery—capstans, winches, rope, etc.
B DECK
106. Covered promenade of the crew and deck equipment for the mooring anchor
107. Third-class lounge
108. First-class cabins
109. Stairway in third class
110. Tourist-class baths
111. First-class cabins
112. Forward stairs in first class

113. Doctor's room in first class
114. Infirmary
115. Waiting room
116. Surgery
117. Hospital
118. Handling space for deck equipment
C DECK
119. Musician's wardroom in tourist class
120. Musician's room
121. Tourist-class cabins
122. Tourist-class dining room
123. Infirmary
124. Second doctor's office
125. Second doctor's room
126. Banquet Hall
127. First-class Dining Room
128. Cloak room
129. Chapel
130. Photographer's studio
131. Dry cleaning
132. Gyroscope
133. Postal agent
134. Sorting room
135. Head of the watch
136. Pages' quarters
D DECK
137. Third-class cabins
138. Third-class embarkation hall and elevators
139. Reception of supplies
140. Crew's embarkation
141. Pastry kitchen
142. Bakery
143. Ice-cream pantry
144. Butcher shop
145. Fish tank
146. Poultry department
147. Kitchen refrigerator room
148. Kitchens
149. Service
150. Coffee urns and service stairs
151. Service dining room
152. Nursery
153. Children's dining room
154. Exercise room
155. Swimming Pool bar
156. Swimming Pool
157. Steward's issuing room
158. Crew's kitchen
159. Automobile embarkation and elevators
160. Mail storage
161. Pages' mess hall
162. Pages' showers and lavatories
163. Third-class baths
E DECK
164. Third-class dining room
165. Assistant engineers' wardroom
166. Main supply room
167. Vintage wine and mineral waters
168. Wine cellar
169. Ventilators for heating and air circulation

170. Engineers' toilet
171. Boiler workshop
172. Quarters, lavatories, and showers for boiler and baggage crew
F DECK
173. Dirty laundry storage
174. Drier
175. Main laundry
176. Cold storage (fish)
177. Cold storage (pork and sausage)
178. Cold storage (poultry and game)
179. Cold storage (meat)
180. Baggage hold
181. Garage
182. Stores
183. Chain well
G DECK
184. Garage
H DECK
185. Cargo hold
BOTTOM
186. Propeller shafts
187. Compartment for 4 electric motors
188. Control bridge for propulsion
189. Compartment for the turbo-alternators and auxiliaries
190. Boilers
191. Double hull

First-class passengers	848
Tourist-class passengers	665
Third-class passengers	458
Officers and crew	1,335
TOTAL	3,326
Length	1,029' (313.75m)
Width	119' (36.40m)
Depth (from the Promenade Deck)	92' (28m)
Gross registered weight	79,280 tons
Power	160,000 horse

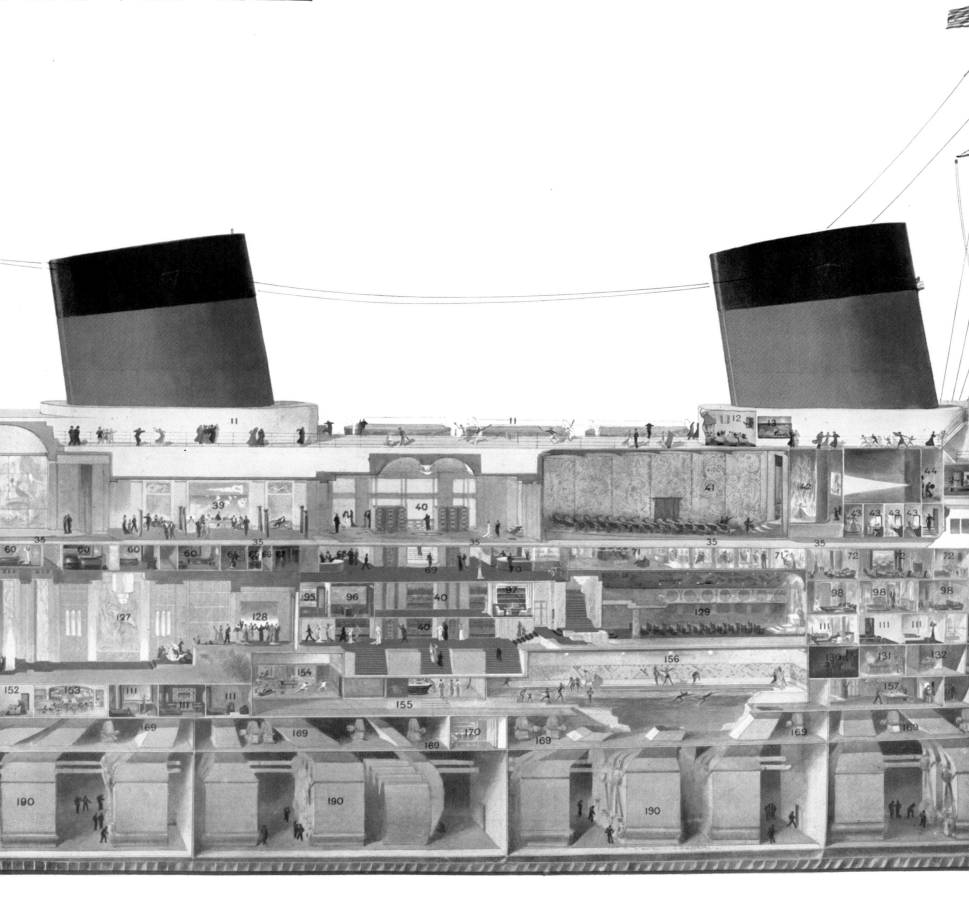

The gallery-lounge

left an Alençon lacemaker and that on the right holding a model of Caen's Saint-Étienne Church. Then there was *Commerce*, whose structure also depended on a pair of facing figures, here like *kores* but actually in the process of folding sails. Just as Saupique had handled his Norman mythologies in a decorative yet tough manner, a sort of Celtic Art Deco, Bouchard endowed his Norman activities with a dignity and a restraint worthy of an artist who dreamed of recovering the grandeur of Phidian Greece and the serenity of 13th-century French Gothic. Here were big, stern lessons for anyone passing through a gallery-lounge beyond which glittered the dark golds of Dupas and the lacquers of Dunand! Should an imaginary passenger of today attempt to re-experience the quality of *Normandie*'s spaces and ambience by merely examining graphic and photographic documents, he would very likely end up concentrating on works that were meant to be viewed rapidly, like elements within an overall décor. But, this said, he could also very well rediscover the intentions and intuitions of the commissioners and the executants who themselves took an analytic, or point by point, approach to the whole.

The gallery-lounge was organized around two large canvases by Ducos de la Haille, mounted at the center of the walls between the Bouchard reliefs. "In the *Conquest of*

Normandie we see the glorious Viking Roland launching upon the Normandy campaign. Frigga, the goddess of nature and fruit and the divine spouse of Odin, guides him and protects the heroes. In the distance, on the Seine estuary, the swift long boats penetrate in great numbers." Facing this composition, "*Norman Peace* makes the rich province bloom between the trees and among the apple blossoms." Readily recognizable were the images of Mont Saint-Michel, Jumièges, and Caen's Abbaye aux Hommes and Abbaye aux Dames. Clearly, Ducos de la Haille provided a synthesis of the iconographic preoccupations of Saupique and Bouchard: the Normandy of the Vikings, of adventure and conquest, of the Romanesque-Gothic flowering, the cathedrals, and the apple trees. "Horses graze in meadows and the warring flotilla of long ships has given way to a light and peaceful flotilla of Norman fishermen." Ducos de la Haille, who had been Prix de Rome in 1922 and in 1931 had decorated the Festival Hall in the Colonial Museum (now the Museum of African and Oceanic Arts), is today a much too neglected painter. Recently rediscovered, his sketches for these compositions — works sold in the United States in 1985 — reveal a rather surprising capacity to fill a large surface with an accumulation of quasi-Mannerist motifs. Strong, local colors, perspective denied in favor of tiered imagery, hyper-realist details contrasted with generalized forms, modeled figures and faces combined with flattened furniture and décor – all the mannerisms that already recall those of Dupas – create a strange world, a world particular enough for us to recognize, if not a style, at least a hand. Ducos de la Haille in painting was very close to Janniot in sculpture. The *Conquest of Normandie*, with its mounted Viking making his entrance across the gallery-lounge like Delacroix's Crusaders into Jerusalem, must have suggested a kind of illuminated tapestry à *la* Boutet de Monvel. In that calm gallery, between Bouchard's Hellenic reliefs with their Normans as still as statues, Ducos de la Haille's coloristic chaos introduced a note of joyous stridency.

The Grand Lounge

Among *Normandie's* great first-class apartments, the Grand Lounge was the equivalent of the Hall of Mirrors at Versailles. The comparison seems all the more apt by virtue of the fact that the Grand Lounge was flanked by tall, rectangular windows, hung with net curtains, five on either side and supposedly open to green pastures of water. In fact, they gave onto the gallery of the Promenade Deck. The central bays were doors providing access to that "concert lounge." But the windows' facing alignment was not the only Versailles touch, since it could also be found in Dupas's décor of etched and gilded mirrors, which amplified – if this were needed! – the allusion to the richest gallery in the richest of all palaces. The wall décor created by Dupas and Champigneulle literally assimilated the Versailles hall by the rarefied technique of treating the Grand Lounge like an immense crystal box. This new Hall of Mirrors was also a new Golden Gallery, which, by the color of its glass, could claim kinship with the great gallery in the Hôtel de Toulouse, long the headquarters of the Banque de France. Some 31 feet tall, the Grand Lounge had a height equal to about two and a half decks, crowned at the top by a sort of flat, or suppressed, vault made possible by the Sun Deck overhead. The vault, unlike the one at Versailles, was left plain, while the walls received the gilding normally reserved for the ceiling. Switched as the order of things may have been, it allowed Dupas to assume the role of a Charles Lebrun.

The Grand Lounge could also be seen in another way, as a sort of temple or church. Its plan had the shape of a Greek cross, since the four corners of the rectangle were occupied on the entrance gallery side by two small lounges, one reserved for women, the other used as a writing room, and on the Smoking Room side by two offices. Four pairs of columns separated the "nave" from its "side aisles." Thanks to proportions most unusual for a ship, even on one of the CGT's masterpieces, and to its strong architectural char-

acter, this salon-church-gallery took on a nobility and a grandeur that were absolutely at one with the ceremonial importance of whatever happened in the Grand Lounge.

Dupas's glass reliefs, aureated, silvered, and painted on the reverse side by the glazier Champigneulle, using "gold, silver, platinum, and palladium" colors, became the *pièces de resistance* of the Grand Lounge. There were four such reliefs, each measuring 21 feet high and 49 feet wide. As revetments for the angles of the cross, they were subdivided into three vertical panels that unfolded or opened out on three surfaces, rather like huge screens, an arrangement that posed extraordinary compositional problems. Champigneulle ended up dividing each composition into a hundred sections, each measuring 4 feet 3 inches by 2 feet 6 inches. From the total decorative ensemble prepared for *Normandie*, Dupas's glass paintings, along with Dunand's lacquers for the Smoking Room, are the best preserved elements. As for iconography, they represent *The Chariot of Poseidon* (gallery port side), *The Rape of Europa* (gallery starboard side), *The Chariot of Thetis* (Smoking Room port side), and *The Birth of Aphrodite* (Smoking Room starboard side).

Here, for the first time, the themes abandoned geographical Normandy for ancient marine mythology and the glory of naval architecture. In this way Jean Dupas (1882–1964) combined the special interests of his friend Expert. Both men were from southwest France – from Arcachon, to be exact, where Dupas moored his own boat and where Expert had been born and later built five seaside villas. Moreover, Expert had a great passion for the architecture of steamships. In a 1948 article, entitled "From the Décor of the 17th Century to the Passengers Liners of Today," Expert recalled, with some nostalgia, the so-called "modern" taste and its somewhat excessive "tendency toward sobriety and a stripped-down look." For him, *le paquebot* constituted one of the last occasions on which grand decorative schemes were programmatically integrated with grand architecture. "Could we speak," he asked, "of modern *paquebot* décor without mentioning those extraordinary decorative monuments that were themselves royal vessels, with prows and taffrails four stories high flanked by quarter-gallery watchtowers, glistening with gilded sculpture, works of the finest masters of the period, with gold brightened by the vermilion of portholes, a blue and black hull under tiers of sails?"

Here, Expert must have been thinking about Dupas's glass panels. For at the very heart of the modern luxury liner, beautiful in its "purity of line, elegance of superstructure, and aerodynamic funnels," the memory of Bérain's sterns or the *Horses of the Sun*, copied from Robert Le Lorrain's relief at the Hôtel de Rohan, glittered with all the gold, silver, and roseate overtones of a dream. Within the architectural

Dupas, The Chariot of Poseidon, now in the cafeteria at the Metropolitan Museum of Art in New York City

sobriety of the Grand Lounge, Dupas's compositions functioned like a miraculously calm, plastic storm.

Dupas — the great master of Bordeaux's neoclassicizing school who, along with Pougheon and Despujols, represented one of the most curious, as well as least popular, currents in French art between the wars — was fundamentally a Mannerist. His long-necked women with the flowing hair looked like reincarnations of the 16th-century Madonnas of Parmigianino. His complex compositions, where everything has been treated with the same intensity, where waves, sails, the bodies of goddesses, and the nostrils of horses have been delineated with the same acuity, make their author appear very much a modern Bronzino. Dupas, the neoclassical *précieux*, who, in an exasperating yet delightful fire-and-ice manner, could combine antique or medieval architecture with the baroque structure of 17th-century ships, knew how to use the irreality of his colors to virtuoso effect, gilding the rocks, trees, and sails of the Thetis composition, for example, while rendering the waves and divinities in silver. These great golden panels have about them a joyousness, a humor, and a sophistication that now seem the very embodiment of the 1930s, a between-the-wars world that, in the middle of the ocean, could appear like an interlude between pleasures. Dupas himself stated that the panels had

been conceived "with the desire to create an abundant, splendid effect," the better "to protest against the indigence and nakedness of the decorative conceptions that were born after the war just in time to invade France at the moment of the 1925 exhibition."

The Grand Lounge, we should remember, was a salon, and everything in it had to be organized around ensembles of chairs. These were distributed about several focal points: six poufs, or circular couches, in the central nave, two of them on the same axis as the great portals, each of these crowned with a Daurat-designed pewter vase, its concealed interior lamp projecting indirect light onto the ceiling. The sconces affixed to Dupas's panels functioned as decorative features, but light so close to the wall served best to animate the ships and marine nudes gliding over the golden glasses. The four other poufs culminated in molded-glass towers, lamps whose vertical succession of corollas reminded everyone of the illuminated fountains with which Expert had done so much to brighten the 1931 Colonial Exhibition at Vincennes. The armless chairs, designed by Rothschild to facilitate both passage and position, were upholstered with floral motifs from the French colonies, worked in Aubusson tapestry from drawings by Gaudissart. In the chairs, colors alternated between gray and red and all gray, since the

Drawing of the Grand Lounge realized during the maiden voyage by Jean Pagès, fashion draftsman for Vogue from 1931 to 1938

Jean Rothschild, sketch for a fauteuil in the Grand Lounge

ground color was an orange-red while the backs were gray. For the windows Jean de Beaumont had prepared curtains ornamented with cherry wisteria on a white ground. Thus, the focal points, with their muted red tonality, served all the better to make the gold, silver, and rose harmony of Dupas's glasses sing out. The sliding door at the end of the nave, giving access to the Smoking Room, had a revetment in the form of a lacquer relief, *Aurora's Chariot*, by Dunand after Dupas. This fire door, fabricated by the metalworker A. Ruhlmann, acted as a prelude to the Smoking Room's dominant material: lacquer.

The Women's Lounge and the Writing Room, those left-over spaces in the angles of the Grand Lounge, had incorporated into their silk wall coverings (white in the portside lounge furnished with an Émile-Jacques Ruhlmann piano, which has just disappeared, and a few other pieces by Ruhlmann, displayed in homage to the great, recently dead designer) two paintings, a kind of art reserved for the most intimate rooms, in contrast to the decorative art that seemed to be called for in the large rooms. Gaston Balande (1880–1971) had painted a strange, panoramic view of Étretat, seen from high on the cliffs, with strong gray and green colors in the manner of Marquet, while Louis Graux (187?–1967) had done a landscape of the Seine's lower valley. Thus, the Norman reference resurfaced in the secret of the small lounges. However, the modern carried the day in Jean Perzel's sconces, whose volutes in rose-enameled glass, well over 3 feet high, were entirely constructivist in their beauty.

Rothschild's large canapé covered with tapestry designed by Gaudissart, set before Dupas's Rape of Europa

General view of the Grand Lounge; lighting towers by Labouret and pewter vases by Daurat

Four Grand Lounge chairs covered with Gaudissart's tapestry (Le Havre Chamber of Commerce)

Jean Dupas, cartoons for the four etched-glass murals in the Grand Lounge, the glass executed by Jacques Charles Champigneulle

The Rape of Europa

The Birth of Aphrodite

72

The Chariot of Poseidon (Louvre)

The Chariot of Thetis

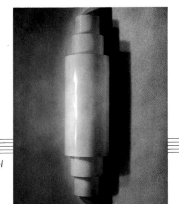

Sconce by Perzel

Small writing room, with Gaston Balande's painting entitled The Cliffs of Étretat

The Promenade Deck

Ladies' lounge; painting by Louis Graux, View of the Lower Seine Valley; furniture by Ruhlmann

The Chariot of Aurora, lacquer panel by
Dunand after a drawing by Dupas (collection Bruce Newmann, New York City)

The Smoking Room

If the Grand Lounge belonged to Jean Dupas and his painted glass, it was Jean Dunand and lacquer that took over in the Smoking Room, for which this artist created four panels: *Horse Taming* (starboard side near the Grand Lounge), *Harvesting* (port side near the Grand Lounge), *Fishing*, and *Sports* (the last two facing the first pair on either side of the stairway leading to the Grill Room). On the reverse side of the door displaying Dupas's *Aurora* appeared *Hunting*, this work, of course, oriented toward the Smoking Room. Swiss-born Jean Dunand (1887–1942) had achieved great distinction for his work on metal, and indeed a case could perhaps be made for his being the only coppersmith active in the 20th century. But in 1912, after an initiation under the Japanese master Sougawara, Dunand began working in lacquer. An avid researcher, he experimented endlessly with unknown techniques and alloys. For the Smoking Room's huge panels measuring 20 feet square, Dunand rediscovered himself as the sculptor he had been at the outset of his artistic career. As a result, the panels became veritable bas-reliefs. With gouge and rasp in hand, he managed to rival his colleagues at work in the Dining Room — Delamarre, Drivier, Poisson, and Pommier.

For the Smoking Room, Jacques Dunand developed an absolutely luscious "Egyptian" manner. This was especially true in *Fishing*, where the boatmen turn their heads in profile and their torsos full front as in the best paintings of the Theban tombs. The artist had a witty way of bringing cultures together, as in the purely Japanese catch being hauled in by the Egyptian fishermen. The steeds in *Horse Taming* owe their heads to equine prototypes on the Parthenon frieze, even though they take flight on wings as in Assyrian reliefs and pile up, seven deep, in the crazy way of Walter Crane. But the governing spirit is solidly neo-antique, without any of the mannerism so dear to Dupas. In *Harvesting* the pair of male and female dancers look as if they could easily have jumped down from the ceiling of the Champs-Élysées Theater. *Sports*, a homage to Coubertin, provides quite a suggestive variation on the modern body. The composition's neo-Greek athletes, throwing javelin, discus, and weights as if at Olympia, display the heads and musculature of contemporary sportsmen; thus, it is not solely the bathing suits that date these figures to the year 1935. The other charm of the bas-reliefs derives from the triumphant polychromy that Dunand succeeded in drawing from his lacquers. He even invented white lacquer by lacing the resins with crushed eggshell. While the dominant tonality may be gold, the black of the grapes in *Harvesting*, the white of waves, and the red of bodies add life and vigor to the grand oratorio of golds.

As in the Grand Lounge, the whole of the decorative effort in the Smoking Room was concentrated on the walls. Here too the tall rectangular windows did not open onto the sea, but could be illuminated from behind. Hearts and eyes warmed by the brilliance within these salons seemed not even to miss the natural elements. What passenger would

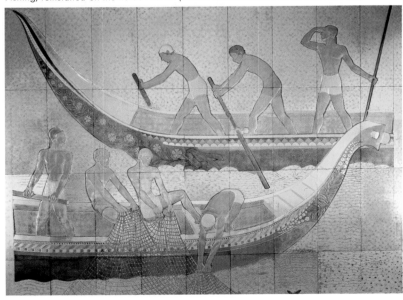

Fishing, *reinstalled on the Île de France (Musée d'Art Moderne de la Ville de Paris)*

Horse Taming, *reinstalled on the Île de France (Musée d'Art Moderne de la Ville de Paris)*

Hunting, *reinstalled on the Liberté (present whereabouts unknown); the doors now hang in Mr. Chow's Restaurant in New York City*

have wanted to escape such Ali Baba caverns? Illumination played an essential role, needed as it was to make the dark gold of the walls glow. A hidden flame radiated through the translucent sides of the alabaster vases set on high pedestals at the center of the poufs. Column strips of light ran up the walls, while on the ceiling, lights almost abstract in shape produced "a new kind of luminosity, the result of tiny crystal

balls fused together in several thicknesses, which radiated among themselves and gave the impression of glass set with diamonds." The comfortable brown-leather chairs suited the purpose of the place and the somnolence of the smoker. Dunand had also created gaming tables finished in lacquer, and here too the new eggshell technique solved the problem of the white needed for checkerboard tops.

Sports *(Musée d'Art Moderne de la Ville de Paris)*

Harvesting *(upper portion), reinstalled on the Liberté (Palais des Congrès de Oissel, Seine-Maritime)*

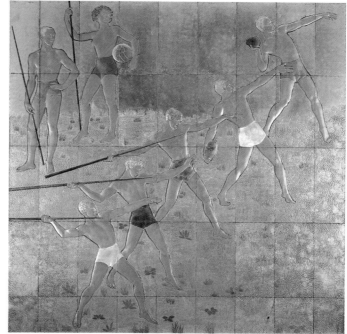

The Stairway to the Grill Room

From the center of the Smoking Room, toward the back, rose the stairway leading to the Grill Room. This straight-line flight, with its five intermediate landings, permitted passengers to make a calm, stately climb the height of a deck, since the Grande Lounge and the Smoking Room were themselves built *à l'italienne* — that is, with ceilings two stories high. Although it had only twenty steps, the staircase gave the effect of real monumentality. At the top stood Baudry's statue — gilded of course — personifying *Normandy*. The figure fixed the axis of this whole suite of grand lounges and seemed to be the culmination of a perspective that joined the Grand Lounge and the Smoking Room in one long continuum. The solution was the same as that found in the classic gardens of Le Nôtre, where statues placed at the extremity of the terrace punctuate what the eye perceives as orthogonals converging toward a central vanishing point. Because the architects had wanted free, open spaces, the better to create wall tensions more resistant to pressure from waves, the statue, along with a few lamp bases, became the only fixed element placed at the center of that extraordinary composition, an avenue that, with the fire-door portal open, stretched over more than 690 feet.

The Baudry statue stood not full face but in profile, so as to provide an interesting silhouette from every side. A rather severe image, it represented a young woman attired in a Greek tunic chastely bound at the waist and falling in long Gothic folds. With upcast eyes, the figure leaned on a kind of wall trellis loaded with the ripe apples of Normandy. The staircase walls were punctuated with the same luminous colonnettes as those which, sunk within staff niches, articulated the walls of the Smoking Room, thereby ensuring visual unity throughout. A watercolor done by Expert, now in the Académie d'Architecture, shows the architect's initial idea for the staircase, which had yet to assume its full amplitude. The columns indicated there would have lent solidity to the staircase, while also making the walls heavier and more congested. Those luminous colonnettes that finally marked off the stairs' steady rise were unquestionably a better solution. This simply reillustrates the role played by light and color in *Normandie*'s interior architecture. Even though clear of projections, the walls nonetheless possessed depth and relief, thanks to their rare materials and rich colors. By its treatment, light traced out and visually defined a kind of transparent architecture.

Léon Baudry, La Normandie, while still in the artist's studio

The Smoking Room

Expert's sketch for the Smoking Room staircase (Académie d'Architecture)

The Café-Grill

The twenty-step staircase led to the Boat Deck and the Grill or Café-Grill, an oval room whose rear bay windows gave onto the sea. Until then a huge absence, the ocean finally made an appearance, at the end of a long and delightful peregrination through the lounges. What influence did the water have on this new space? Certainly the décor, conceived by Marc Simon, went through a sea change. Here, the tables and chairs, for instance, were made of stainless steel, and although covered with the leather required in first class, the furniture was truly "modern," with nothing of the Ruhlmannian richness seen elsewhere but, rather, with a Bauhaus functionalism worthy of Mallet-Stevens. However, on the pigskin-covered walls near the staircase, there were luminous columns of tiered corollas that rhymed quite well with the opulence seen earlier. Still, the atmosphere was of a totally different nature, as if purified by proximity to the sea and its spray. The ceiling lights with their reflecting spirals and bars assured abstraction a solid presence on the ship.

The "all-black" Grill displayed an "enormous cast-metal plaque" in which Hairon, "with an Assyrian verve, depicted the pleasures of capturing and raising animals normally meant for the spit, from wild boars to rabbits and ducks, as well as deer and lamb." Such a theme was meant to stimulate the appetite while providing a feast for the eyes. The bar was made of glass embellished with engravings of vinous subjects based on paintings by Max Ingrand. Thus, Ingrand and Hairon were supposed "to create a gay, insouciant atmosphere conducive to the enjoyment of the good products of France." This may have been too much to expect of

Charles Sarrabezolles, The Spirit of the Sea *(presently in front of the CGT headquarters in the port of Le Havre)*

Hairon's cast-metal relief in the Grill Room

left: *Paul-Élie Gernez, The Honfleur Roads, hung in the Bridge Room*
opposite: *Paul-Élie Gernez, Bouquet of Flowers, Flowers and Shells, and Flowers, all hung in the private dining room of the Café-Grill*

View from the terrace of the Embarkation Deck

The Café-Grill, designed by Marc Simon

them in the Grill Room's spare and totally nautical environment, where nothing could distract from the view of the sea. Moreover, the bars, whatever their decorative qualities, attracted mainly the knees of thirsty passengers, not their eyes. Max Ingrand's talent would find more scope and fare better in the hairdressing salon.

In back of the Grill Room, in the spaces between the Embarkation Deck and the Smoking Room stairwell, the CGT had inserted a private bar and a bridge room decorated with paintings by Paul-Élie Gernez (1888–1948), a very respectable artist, briefly touched by Cubism, who at the Galerie Druet exhibited the Honfleur landscapes and flower paintings for which he was best known.

From the Smoking Room door giving onto the sea, another stairway, this one open-air and divided like an inversion of the model at Fontainebleau, led down to the Terrace Bar. From here first-class passengers had spread before them the spectacle of the whole series of terraced decks cascading toward the ship's stern. The arrangement gave the lucky few visual access to decks reserved for the other classes, without themselves being subject to observation from below, as well as to the sea from the highest and widest vantage point. The layout of the rear sundeck was quite remarkable, with its stationary banquettes arranged in two zigzag rows, which, among the easy, echoing curves of the various decks, introduced a nervous, dynamic note. At the center stood six lamp posts, some 16 feet tall and designed to illuminate the aft deck, but also indispensable for docking by night. Apart from their utility, these lighting stanchions, with their stacks of four bulbs each, functioned somewhat like the Cubist trees of Mallet-Stevens and the Martel brothers at the 1925 Exhibition. Strange objects originally justified by their pure

The waiting room in the hairdressing salon; carpet by Alavoine and etched glass by Max Ingrand

plastic beauty, they seemed all the more remarkable for being essential to the ship's survival. The Sun Deck was also to have been graced by Sarrabezolles's *Spirit of the Sea*, but vibrations made it impossible to install the sculpture, the image of a fish-tailed marine god, whose absence left the place to its basic purity. Like Dupas in the Grand Lounge, Sarrabezolles reconciled the modern liner with an antique vision. Obviously, there could never be enough delights and surprises for first-class passengers.

The First-Class Public Rooms on the Lower Decks

Corresponding to the grand suite of chambers on the Promenade Deck, by Bouwens and Expert, was another, in the depths of the ship, designed by Patou and Pacon and devoted to what may have been the most important function of a smooth crossing aboard a floating palace dedicated to the eternal glories of France: the Dining Room. Pierre Patou (1879–1965), like Bouwens, had long been familiar with the interior architecture of passenger liners, since it was he who did the dining room on the *Île de France*. At the 1925 Exhibition, he had also created the "Town House of a Collector," the very theme of which never ceased to enrage those who wanted the modern decorative arts to be, if not minimalist, at least democratic. In this pavilion, with its Ruhlmann ensembles, Patou had shown a Hoffmann-like virtuosity in his organization and penetration of interior spaces. Still, the composition, with its pure volumes, adhered to the laws of symmetry and made obeisance to the key monuments of classical architecture. Patou, a moderate and even-handed modernist, faithful in his friendship and professional dealings with artists he appreciated, has recently been rediscovered as one of the most interesting architects of the period. Some of his buildings, such as the Boulogne town house for the painter Lombard (1928), are among the era's most refined and modernist of terra-firma *paquebots*, which the 1920s and 1930s, with their sense of exact space, simultaneously subtle and sensational, loved to put up. Having been the collaborating architect of steamships, Patou understood them so well that the best part of his creative output could be said to owe its exceptional quality to the myth of the luxury liner.

Henri Pacon (1882–1946) could also claim a pavilion at the 1925 Exhibition, that of the review *Art et décoration*, which had been like an experience in the fitting out of passenger ships. Moreover, the highly streamlined *Île de France* (1926–33) had been his work. Of the four master architects in charge of *Normandie*, Pacon was without doubt the most unabashedly modernist. Between the wars, he became the great architect of passenger stations, having prevailed at Le Havre, with the help of Raoul Dautry, over a project by Lemaresquier to build a concrete structure notable for its immaculate volumes and powerful corners (1929–32). The Pacon-Patou team was certainly more homogeneous and solidary than that of the one upstairs. While Expert pulled ahead of an aging Bouwens, Patou and Pacon worked so closely together that it would be difficult to separate the hands of one from those of the other.

Information Center and shops on the Main Deck

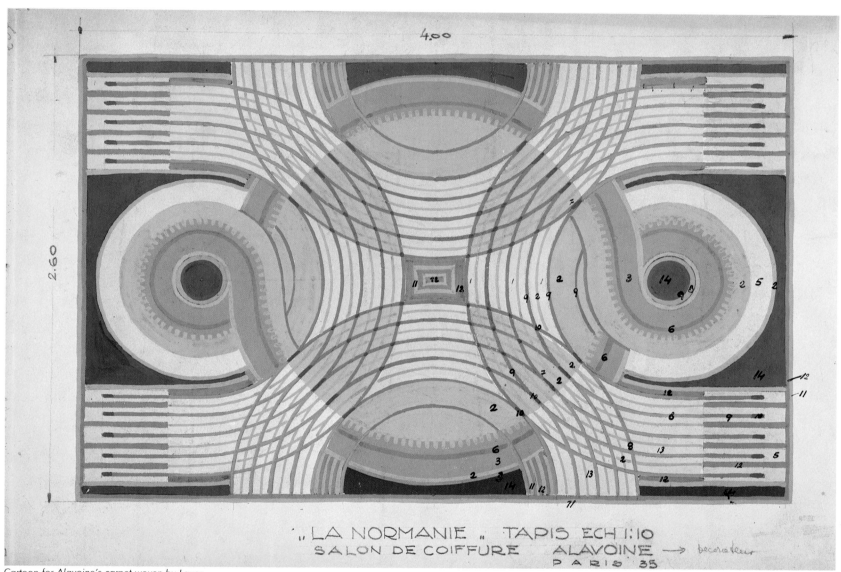

Cartoon for Alavoine's carpet woven by Lauer

The Hall

The first level of Hall — the Upper Hall that is — gave access to the Theater and the enfilade of lounges. The Hall at the next level down was reserved for the services most immediately required by passengers. It constituted the Main Deck, which was, primarily, a cabin deck. Thus, on this intermediate floor could be found the Information Center, with its attentive and discreet staff, the very Parisian vitrines of the Bon Marché, the hairdressing salon, the flower shop, and the office of France's state tourist service and railways. In terms of its décor, the area was kept modest, as it should

have been, in order not to take away unnecessarily from the splendors both above and below. The Information Center, with its circular projection, its counter of Rio rosewood, and its sign lettered out in the streamlined manner of the time, evinced an honorable and sufficient modernism, the product of designers Michon, Pigé, and Peigné.

On the forward side, several steps led up to the Chapel, located in the same vertical line as the Theater. On the landing, just opposite the Dining Room, hung François-Louis Schmied's *Norman Knight*, based on the Bayeux Tapestry and a work that brought the history of old Normandy to the depths of the ship, just as the *Viking* of Ducos de la Haille did for the vessel's upper reaches. Schmied was primarily

The Chapel, with a vault painted by Lombard and walls painted by Voguet

an illustrator, and the drawings he did after Jouve for the *Jungle Book* — the Jouve whose thirsty Hué elephants and tigers adorned the Reading Room upstairs — were considered, with good reason, to be masterpieces of technique. The *Norman Knight* also emerged as a technical marvel, being an enormous champlevé enamel on cast iron in which Schmied had re-created his own woodcuts. (Several years ago the piece was sold at auction in the United States.) Actually it was part of the program for *Normandie* that the decorative applications of new processes should be demonstrated. Thus, Ingrand's etched glass, Dunand's lacquers, and Dupas's glass paintings celebrated the encounter between artists and ambitious experiment. Even though the composition may have been borrowed from Miklos, as Félix Marcilhac said, the *Knight* surely takes it aesthetic value mainly from the technical skill the work evinces. It is not at all certain that Schmied's own art would benefit by such enlargement.

The Chapel

The panel bearing Schmied's *Norman Knight* could be slipped aside to open the way into the Chapel, an ecumenical place designed for both Catholics and Protestants. Sliding doors made it possible to conceal the Martel brothers' altar during services not requiring it. In his painted decorations Voguet had employed a reconciliatory iconography, free of controversial scenes and subjects. Instead, he devised rather philosophical or altogether symbolic compositions, in which five Prophets appeared on the right and the Evangelists with Saint Paul on the left. The form of the Chapel, with its barrel vault and vestigial side aisles, was meant to evoke the feeling of a traditional Christian church. The floral wreath surrounding the Christ figure behind the altar could be seen as a stylization of Baroque glorioles. Meanwhile, the floral motifs on the vault introduced a strange note of freedom in a decorative environment essentially geo-

metric in character. Of all the public rooms on *Normandie*, moreover, this was the only one, other than the Banquet Room, with overhead decorations, since the general scheme of the ship had been to make the ceiling a bare, reflective surface for indirect lighting.

The Chapel also contained an authentic masterpiece, the Stations of the Cross by Gaston Le Bourgeois (1890–1946). Ten of the original fourteen pieces survive and now adorn the Saint Thomas Aquinas Church in Le Havre. A second version also exists — thanks to André Marie, his family attachment to the CGT, and his passion for sculpture, as well as to help from the sculptor himself — and it can be seen in the church at Barentin. Le Bourgeois, who was also a very witty *animalier*, had carved his fourteen stations in dark rosewood. Placed in marble niches, the cruciform panels presented alternating variations of Christ seen close up, simple inscriptions, and figural scenes, all realized in an allusive if not symbolic manner. In their expressionist handling, these wood sculptures — really engravings, since the carving is very shallow — exude a kind of power and feeling that may have seemed rather alien in a luxury liner dedicated to pleasure and escape from all terrestrial problems. Shutters, inscribed with simple texts and a cross, made it possible for the insistent presence of the suffering Savior to be hidden during Protestant services.

The altar and tabernacle, the candelabra, organ loft, and liturgical furniture were all by the brothers Joël and Jan Martel (1896–1966). Thus, the modernists had decidedly found a home in the Chapel, just as Chauvin had established a beachhead for abstraction in the swimming pool. The Martels, those great friends of Mallet-Stevens, who designed their residence-studio next to his in the street now called the Rue Mallet-Stevens, managed during their long career as sculptors to think through and reinterpret virtually all the great plastic experiments of the 20th century, from Cubism to abstraction. On *Normandie*, the Martels counted among

Maquette for Schmied's panel (collection Félix Marcilhac)

The Norman Knight, by F. Schmied (auctioned by Sotheby's in New York on June 13, 1981)

A Perzel sconce for the lateral stairs

the few representatives of the UAM, an organization they had helped to found. On the organ loft, they depicted Christ calming the waters; on the altar panel, Christ in Glory with angels carrying the instruments of the Passion; on the tabernacle doors, the Mystical Lamb and, finally, Christ on the Cross. Throughout the series the relief work was so shallow, fine, and yet crisp that light seemed simply to glide over the surfaces, at the same time that it picked out the imagery in sharp, clear profile. Thus, the highly synthetic sculpture of the Martels revived the old problem of religious hieratism. The Christ on the Cross, with its characteristic treatment of the torso as an arrangement of interlocking volumes, showed the degree to which the Cubist lesson had made a lasting impact on Jan and Joël Martel. Here the artists seem closely akin to Archipenko. Working from the Martels' drawings, the great Parisian silversmith Puiforcat had crafted the ciborium, chalice, holy-water font, altar cruets, and censer, all conceived as assemblages of circular volumes and realized in silver and ivory. The Martels also prepared the geometric and symbolic designs for the chasubles, which were then sewn and embroidered by Mlles Hélène Henry

and Clery. Thus, the Chapel — thanks to Le Bourgeois, the Martels, and Voguet not having fallen from grace — emerged as one of the most remarkable of all the aesthetic successes on board *Normandie*. Oddly enough, it makes sense that this sanctuary had been concealed by the lay image of a Norman Knight, for, after all, *Normandie* was not a clerical ship.

Jan and Joël Martel, bas-relief for the organ loft

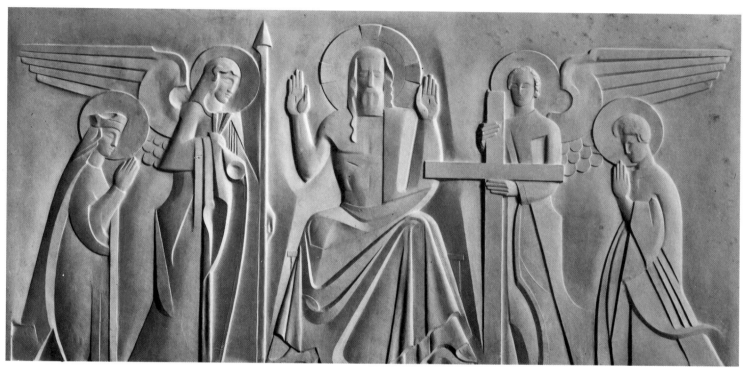

Altar bas-relief, bells, and cruets by the Martel brothers

Gaston Le Bourgeois, The Way of the Cross,
in dark rosewood, now in the church
at Barentin

The Dining Room

With Schmied's sliding panel closed, the door facing it on the opposite side of the landing, a work by Subes, attracted considerably more attention and movement, since it provided access to the Dining Room, where earthly meals were more often celebrated on this paradise-boat than the Eucharistic Supper across the way. The period had a pronounced taste for great, monumental portals in metal. The two exterior panels, measuring 20 feet high, included ten medallions representing Norman cities, making a project that integrated the arts of both metal and medals. On their other side, the doors had been decorated with arches, shells, and waves, themes reminiscent of those on the elevator grilles. In its size and amplitude, the portal was fit for a church, and so whereas the Chapel had hidden itself from the passengers, the Dining Room proclaimed its presence in full pomp. The medallions of Le Havre, Dieppe, Alençon, and Falaise, with their steamship and fortifications, could almost be read today as symbolic litanies of the Virgin, the vessel, the ivory tower, etc. This shift in meaning follows quite naturally, given the extent to which the very ambitiousness of the doors make one think of those splendid prototypes at the Florence Baptistery.

Passengers entered the Dining Room by way of a very grand staircase – a *grande descente*. This took them down a deck, which was necessary given the fact that the Dining Room had an elevation equal to three decks. But since this was a theater where the real performance took place in the auditorium, the arrival by descent permitted the actors and actresses, who were also the diners, to make their entrances brilliantly spotlighted. The dimensions of the Dining Room were an unbelievable 282 feet long and 28 feet high, providing space for 700 chairs at 150 tables. If space is the supreme luxury of boats, this Dining Room, situated at the aft end of the ship, thus near the service quarters, and devoid of outside windows, was like a miraculous grotto, an Ali Baba cave, its walls scintillating with Labouret's molded or hammered glass slabs. Whereas on the Promenade Deck, Bouwens and Expert had expanded, contracted, and varied their spaces, Patou and Pacon would maintain the strict volume of a rectangular parallelepiped, its simple geometry reinforced by a coffered ceiling. Thirty-eight monumental sconces, almost 16 feet tall, measured off the walls like engaged columns. Within the room itself, twelve Lalique "fire pots," towering 10 feet high, radiated light and punctuated the space at regular intervals. Tables stood in ranks parallel with the long axis of the room. In contrast to the Grand

Medallions by Subes, now mounted in portals at Our Lady of Lebanon in Brooklyn, N.Y.

opposite: Raymond Subes's great bronze portals leading to the Dining Room

Perzel ceiling light in a private dining room

Lounge and Smoking Room, where the sitting furniture was arranged in clusters and islands, everything in the Dining Room adhered to a strict order. In *Normandie*'s first class, the culinary rite was celebrated according to the purest protocol and with unflinching formality. The little round tables lined up as if every dinner constituted a state occasion.

At the extremities of this rectangular hall, the plastic arts made their presence known in bas-reliefs measuring 20 by 13 feet. Marking the entrance, on the flanking walls at the bottom of the stairs, were, on the starboard side, *Art in Normandie* by Raymond Delamarre (Prix de Rome, 1909) and, on the port side, Léon Drivier's *Sports and Games*, both bas-reliefs done in stucco (stone would have added unnecessary weight) and gilded, "to be in keeping with the room and able to benefit from the blaze of light." At the other end of the hall, Pierre Poisson paid homage to *Maritime Normandy* and Albert Pommier to *Terrestrial Normandy*. Owing to the split commission, unlike the situation in Dupas's Grand Lounge and in Dunand's Smoking Room, the CGT representatives had spelled a few things out for the artists. At the center of each composition, for example, there had to be at least two large standing figures. Moreover, the iconographic program was Norman, except in the curious instance of the sports subject. And inasmuch as it was clearly necessary to maintain a degree of generality, for passengers who were not, after all, specialists in the history of Normandy, the themes repeated those already given to Bouchard and Saupique on the deck above!

Delamarre, whose real talent lay in medals, created his relief by carving directly into the stucco material. To illustrate the arts in Normandy, he inserted direct quotations, as of the horsemen from the *Bayeux Tapestry*, or reinterpreted the jamb figures from Caen's Abbaye aux Hommes or the Rouen Cathedral in the corresponding styles. Léon Drivier (1878–1951) modeled his panel and endowed his figures with considerably greater relief. Resisting the realism that had seduced Dunand in his treatment of the same subject, Drivier adopted supposedly antique, Olympian nudity for his canoeists and polo players. A Rodin student converted to classicism, he had retained at least one of his master's principles: "Guard against flatness; volume must project from the plane." By comparison with the Delamarre relief, where nothing projects, the Drivier piece offers the pleasure of a totally different sensibility.

At the other end of the Dining Room, in this encounter between 1930s art and the bas-relief, Pierre Poisson (1876–1953) paid tribute to Normandy by invoking Mercury and Venus and treating them with an almost Canovian grace. On the facing wall, Albert Pommier, who too was a medalist,

Raymond Delamarre, The Arts and the Regional Monuments

Janniot's bas-relief on the back wall of the Banquet Room

piled up, without regard for perspective, all the attributes of terrestrial Normandy, from apple trees to cows. But all these bas-reliefs were still not enough for the Dining Room, and so, at the far end of the hall, surmounting the Captain's table, stood the verdigris bronze *Peaceful Normandy*, a statue by Dejean that succeeded in asserting the superiority of freestanding sculpture in a world of bas-reliefs. "That vertical was necessary in order to dominate the low elevation of the tables and chairs." In this temple consecrated to French gastronomy, a giant, protective goddess — Athena Parthenos — was desperately needed, and the figure the room got measured 13 feet tall.

Eight small dining rooms opened onto the large one, each of them decorated by a single painter. Mme Chantaud-Chabas, the wife of the better-known Chabas, had done allegories of cider, milk, harvests, and fishing; Louis Degallaix, *Spring*; Léopold Lévy, *Summer*; Josué Gaboriaud, *Autumn*; Mathurin Méheut, *Winter*; Joseph de la Nezière, famous Norman monuments; Edy Legrand, *The Harvest*, *The Norman Woman*, *The Orchard*, and *The Sea*; Bouchard, *Fruits of the Colonies*: oranges, coconuts, dates, and bananas, each borne by a native from the country of origin. The series would not seem to have harbored any great masterpieces.

Behind the Dejean statue, a staircase, corresponding to the one at the other end leading down from the Hall, took

Georges d'Espagnat's ceiling for the Banquet Room, representing sixteen personifications of Dance, Music and Painting (Museum of Irreplaceable Artifacts, New York)

The Dining Room, with Dejean's Peace standing before Janniot's bas-relief at the far end; along the sides, Szabo's bronze doors giving access to eight private dining rooms

The children's dining room with décor by Jean de Brunhoff and furniture by Jean Philippot

passengers through Szabo's gilt-bronze doors to the Banquet Room, a space with a lower elevation than that of the Dining Room. In a niche at the back stood a gilded bas-relief by Alfred Janniot, the pope of such stone tapestries, those huge bas-reliefs which, between the wars, the artist proliferated from the Colonial Museum to the Palais de Tokyo. It was Janniot who understood, perhaps better than anyone else, how to organize motifs in tiers, without regard to perspective, and fill the void throughout a planar field. The title of his subject: *Normandie, in the brilliance of her history, spreads the beauty of her soil from the banks of the Seine to the shores of the sea.* This allegorical Normandy — composed of themes already seen from the iconography of the province, its apple trees, beasts, and boats — offers a flavorful mixture of realism and antique grandeur that became a Janniot hallmark. Between the Seine and the Channel, Normandy-Pomona protects women wearing the beautiful native dress of Caux, Braye, and Auge. With Drivier, Delamarre, Poisson, and Pommier here assembled about Janniot, and all to be reunited for the Palais de Chaillot commission, the revival of bas-relief in France between the World Wars had its sanctuary in *Normandie's* dining halls. In the Banquet Room, Georges d'Espagnat's brilliantly colored and activated ceiling, high above walls of old rose, made a perfect complement to the warmth expected of a banquet.

The décor of the Dining Room very much included the treatment of tables. The Christofle firm had provided a *ménagère*, or table service, consisting of 45,000 pieces of silver, and Daum almost 50,000 pieces of glassware, "the cost of which we leave, without comment, to the imagination of housewives." However, the statement emphasized that the silver possessed "that somewhat massive strength and so-

lidity typical of present taste." The CGT monogram, in its pure geometric simplicity, was consistent with the silver's general stylistic character. Such formal qualities were also to be found in the glassware made of Daum cut crystal, whose deliberately compact shapes and squat bases were designed to prevent spillage in rough weather. The only decorative feature was a streamlined set of company initials on the foot.

On the deck below, the children traveling in first class enjoyed an advantage that everyone in first class might well have envied: a dining room designed by Philippot, with walls displaying elephants painted by Jean de Brunhoff, the father of "Babar." The metal chairs were among the most modern on the ship, as if children deserved a preview of the furniture they would know as adults in the second half of the 20th century.

The Swimming Pool

The Swimming Pool got tucked in under the Chapel. Technologically, there had never been anything like it, for the facility required "establishing within an environment constantly subject to vibrations . . . an enormous mass of water, itself in movement." Nor could anything compete with it in sheer magnitude, since the objective was to give "the world's biggest passenger liner the biggest swimming pool ever created on board a ship." Of all the spaces on *Normandie*, that given over to the pool was the one in which high modernism would win out unequivocally. In a luxury liner devoted to resurgent classicism and moderated contemporaneity, the pool room became the very tabernacle of abstraction. Dupas, Dunand, Poisson, Drivier, Janniot — all would be summarily dismissed in favor of an unchallenged "element of sculptural composition realized in antique bronze

The Swimming Pool

Jean Chauvin's luminous "fountain" and Victor Menu's decorative frieze

by M. Chauvin." In his time, Jean Chauvin was possibly the foremost French exponent of abstract sculpture. But this said, his special "element" remains nonetheless difficult to describe; moreover, it must also be discovered in devices designed to hide light sources, which gives his work the character of lamps or light fixtures. In such instances, abstraction became inextricably bound up with the utilitarian.

The arrangement of the pool in a graduated sequence of depths, each marked by rubber posts or "bumpers," made the pool somewhat like a water buffet. Measuring 82 feet long and 20 feet wide and inserted in a liner where sports held a conspicuous presence, not only on the walls (e.g., the works of Dunand and Drivier), but also in rooms reserved to them, the pool was one more aspect of that deliberate assimilation of the palace into the luxury liner. The role it played on *Normandie* was that of the basin fountain in the classical gardens of, for instance, Le Nôtre, the nobility this implied reinforced by the bluish tonality of the tank tiles covering both walls and vault. Completely encircling the pool and its walkway was a 16-foot-high frieze of animal themes, worked in Sèvres stoneware tiles from designs by Victor Menu.

The Public Rooms in Tourist and Third Class

The 750 so-called "cabin" or first-class passengers could be seen as the aristocracy of the realm, in contrast to the 625 "tourist" and the 340 "third-class" passengers making up the lower "orders" on board *Normandie*. This luxury liner was clearly made for the first class, and indeed the passengers booked at that level constituted the greatest number carried by the CGT's flagship. Even so, an effort was made on *Normandie* to achieve an equality well above what might

Tourist-class lounge, following the alterations made in 1936, with a wall painting by Mme Chantaud-Chabas

have been determined by a formula based exclusively on the mathematical power of the lowest common denominator. The public spaces in first class, so lavishly and deliberately reproduced in the literature distributed at the time of the ship's entry into service, were certainly not totally inaccessible to others on board for crossings. Moreover, they were not meant to insult the poverty of emigrants, like those of the 19th century whom Ford Madox Brown painted, spattered and soaked by the ocean's salt spray. Rather, the glories of first-class *Normandie* represented a promise of the fruits to be harvested from an alliance between the old world and the new.

Normandie's planners took great pride in the fact that, relative to all precedent, they had expended great care on the spaces allotted to the second and third classes. Of course, it must have been frustrating to travel so near and yet so far from the lacquers of Dunand and the golds of Dupas. On the other hand, a pure, if not hard, modernism was certain to prove more satisfactory to tourist-class passengers than to those in first class. Herein lay one of the charming paradoxes of *Normandie*.

The tourist-class dining room, with its 360-seat capacity, was located on C Deck toward the stern, just behind the first-class Banquet Room, an arrangement dictated by the proximity of the kitchens on D Deck. Aligned at right angles to the first-class Dining Room and athwartships from port to starboard, it rose at the center to the height of two decks, which gave the effect of considerable grandeur. The central dome was supported on a bundle of gilt-staff columns encircled by a serving buffet, a curious arrangement explained

Tourist-class staircase with a view onto the Main Deck

The bar in tourist class

The covered promenade in tourist class

The dining room in tourist class, with décor by Rousseau

Decorative panel by Claire Valière

The information center in tourist class

by the fact that the columns concealed conduits. Thus, the monumental prevailed in tourist class as well as in first. The walls were clad in pale ash, and the chairs made of wood combined with metal, the same metal allowed to first-class passengers only in the Smoking Room but given more generously to the other classes. Legas, Maurice, and Jamin were the collaborating decorators.

The third-class dining room, designed by Rousseau, was also located in the rear part of the ship, this time on E Deck just under the kitchens. Here again, the central section rose to a steeper elevation, the better to ennoble the space and make it breathe. Crowning the "stepped-up" dome was a light fixture of almost Mondrianesque design. Now, luxury resided in geometric rigor and in the crisp forms of the luminous structure.

The tourist-class lounge, located on the Main Deck in the ship's aft section, had been created by Schmit et Cie in a "harmony of white and rose." And it too had the central dome that seemed to be an almost typological feature of the public rooms in tourist class. White sycamore provided the material not only for the wall revetments but also for the chairs, the latter covered with Aubusson tapestry with the same floral motifs as those in first class. This decorative theme recurred in wall hangings of "rose-stone fabric" suspended from the cupola, whose "square" drum was mounted with glass pieces etched by Ingrand. Compared with the Grand Lounge in first class, the tourist lounge differed mainly in its simplifications, in the shift from gold to rose (a color that had been merely an accent in Dupas's panels), and in the elimination of art works, which now, where there were

The recreation deck

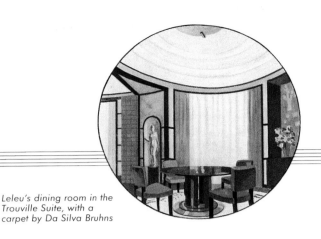

Leleu's dining room in the Trouville Suite, with a carpet by Da Silva Bruhns

any, became practically anonymous or appeared overhead. In this environment, modernity and economy joined together in easy alliance. A multipurpose facility, the tourist lounge could be transformed into a chapel, a cinema, or a dance floor. As in first class, the tourist lounge had a companion room for writing, its décor derived from maple and wild cherry wood, characterized as "light, feminine, and gay," and a bridge room, finished in "white and pale green, *en avodiré verni*." This space was "endowed with an intimate retreat and a curved bar in brown lacquer with sides of varnished sycamore," it too designed by Schmit et Cie.

The third-class lounge, conceived by Noyon, gave evidence of still greater reductiveness, but, in compensation, it enjoyed a luxury denied every other class — a view directly onto the sea — since the space was located at the very end of B Deck. And the tourist smoking room, on the Promenade Deck, enjoyed the same advantage as that claimed by the first-class Grill Room on the Embarkation Deck — a panorama overlooking the vast field of water that a giant had just plowed. Laid out horseshoe fashion, walnut-paneled, and cinctured by a row of columns, this smoking room was comparable, within the *Normandie* cathedral, to the ambulatory of a Gothic choir. The furniture came from the studios of Marc Simon. And so, the reader of *L'Esprit nouveau*, the supporter of the UAM, or the fanatical admirer of Le Corbusier did not need to deny himself travel on *Normandie*, provided only that he take the more economical accommodations available in tourist and third class.

The Four Luxury Apartments

Four deluxe apartments, designed by Leleu, Süe, Montagnac, and Dominique and meant for the special few who could claim them by virtue of great status or great means, symbolized the triumph of French decorative art on board *Normandie*. They represented a "rich" version of the normal solutions devised for the various cabins and served to give them all a certain tone. The apartments prepared by Leleu and Süe were located behind the Sun Deck and cantilevered over the Embarkation Deck, which gave them the advantage of a private terrace with access to the double spectacle of the sea and the whole cascading sequence of aft decks. As in modern villas, the masters were placed at the summit, closer to open air.

These *grand luxe* apartments comprised several rooms. Far from ignoring the realities of the space, Jules Leleu had conceived the Trouville Suite (Sun Deck, starboard side) as a variation on oval and semicircular plans derived from the rounded shape of the rear Sun Deck. The oval dining room

The salon in the Trouville Suite, with an Aubusson tapestry executed by Lauer from the cartoons of Anatole Kasskoff

102

Süe's salon for the Deauville Suite

was lined with ivory Moroccan leather, the chairs covered in vivid green hide, and the boiseries and sliding doors lacquered in brown or gold. On the curved walls of the salon hung Aubusson tapestries representing Kasskoff's figures from Greek pastorals. The chairs, meanwhile, had been veneered in burled ash and upholstered in a bronze-colored satin. Such precious materials and exquisite colors, the lacquers and gold — all brought into the Trouville Suite the very atmosphere of the first-class Grand Lounge and Smoking Room. Without compromising his taste for pristine forms, Leleu had so inflected the architecture of his furniture that the shapes — especially in the salon canapé — echoed those of the walls and bays. This formal theme was also recapitulated in the abstract sinuosities of Da Silva Bruhns's carpet on the salon floor.

In his Deauville Suite (Sun Deck, port side), Louis Süe had to deal with the same problem, which he too solved by choosing an oval plan for the salon. The apartment that resulted was "blond and gay, and extremely well arranged." In a special touch, Süe had dreamt up a small burled-ash neo-Louis XVI chair upholstered in the tufted Napoleon III fashion, an all-blue piece that contrasted wittily with the salon's Aubusson-covered "comfortable" armchairs and canapé. The overall tonality was rose-beige. The bedroom had ivory-lacquered furniture, gondola beds, and bronze-colored satin covers, which altogether made a restrained, less grandiose ensemble — and a tribute from Süe (his partner Mare had died in 1932) to the continuity of styles.

The Trouville dining room

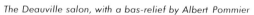

The Deauville salon, with a bas-relief by Albert Pommier

The Deauville bedroom, with an Aubusson tapestry executed by Lauer from cartoons by Louis-Marie Süe, entitled Le Château de Couterne

The Rouen salon

Rouen's bedroom by Dominique

The dining room in the Caen Suite

Montagnac's bedroom for the Caen Suite

The Caen Suite's bathroom

Two of Dominique's bedrooms for the Rouen Suite

In the Caen Suite (Main Deck, port side) Pierre Paul Montagnac gave vent to his taste for rare woods and paneling in the same material as the furniture: Rio rosewood in the dining room and salon, Makassar ebony in the bedrooms, and sycamore everywhere else. It was "the style of the perfect cabinetmaker." The red satin of the bedrooms and salon and the green leather of the dining room were colors that by their very strength brought great dignity to the whole. Understandably, it was Montagnac's Caen Suite — an "en-semble whose tact and aristocracy belong among the finest creations to be found in the French tradition" — that was chosen for Mme Albert Lebrun, the wife of the President of the Republic, during *Normandie's* maiden voyage across the Atlantic.

The Rouen Suite (Main Deck, starboard side) was re-

markable for the extremely refined use that Dominique made of materials: walls lacquered blue and silver in one bedroom, covered with pigskin in the salon, and with parchment in the dining room, the better "to retain a sense of traveling by sea." Dominique, the firm founded by André Domin and Marcel Geneviève, was unquestionably the most avant-garde of the four talents assigned to the deluxe apartments. Along with Pierre Chareau, Pierre Legrain, and Raymond Templier, Dominique had been part of a "group of five," whose spirit differed somewhat from that of Leleu and Süe, who tried to reinterpret and modernize the grand tradition. Thus, Rouen had the simplest furnishings of any among the four luxury suites. Here, as in the first-class cabins, Dominique did a lot with Manyfil fabrics, created by Rodier and presented as masterpieces of textile art. The consciously reductive motifs made the quality of the materials seem all the more extraordinary. Dominique's purism was absolutely at one with the most natural of silks and wools, all hand-loomed. In keeping with this, the firm employed light fixtures with radically modernistic forms from the studios of Jean Perzel. Ten deluxe apartments on the Main Deck completed the Norman cities series. Among these, Laprade did Alençon; Carlhian, Bayeux; Jansen, Coutances; Pascaud, Dieppe; Fallot, Fécamp; Huet, Prou, and Chevalier, Lisieux; Sibu, Mont Saint-Michel; Tchumi and Vermeil, Honfleur; Nelson, Jumièges; and Carlu, Le Havre. Two of the suites continued the old historicizing tradition that, until then scarcely felt on *Normandie*, had been dominant on the pre-1914 ships. Carlhian, who did so much to introduce the French 18th century into the great American houses, had made the Bayeux salon into a Régence and Louis XV affair, while doing the bedroom in Louis XVI. Camaïeu motifs in the manner of Pillement ornamented the boiseries. A kindred spirit was Nelson, who in Jumièges had selected motifs from the panels made for Mme de Pompadour at Meudon. The other deluxe apartments reflected the various tendencies of their respective decorators and differed from one another mainly by the relative importance given to wall revetments and ceiling decorations, as well as by mood and stylistic variations.

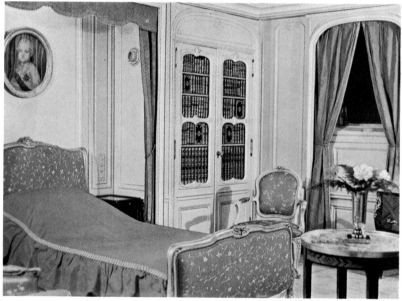

Nelson's bedroom for the Jumièges Suite

Maquettes for the Bayeux salon and its furniture by André Carlhian (collection Robert Carlhian)

Jacques Carlu, the future architect of the Palais de Chaillot, gave Le Havre a salon based on curve motifs: a stuccoed ceiling with the *trouvaille*, or windfall, of a central oculus serving as a light reflector directly above a small table, itself round, and chair arms that reinvented and transposed traditional Louis-Philippe furniture. Carlu's classicizing taste found expression in tables supported on bundles of columns, in statue bases, and in neo-Greek pictures from the Dupas-

The Le Havre salon by Jacques Carlu

The Honfleur salon by Huet-Tchumi-Vermeil

Jansen's bedroom in the Coutance Suite

The salon and bedroom in the Alençon Suite by Laprade and Bazin

106

Jean Pascaud's salon for the Dieppe Suite, with a decorative panel by J.G. Domergue

Follot's bedroom for the Fécamp Suite, with decorative panels on the theme of Provence by Georges Lepape

The Lisieux bedroom by Prou-Chevalier

The Mont Saint-Michel bedroom by Sibu

Service corridor in first class

Dufet, Bureau, Fréchet and Rothschild, Chevalier, Groult, and finally, Ruhlmann, who was to die in 1933. Eventually there would be forty different types of cabin: nine for the terrace cabins, eleven for the salon cabins, eleven for the bedroom cabins, and nine for the interior cabins. Among the 439 cabins in first class, 117 were inside accommodations without direct access to the sea, while 322 had portholes.

Cabin by cabin and class by class, the guiding principle had been *luxe generalisé*, whether it was a matter of space or of finishing. Thus, the third class on *Normandie* had to be the equivalent of "first on many passenger ships." As in its public spaces, tourist class offered cabins that, owing to the simple economy of materials and meters, were the facilities on *Normandie* most nearly in tune with the modernism preached by the UAM and Mallet-Stevens. In terms of such minimalism, the cabins that today seem particularly impressive would include the first-class units designed by Blanche J. Klotz, as in, for example, her bedroom-cabin-salons in sky-blue-lacquered aluminum. The wall décor consisted entirely of parallel stainless-steel bands of different lengths, an arrangement that resulted in a genuinely abstract, purist composition. The metal chairs were by Fibracier and the blue and rose fabrics by Hélène Henry. Metal had also been used by Lucie Renaudot in her Type B bedrooms and her Type C salon cabins, where butternut, moiré sycamore, and white-maple panels were attached by metal strips in a way to give the rooms an armature-like structure. Matched to those on the walls, the woods used in the beds were also enhanced with metal features comparable to the wall strips. Renaudot, as well as Klotz, liked to combine rigorously purified, minimal furniture with the abstract curves of sculptural ceilings, the latter with integrated light fixtures.

Among the decorators with modernist sensibilities, Michel Dufet deserves special note, since he took charge of fitting out forty first-class cabins in all the various categories — terrace, two-bed, salon, and interior. Although in 1930 he had created zinc furniture for the Compagnie Asturienne, Dufet used only wood for revetments on *Normandie*. His Type B cabin-bedroom with two beds was entirely paneled, from floor to ceiling, in varnished zebrano, the material repeated in beds, chairs, cabinets, and desks, which were themselves integral with the wood paneling. Applied horizontally, the wood strips made an uninterrupted linear continuity around the room. The "abstract-concrete" arrangement completed the décor for this room, in which the bed's headboard was left bare of everything but reflected light. Several of Dufet's signature touches could be found from one cabin to another. There were, for instance, those high

Pougheon school. In Follot's Fécamp, it would seem to have been the talent of Georges Lepape — the source of so much humor in those gouaches for the *Gazette du Bon Ton* and the pictures with provincial subjects delightfully Cubified — that brought such a fresh and surprising touch of gaiety. Even the large fauteuils designed by Follot — rather like bergères-bibendum — partook of a euphoria in which beams and bosses came together in gentle alliance. The most modernistic of the apartments was Honfluer, where Tchumi and Vermeil used steel bands to cut the boiseries into horizontal registers, all the while that the velvet furniture remained a bit traditional.

The Cabins

Following a competition, the various cabins had been assigned to fifteen decorators, who would be joined by still other designers — Follot, Pascaud, and Printz. Besides Mmes Klotz and Renaudot, the winners seem to have been Prou, Rapin, Montagnac, Dominique, Perreau, Thery, Bouchet,

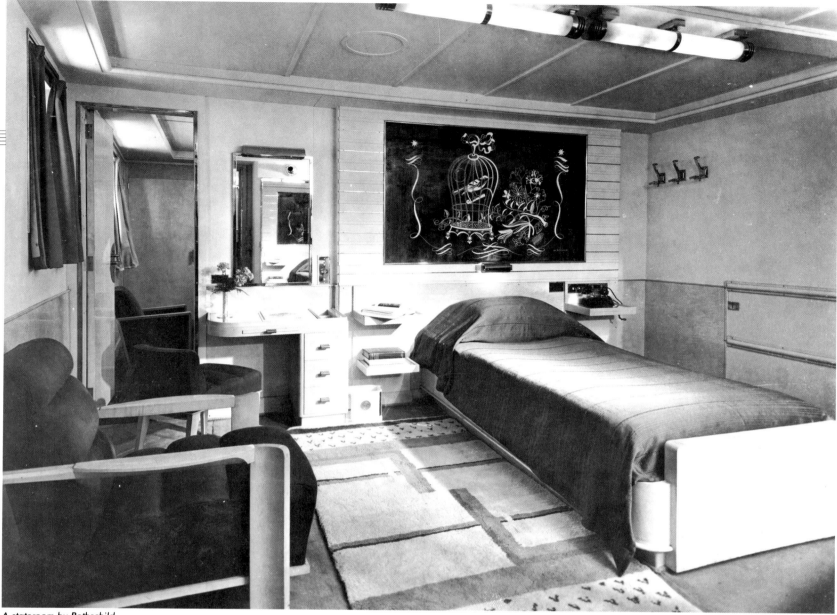

A stateroom by Rothschild

bed railings in curved metal, which, within Dufet's floating wood boxes, seemed to echo the ship's own railings; also the convex shape of the furniture's projecting corners, designed to reduce the danger to occupants during rough seas, even on board what was the most stable of ships. The beauty

of these modified right angles was consistent with other such easements. Dufet had called for "vivid, gay colors like orange, blue, coral, and related variations [that are] both tense and tender." Thus, in one cabin Dufet set off furniture in varnished white maple against vermilion lacquer walls

A stateroom by Bouchet

A terrace stateroom by Domin

painted with carefully spaced tiers of cascading vegetable motifs, the latter simplified by Le Bucheron *à la* Matisse.

Bouchet, who too worked with Le Bucheron, used pale woods, "avodiré, platan, perofa, wild cherry," but, even more, "dark, warm-toned woods," such as rosewood or American mahogany, whereas Dufet had a pronounced preference for very light-toned materials, white sycamore, burled ash, etc.

Other decorators, such as René-Jean Prou from the Pomona studio at Bon Marché, Jean Rothschild and André Fréchet, André Domin, Marcel Perreau, and Léon Bouchet simply transposed to *Normandie*'s cabins decorative ensembles, essentially unchanged, from their stock in trade on land. The charm of *Normandie* — even if some would call it a flaw — lay precisely in that transfer on board of the decorators' stands normally seen at the annual Salon. The relative vastness of the first-class cabins did in fact allow their designers to arrange corner groupings and place beds side by side as at home. The opportunity and challenge were somewhat comparable to those presented by bedrooms in grand hotels by the sea. Thus, Léon-Émile Bouchet made the armoire-closet into the sort of showpiece furniture that gives such pleasure to lovers of the Art Deco style. Fréchet and Rothschild mixed a streamlined bed with chairs styled in that moderno-Louis XVI manner which had been one of the most attractive developments to emerge from the 1920s' delightful "return to order."

Just as generals find their places in history more readily than unknown soldiers, the cabins in first class certainly remain better known than those in second and third classes. And these were, of course, less photographed and less reproduced in the media. Moreover, they offered less variety in their décor. Given more restricted spaces to work with, the decorators resorted to ordinary stacked bunks, which, however, could be real beds, since wood, perhaps *the* great luxury of *Normandie*'s interiors, was widely used in these cabins. Here, the occupants had only one armchair, albeit upholstered in velvet and good enough to hold its own, if necessary, in more expensive cabins. Here too, wiring and conduits had been much less carefully concealed than in the better accommodations. Wash basins projected with unabashed nakedness from the wall between bunks. While vegetal motifs ornamented the walls, metal, so dear to the UAM, had the right of place in third class. Thus, when fabricated of metal, the bunks were solid bits of architecture made of curves and straight lines. With this came at least the one wood chair, which, however modest, gave symbolic presence to the sumptuosity of cabinetwork and upholstery. Bare light bulbs dropped directly from the ceiling, but the luxury of a bouquet of real flowers placed on the shelf over the wash basin, no doubt for photographic purposes, gave this third-class cabin what art could not afford to provide.

Normandie: Truly a Monument to the Art of Her Time?

The splendors of *Normandie*, during the ship's planning stage and at the time of her maiden voyage, gave rise to an argument that has not abated even now. Was this liner, which won the mythical Blue Ribbon for speed and achieved technological perfection, truly the standard-bearer of French art and quality as her apologists so eagerly claimed? To turn the fable around, did the bird's plumage come up to the song? Is it possible that this "avant-garde" ship was in fact the last survivor of an older age, somewhat like a knight in shining armor wandering into modern shell fire? Hardly had *Normandie* made her debut when she came in for criticism from one of the best of the French "moderns," Robert Mallet-Stevens. In the midst of the general enthusiasm, Mallet-Stevens let his opinion be known in a 1935 issue of *Architecture d'aujourd'hui*, and it was prophetic. The power of Mallet-Stevens's influence at that time should not be exaggerated, for, like that of Le Corbusier, it spoke for a minority view, but it was the voice that posterity would listen to, for a long time at least. Only today, with the reaction against the absolutist, puritanical attitudes of the postwar years and the 1950s, has it become possible to regard *Normandie* more objectively and give honest consideration to her place in the history of French art, or of art in general.

The point of departure for this reconsideration should be Mallet-Stevens's criticisms, which were twofold. First, *Normandie* was not a boat of sufficient technical daring, either in her design or in her choice of materials. She did not, for instance, invent what would become the decorative style of the late 1930s or of the second half of the 20th century. Instead, the ship exploited and revived formulas that had been advanced in 1925, which, because too timid or too familiar, could not carry the torch for "modernism." According to Mallet-Stevens, *Normandie* did not deserve to be stamped with the trademark "France." "Was this floating exhibition really a reflection of contemporary art?" asked the critic. "We hasten to say no. A good many bits of that enormous ensemble have a pronounced 1925 look. Too often, while wandering about on board, one has the impression of viewing a retrospective." Mallet-Stevens would have preferred that *Normandie* present a totally unexpected profile, a "new silhouette," without smokestacks and certainly without that third one, a fake which the engineers had thought

A stateroom by Lucie Renaudot

A pair of staterooms by Mme Klotz

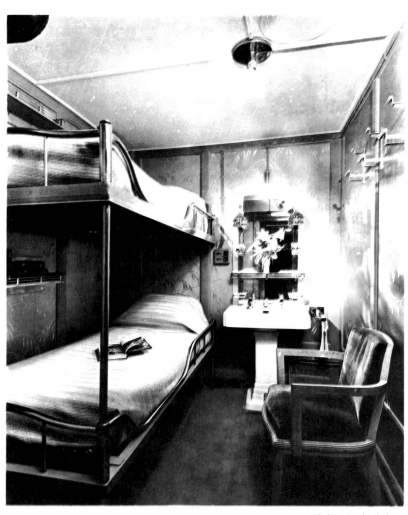

Cabins in third class

Cabins in tourist class

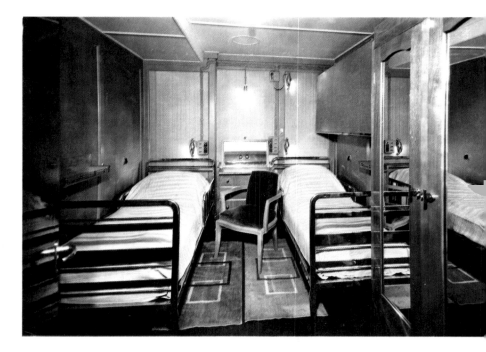

essential to the ship's image. Accusing the maritime engineers of being behind the times, he regretted that the propellers were not mounted laterally. "*Normandie* 1935 could have been to *Normandie* 1885 what an aerodynamic automobile is to a taxi at the Marne" (referring to the Paris cabs commandeered to help hold the German army at the Marne during a decisive battle in World War I).

Second, Mallet-Stevens attacked the use of wood or uselessly luxurious substances at the expense of what should have been the dominant material, the only truly imperishable and nonflammable material: steel. The OTUA (Office Technique pour l'Utilisation de l'Acier) had in fact just asked "several artists of the Union des Artistes Modernes to do a study of steamship cabins in steel." Those chosen were Chareau, Barbe, Gascouin, Herbst, Jourdain, Louis, Pingusson, and, of course, Mallet-Stevens. The results of this creative effort appeared at the Salon d'Automne in 1934, and a publication of the OTUA, brought out in 1935, outlined their proposals, which, in essence, were offered as object lessons for the work under way on *Normandie*. Reviewing the history of "art on board passenger liners," Mallet-Stevens recalled how décor had over the centuries passed from the exterior to the interior of ships, from the huge sculptural poops of 17th-century vessels to the lounges of luxury liners. According to the author, this transformation had been accompanied by an ineluctable shift in material, from wood to steel, which had claimed the hull but not yet the internal structure and furnishings — an intolerable contradiction for the modern rationalist. Following the system of "wood hull — wood furnishing" should come "steel hull — steel furnishing." Then Mallet-Stevens added: "After the adoption of mechanical locomotion, the great progress in matters of navigation should be the incombustible ship." For this critic, *Normandie*, in which so much of the interior had been given over to marbles, glasses, and rare woods, was too remote from the all-steel ship, his idea of the true modern liner.

Then, as a final, overriding argument, the decorator teams selected for *Normandie* were deemed incapable of "using steel in a way to make lodging at sea attractive, gay, bright, and comfortable." The Salon d'Automne exhibitions, mounted in response to the OTUA's invitation, provided an example of what should have been done on the new ship. The criticism thus culminated in an indictment of the men responsible for *Normandie*, of those who had failed to engage artists competent to take a genuinely contemporary approach. Acknowledging the absent, Mallet-Stevens mentioned "Barillet, Burkhalter, Chareau, Dourgnon, Gascoin, Herbst, Francis Jourdain, Lambert-Rucki, Léger, Lurçat, Prouvé, Salomon," all active, if not exactly famous, members

of the UAM. And so, one could well imagine another *Normandie*, with fittings by René Herbst, Pierre Chareau, and Jean Prouvé, with décor by Fernand Léger and the Delaunays, and with architecture by Mallet-Stevens and André Lurçat! In Mallet-Stevens's view, this *Normandie* would have been *the* modern liner, the ship for the 1930s through the 1960s, a vessel that could properly symbolize the passage into the second half of the 20th century, whereas the CGT's *Normandie* had come forth as a "retro" liner, a prolongation of the 1925 show. Were it not for the time it takes for terms to catch up with chronology, the boat could have been dated 1910, the moment when the taste subsequently known as Art Deco actually came into being.

This judgment, which became the dominant view for almost forty years, has at last been challenged. A fantasy ship conjured through the medium of surviving evidence rediscovered at auctions and quickly installed in the world's greatest museums (the preeminent symbol of this came when the Metropolitan Museum in New York acquired one of Dupas's glass panels), or revisualized from the images in old travel brochures, glitters anew under the fires of nostalgia and dream. The time in purgatory, required of boats as of writers, has passed. Now, with the dogmas of the Bauhaus and the so-called International Style under indictment, brought by the new "post-modern" age, *Normandie* is eagerly cited as the floating, if not living, proof that other solutions were possible. Just as the Palais de Chaillot — designed by Jacques Carlu upon his return to France from the United States, where he had been professor at MIT before he was replaced by the Bauhaus heroes fleeing Germany — has reemerged not as a flat attempt at a neoacademicism, but as the example of an architecture that wanted to reconcile modernity with classical tradition, the interior décor of *Normandie* strikes us today as a manifest desire to discover an equilibrium between the exigencies of Le Corbusier's "machine for living" and the prolonged ostentation of Art Deco. It gives definition to the part France played in a *style 1935*, the same style that would characterize the Paris World's Fair of 1937 and the New York World's Fair of 1939. The storm that broke in 1940 would capsize both the boat and the sensibility she embodied, but the historian knows that in the cavalcade of styles, there was and will remain, if not a style, then certainly a *moment Normandie*.

This said, there is no reason to confuse a program for decorating a ship with an exhibition staged as a manifesto. Regardless of what may have been voiced or written, *Normandie* did not claim and did not need to be a complete demonstration of the modern French art of her time. The passengers were certainly delighted with the art the ship offered them, and they did not expect it to deliver an avant-garde message. The art simply illuminated the pleasure of being there, in a world that synthesized the ambitions of the 1930s. Claude Roger-Marx has expressed the limits of the genre quite well: "A liner is neither a museum nor a palace; it is an instrument of transport at the same time that it is also a hostelry. Security and comfort — these are its primary virtues. Afterwards come the art of diverting, or of ornamenting the time, in a charming way. Thus, it has less to do with decoration or with beauty in the absolute sense than with a fantasy about the present. Painters and sculptors capable of bowing to particular exigencies step in as illustrators." It would surely be useless to pretend that Jean Dupas was a misunderstood genius who could put Fernand Léger in the shade, but it would also be pointless to hold him in contemptuous disregard as has been the case until recently. Actually, the artists assigned to *Normandie* understood quite well how, within the limits of a decorative scheme, to please a special audience and how to express a taste sure of its own ambitions. They demonstrated that the *paquebot* style so often imagined for the 20th century could magnify other values than those extolled by Le Corbusier in his 1920 articles for *L'Esprit nouveau*.

Contemporaries were taken aback by the apparent contradiction between the *styles paquebots* that never ceased to be proclaimed and contrasted to one another. There was, for instance, the style that could be seen most often on land, in such buildings as the Hôtel Latitude 43 at Saint-Tropez, built by Pingusson in 1932 and offering a rigorous kind of architecture more like a sanatorium than a palace. Then, there was the style evident in the liners themselves, which, from the *Île de France* to *Normandie*, seemed to have nothing in common with that minimalism of surface and ornament which the "modernists" saw as consistent with the technological efficiency of the airplane, automobile, or steamship. "The passenger ship should be decorated, fitted out, and furnished as a passenger ship," Mallet-Stevens declared. On the other hand, Claude Roger-Marx insisted that the originality of *Normandie* lay in her very refusal to be overly subservient to physical and functional realities: " 'But where is the boat? . . . I want to see the boat,' cried a little boy, wonderstruck at the winter garden, the game room, the swimming pool, the library, the halls, the immense lounges he had been taken to see. This charming anecdote sums up the paradox presented by these floating cities, in which everything has been organized to make the passengers believe they have not left their normal environment. . . ."

The boy could not have known that the ship so unlike a boat was a failure in the eyes of those who wanted houses to look rather too much like themselves. Misunderstanding abounded when it came to the notion of a *style paquebot*. On the one hand, *Normandie* was the ship which ostensibly rejected that simplicity and efficiency thought to be the virtue of modernity. On the other hand, *Normandie*, by her success in combining luxury and security, should be sufficient proof, even to the apostles of maceration, that poverty and modernity were not indissolubly linked. Jansenist rigor and the Jesuit style had detested one another, but by their very opposition they also defined the reality of 17th-century France. For us, Philippe de Champaigne does not exclude the possibility of Rubens, and vice versa. By the same token, it should be acknowledged that in the 1930s *Normandie* represented a trend just as coherent and interesting as that which would go on to triumph after the Second World War. On one side there was Mallet-Stevens who called for a "new, special style, and it is, moreover, that of the steamship." The qualitites he wanted were "a minimum of clutter, painted but not concealed materials, easily washed surfaces, electrical wiring in bare, unenclosed tubes, strongly asserted ventilation, mirrors clearly reflecting one's image (even in the lower classes) and optically expanding the unavoidably limited spaces, sanitary fixtures that are practical, simple, and honest in color, no decorative motifs (at least in cabins), motifs that can obsess the sick. . . ." On the other side, the architects of *Normandie* demonstrated that within her closed world a ship can also dramatize "that most incomparable of riches," space, employ the most varied and impressive of materials, from marble and steel to wood, deny the pointless display of plumbing, a parody of that other myth known as "the machine for living," and give free reign to décor, despite the dictatorship of Ripolin and whitewash. *Normandie* simply denied the "inevitability" of evolution.

Now that modernity has taken its place in the march of time — certain as always of the morality of its solutions, especially that "standard," the key word so dear to Le Corbusier, which tyrannically usurped the place of the classical orders and proportions — *Normandie* stands forth as an outpost of freedom, offering the possibility of escaping norms and uniformity. "Inevitably," so ever-present in the language of Mallet-Stevens, was an adverb never used by those who wanted to reconcile history with modernity and repair the linkage of the ages. To understand the exasperation — the indignation — that *Normandie* aroused among the pure and tough (whom the ship's fire must have struck as just vengeance wreaked by the new gods), one should reread the chapter Le Corbusier devoted to ships in *Vers Une Architecture* (1923): "The passenger liner is the first step in the

realization of a world organized according to the new spirit." Ten years later, *Normandie* challenged the tablet of laws handed down by the new spirit and particularly its optimistic belief in the serial. "Style," Le Corbusier had concluded, "is a unified principle that informs all the works of a period and produces its characteristic spirit." *Normandie*, however, proved that the power of the principle did not have to be dictatorial, that solutions could be found by means of the highest, and not exclusively by the lowest, common denominator.

It should be clear, in any event, that for those who conceived her, *Normandie* was not a timorous ship. If they decided against an exclusive use of steel, it was done consciously and without regrets. In 1935, when Jean Marie, the CGT's manager, described the liner for *Je sais tout*, he of course stressed the extraordinary precautions that had been taken against fire — more frightening than a storm — but for him "the marbles, the onyx, and the glass works" offered the double advantage of incombustibility and a beauty that *Normandie* should not be without. Why reject Aubusson tapestries as long as they could be "fire-proofed"? Similarly, if the architects of *Normandie* used glass so freely, it was because the material offered incombustibility as well as a substance "so rich in clarity, so mercurial in its effects, so singing in its brilliance, so harmonic in its purity that it is almost alive." The luminous enchantment of *Normandie*'s Dining Room, with its Labouret glass walls, was simultaneously a hymn to safety. The great ship's apartments and cabins simply thumbed their nose at Mallet-Stevens's allegations when, in a statement to *Paris-Soir* in 1933, the critic took rather easy advantage of the emotions generated by the fire on the *Atlantique* to lobby steamship companies and passengers in favor of metal. "The more it provides an extra margin for safety," he said, "the more the lover of exotic woods and varnished marqueteries will be happy with a plaque of chromed steel, once he knows his life depends on it." But experience had shown that metal shells could withstand fire very little better than wooden structures. And the future would lie in alliance more than in an implacable war. Moreover, the so-called technical arguments always concealed tenets that were basically aesthetic. "To those who say, 'safety, not luxury,' we reply, 'luxury and safety,'" Olivier Quéant stated in the April 1933 issue of *Art et industrie*. The luxury was certainly the sort expected and deserved by the 850 passengers in *Normandie*'s first class. Above all, it denied that "ornament is a crime," the famous formula which, even though a distortion of what its author, Adolph Loos, actually believed, would become one of the rallying cries of the new architecture.

The tempered modernity of *Normandie* should never be confounded with a retardataire 1925 mode, as some contended. A comparison between the *Île de France* and *Normandie*, both of which employed the same artists, simply makes the difference seem all the more striking. There is as great a difference, for example, between the Régence style and the Louis XIV style as between the first-class lounge on *Normandie* and that on the *Île de France*. Clearly, the spatial disposition and décor of *Normandie*, relative to the great sea queens of the 1920s, seemed to establish a new *style paquebot*, even if it were nothing more than the emphasis on horizontality. Whereas on the *Île de France* the architects had taken over the steep halls of the great department stores, with their staircases and galleries, and then turned them upside down, *Normandie* offered horizontal perspectives and longitudinal avenues. The group of four — Bouwens-Expert and Patou-Pacon — were the counterparts of Faure-Dujarric at the Trois Quartiers store in 1931. And it was precisely in the March 1932 issue of *Architecture d'aujourd'hui* that Louis Faure-Dujarric defined the modern department store as a "machine for selling" that no longer needed "halls several stories high" and staircases. To this *grand déballage* — or "great spread" — of merchandise, he preferred that objects be presented "in an impeccable arrangement." The arrangement of the large public suites on *Normandie*, with their horizontal succession and their assignment by function, was symptomatic of the shift toward a 1930s taste. In her architectural conception at least, *Normandie* could very well be on the side of the modernists, of those, at least, whom we recognize as such.

Normandie could never be confused with either of the two principles that, according to Mallet-Stevens, governed the decoration of passenger ships: "On the boat reproduce the style of the country to which the boat belongs or re-create the style or styles of the countries visited by the ship. . . . I do not think the decoration of future ships will depart from these principles: country of origin or country visited." Here Mallet-Stevens was responding to Georges Philippar, president of the Messageries Maritimes, who in an instructive conference in 1926 had actually suggested that more inspiration be sought "in the particular styles of the regions served." Thus, for *Mariette Pacha* and *Champollion* "the characteristics of the architecture of pharaonic Egypt" had been adopted, "combined with the pure lines of French modern art"! It had even been suggested that borrowings be made "from our dear old regional French heritage." For example, "the smoking room on *Athos II* would be Breton. Thereafter would come Provençal, Norman, Alsatian, and Basque smoking rooms. . . ." It was Georges Philippar who thought only

Expert's French Pavilion at the 1939 New York World's Fair

overleaf:

The aft Sun Deck
(one of the plates made for the publicity brochure)

"modern" styles posed the risk of early obsolescence and that it would be much better to adopt "a clearly classified and somewhat old style." But the Messageries Maritimes were not the CGT, and Presidents Dal Piaz and Cangardel did not sail on the same ships with Philippar.

Certainly *Normandie* did not represent an attempt to revive a French historical style. And here it is important that an iconographic program not be confused with stylistic choices. The references made on *Normandie* to cathedrals, châteaux, meadows, and apple trees in no way implied an assemblage of "classical European styles" or the best architectural examples of that region. Nor, clearly, did *Normandie* fall under the sarcastic label of "yacht style," which Mallet-Stevens quite justly mocked for its "mahogany cabinetwork, polished copper, portholes, gently curved walls, low ceilings, and steep, narrow ladders." The challenge of *Normandie* lay elsewhere, in the modernization and adaptation of the new taste so powerfully revealed in 1925, in the purification of its formulas, and, moreover, in the retention and defense of certain of its values then under attack. From this point of view, the 1935 classicism of the *Normandie* décor constituted an original creation, the source and foundation of which were *Normandie* herself. As a consequence, one can truly speak about a *style Normandie*, of which the Palais de Chaillot and the 1939 New York World's Fair produced other versions.

The French pavilion at the New York World's Fair did not, it would seem, find any better solution than a further development of the formulas worked out on *Normandie*. Expert and Patou, the principal architects of the two large suites of public rooms in first class, had joined forces across the Atlantic. Other familiar names also reappeared. The "Salle des Métiers d'Art" had been assigned to *artistes décorateurs*, the very kind of creative folk preferred by the CGT for *Normandie*. The "Rotonde d'Honneur" was "an immense hall, conceived as a park, with monumental staircases, plinths supporting the recent work of our sculptors, and floral motifs and fountains. All perspectives converged toward a loggia, set like a small temple in a garden and ornamented on the interior with an immense lacquer realized by Jean Dunand after the cartoons of Dupas." And so Dunand and Dupas, the two heroes of *Normandie*'s Smoking Room and Grand Lounge, had also been reunited. On the ship, Expert had created an urban perspective; in the 1939 pavilion he inserted a composition like that of a French garden, complete with sculptures and fountains. Here the graduated stairs recalled the "grand steps" of the fountain front at the Palais de Chaillot. The contrast between the structure of the pavilion, with its huge, continuously glazed rotundas, and the architectural treatment of the interior spaces recalls that in *Normandie*, between the ship's impeccable profile, its "pure, crisp, clean, solid architecture," as Le Corbusier would have said, and the decorative invention of the suites and cabins.

The third, nonfunctional smokestack that brought *Normandie* so much ridicule had appeared indispensable to the ship's planners. It stood as a symbol, mocked but moving, of the plenitude of ornament that had been considered the vessel's Loosian crime and that today has earned a pardon. Jean Marie, the head of France's Marine Engineering who played such an important role in the liner's conception, did not suffer many pangs of conscience: "Breaking free of her scaffolding, *Normandie* looked like a great work of French genius, perhaps the masterwork of our generation." Despite the excess of chauvinism and the rapture, Jean Marie may not have been wrong. The time has come again to take *Normandie* out of the dry dock of oblivion and remember that this ship proved a worthy vehicle of a decorative style that itself became one of the victims of World War II.

LIFE ON BOARD NORMANDIE

CLAUDE VILLERS

Life on Board *Normandie*

May 23

All the gilded pomp of the Third Republic was a show, represented by bearded officials in tailcoats and top hats. They made their way on a large red carpet between two rows of helmeted guards, sabres glistening in the sunshine. There was the click of heels and a roll of drums under the great glass covering of the Gare Saint-Lazare. That morning, May 23, 1935, Albert Lebrun, President of the French Republic, was about to board a special train for Le Havre.

At exactly 9:10, the trumpet call "To the Battlefield" nearly drowned out the first puff of the presidential locomotive which was starting on this extremely short trip. Standing at the window of his compartment, the Head of State waved to the celebrities and press who were gradually disappearing in great waves of smoke and steam.

Albert Lebrun had a great personal interest in this trip, which enhanced his ceremonial role, and he was impatient to explore the liner that many were declaring to be a true wonder of the seas. A former student at the École Polytechnique, he was eager to verify personally that the colossal investment by the government he headed was one which made sense.

The maddest rumors and the most contradictory information possible were in the air about this giant of the waves which was supposed to give France supremacy on the high seas. In a country where opinion is divided on absolutely everything, there were as many pro as contra *Normandie*-ites. For months, even years, they had been expressed in long, contradictory columns in the daily press. The disagreements started with the very name: should it be *Le Normandie* or *La Normandie*. Even the Académie Française studied the grave problem. Obviously this also had political shades, since masculine was considered liberal, feminine, conservative. Centrist France (which was in the majority) preferred to have just *Normandie*. More serious disagreements raged about the extremely high cost, subsidized largely by the state. Everybody had different ideas. Should such an adventure have been started in the very jaws of a dreadful economic crisis? In Paris, the comedians on the boulevards had nicknamed the ship "the floating debt."

President Lebrun was aware of the skepticism of the French people and of the divisiveness of the issue. But he also knew that, as the launching approached, the publicity department of the French Line was revealing new information and creating great excitement. Bit by bit, public opinion was turning

Viewed from the port's tidal gauge, Normandie at her quay in Le Havre

in favor of the great ship. An accumulation of praiseworthy reports, flattering pictures, and astonishing statistics — all wrapped in superlatives — had started to make the liner a subject of national pride.

Think of it! The *tricolore* would soon fly from the largest liner in the world. Not only the largest and most beautiful, but also the most French, especially in her gastronomical distinction. It was this very nationalistic sentiment that Albert Lebrun was to evoke in his speech that evening.

Normandie is an accomplishment of an essentially national nature. There is not one province, one great city, one major industry or one major art form which has not made its contribution. Under the *tricolore* France will be displaying the world of tomorrow on the high seas, a world extremely French in its logic and variety.

The President knew the force of his words. Soon they would flow off his lips with the ease of a former actor who was not quite used to the microphone. The entire country would tremble with pride at this dramatic moment.

Indeed, that day, throughout the world, *Normandie* made the front page. The surge of world interest in the ship was nerve-wracking for those in charge of her success, from the directors of the French Line down to the workers who were still busy finishing the work inside the ship. While the presidential train was on its way to Le Havre, on board ship there was a last-minute rush, and panic. Some of the cabins were far from being finished; the Grill Room wasn't ready; carpets were missing in certain corridors; knobs were missing on cabinets; electric wires were sticking out of walls; the librarian had just started to open cases containing more than 4,000 books which were to fill the solid wood shelves; and the head stewards were having a meeting to settle the last details concerning the arrival of the first guests.

On board an ordinary ship, everybody knows what he

should do, at least as far as running the engines and navigating safely are concerned. On an ocean liner, everything is more complicated. Besides the mechanics, the well-being of the passengers must be assured on all levels, and most of the travelers are used to the same impeccable service whether at home or on the high seas.

Except for emigrants, the travelers of this period lived surrounded by servants, either at home or in the palace hotels in which they spent a good part of the year. For any self-respecting steamship line, a boat is not only a means of transport but also — and above all for the French line — a floating hotel. And what a hotel *Normandie* was. Let us follow Jean Marie, the French Line's president, in some breathtaking figures:

It is not a floating city, *it is a capital city*

The general staff will include — in addition to the Captain, the staff commander and the second captain — 9 bridge officers assisted by two student officers. There will be 17 mechanical officers helped by 19 assistants. The total crew for the bridge and machine room will not exceed 292.

On board there will be 3 doctors, 2 nurses, 30 electricians, 7 printers, 9 hairdressers, and 16 musicians.

187 cooks and assistants will be assisted by 9 butchers, 6 wine stewards and 10 bakers, all of whom will make the kitchens a hive of activity.

628 stewards, 25 stewardesses, 108 sailors, 15 ships boys, and 20 pages will satisfy all the personal needs of 2,000 passengers.

The serving equipment will include more than 2,000 carafes, 57,000 glasses, 56,000 plates, 28,000 cups and saucers. The silver will consist of 770 coffeepots, 12,000 knives, 15,000 spoons, 14,000 forks, 2,000 serving platters, 2,800 plates, 1,160 milk pitchers, 600 flower vases.

The linen includes 38,000 sheets, 14,500 tablecloths, 130,000 dinner napkins, 48,000 tea napkins, 6,000 bathmats, 150,000 towels, 16,000 kitchen aprons, 45,000 cleaning cloths, 5,800 blankets.

And now, let us talk about the belly of our giant.

On each trip, the ship must carry 70,000 eggs, 7,000 chickens, 65,000 pounds of potatoes, 35,000 pounds of meat, 15,000 pounds of fish, 200,000 pounds of ice cream, 24,000 liters of table wine, 7,000 bottles of vintage wine and champagne, 2,600 bottles of liqueurs, and 9,500 bottles of mineral water.

The bakery is equipped with two ovens capable of making 180 loaves at a time, or about 3,000 pounds of bread per day.

The kitchen has 30 burners and 32 ovens all of which are electric. They measure about 50 feet long by 6 feet wide. The kitchen itself is 200 feet long and includes cold tables, hot tables, and even a mechanical pump for oil and vinegar.

Je sais tout, **May-June 1935**

Meanwhile, the purser and his assistants passed muster on the most hidden corners of the liner, carefully noting everything unfinished, all imperfections, and gathering together the people responsible in order to remedy immediately any situation which might disturb the future guests in any possible way. In the grand Hall on C Deck, filled with bronze, onyx, mirrors, and marble, Louis Courteau, to all effects and purposes the chief receptionist, the *concierge* of the liner, was holding a conference with his assistants and the team of Georges Le Barzic, head of baggage. The Hall was, in fact, the principal entrance to the ship. The two groups were responsible for embarking passengers and getting them — and their trunks and valises — to the cabins which had been allotted according to a well determined hierarchy based on the importance and rank of the guest. In any case, complaints would not be lacking, and any final decision would be taken by Chief Purser Villar. It was his job to calm the ruffled feathers of anybody who felt unfairly treated. On the gangway, Ollagnier, the second Chief of Reception, was reviewing a batallion of grooms in bright scarlet jackets and caps. Not one polished button was missing, shoes were shining, hands and ears scrubbed, and nails cleaned.

Not far away was the majestic Dining Room. Head waiters, wine stewards, galley chiefs, and chiefs of protocol were assembled, around their boss, the head maître d'hôtel, Olivier Naffrechoux, who had twenty-one years of experience on nearly all the ships of the French Line. Like Chief Steward Villar, Naffrechoux also had an international reputation.

In a small booklet published by the CGT shortly after the first crossing, Henry Champly wrote:

At the beginning of every crossing when anyone of note from America, England, or France walked down the staircase of the First Class dining room, Naffrechoux's memory started working away. 'It's two years since we have had the honor of seeing Monsieur among us. I do hope you are in good health. I remember that Monsieur wanted to lose some weight, and see you have succeeded. Perhaps Monsieur doesn't yet know that his friend, Mr. X, is on board. I have taken the liberty of sitting you at the same table.'

'How astonishing that you recognize me.'

'It would be a great shame if the French Line didn't remember the most faithful passengers on its liners. Monsieur will have a magnificent trip, as always.'

This might seem like flattery, which of course it was. However, it was also a way of creating faithful clients.

On this day of May 23, 1935, an hour of meetings in the kitchen had been held. Already the pots were on the burner

President Albert Lebrun reviewing troops   of France's 129th Infantry Regiment

and Chef Gaston Magrin was going from one work station to the other giving an order or a piece of advice to all his men who were responsible not only for the Presidential Gala Dinner but also for feeding the crew.

On the Promenade Deck there was a drama in the Theater. Not on stage but in the auditorium, and it was in the form of acoustics. In the third row, Gaby Morlay and Victor Boucher could hardly be heard. Trébor exploded with anger. How dare they make him responsible for the first theater ever on a liner — indeed on the world's most beautiful liner — if nobody was even able to deal with deficient acoustics. Happily, technicians arrived posthaste and swore to the gods that everything would be ready by showtime. But they were swamped with work. They had to install microphones in the Dining Room and lounges for the official speeches and help their colleagues on radio who were covering the presidential visit and the inaugural ceremonies.

Several live broadcasts were sent from the ship by state radio: at 5:15 P.M. and 6:45 P.M. on Radio Paris, when Jean Antoine, Georges Briquet, Alex Surchamps, Dehorter, and Alex Virot were to follow and comment on the President's visit, and at 9:15 P.M. on Radio PTT, when Paul Chack was to present the President's speech and the whole evening's theatrical entertainment.

At that moment, all the radio reporters and a gang of journalists were meeting President Lebrun as he got off his train at Le Havre station. At the dock also were all the officials of the city and province: Le Beau, prefect of the Seine-Inférieure (today the Seine-Maritime); Léon Meyer, deputy mayor of Le Havre; senators, deputies (among them René Coty, a future President of the Fourth Republic), generals, admirals, and endless presidents of countless organizations, associations, or companies.

After the first speeches and the first *Marseillaise*, the group gaily crossed through Le Havre. A large crowd was amassed on the sidewalks to greet the President, while the cannons roared and all the bells of the town rang out. Flags waved in the breeze, and the wind and the sun added to the festive atmosphere.

Our eyes, mouths, and ears are full of *Normandie* as nobody is talking about anything else. That is true popularity, the popularity of a dictator. Le Havre killed the fatted calf.

The newspapers say it's the giant of the seas, a Titan, a steel monster, and any other epithets that might evoke a respectful fear in faint spirits, the same fear that in ancient times was directed toward known and unknown Molochs.

Her crushing silhouette is thrown straight at us, nonstop. And everybody says 'Oh!' just like that.

Around her, the crowd is silent, although they know all about

her already. They are admiring, confused with respect, dulled as if in front of an overpowering chief of a primitive people. A floating town? No, but certainly a monstrous and magnificent dream.

Madeleine Jacob, *Vu*, May 1935

Before the dream could become reality in the presence of the French Head of State, President Lebrun had to satisfy several on-land obligations. At 11:30, inspection of the honor guard of the 129th Infantry Regiment was followed by a wreath-laying at the War Memorial (Poisson's monumental sculpture), a visit to the hospice, an interminable banquet at City Hall for 365, followed by the usual speeches.

Finally, at 4 o'clock, the official party boarded the *Minotaure*, the French Line's largest tug, to review the Navy buildings, visit the port, inaugurate a refinery, visit the south jetty and the south station of the Compagnie Industrielle before reaching the completely new Gare Maritime of the CGT. This was a vast work designed by the architect Cassan, consisting of a glass curtain suspended from a cast-iron vault long and broad enough to cover three whole trains at the very foot of the ship and topped with a strange tower about 80 feet high (baptized the "Tidal Gauge"), which, thanks to large illuminated figures, permitted pilots and captains to ascertain the tides from a good distance before entering the basin.

Finally, at exactly 6:00 P.M. , the President and his suite reached the gangway leading into a *Normandie* draped in the French flag. Governor General Olivier, chairman of the board, and M. Henri Cangardel, president of the CGT, Captain René Pugnet, the only master (after God) of *Normandie*, his assistant, Commander Pierre Thoreux, and all the general staff were present to greet the French President, accompanied by Mme Lebrun, who was to christen the ship. Then Chief Purser Villar conducted the President and his wife to the deluxe Caen Suite designed by Montagnac, so that they could rest before touring the liner.

At this time, in the kitchen, Chef Gaston Magrin was everywhere at once, urging on his cooks and their helpers, all the while supervising the unloading of a special supply train which had just arrived from Paris full of the absolutely freshest possible victuals. The liner *Paris* had just arrived from New York, bearing typically American food, unfindable then in Europe, and essential to satisfy the Anglo-Saxon appetite: breakfast cereals, maple syrup, ketchup, corn on the cob, cranberry sauce, buckwheat flour for pancakes, and other such delicacies.

The *Paris* was a large ship, but coming alongside the new giant of the seas, she seemed suddenly tiny and very modest. The crowd amassed on the dock could play at comparisons, definitely to the detriment of the *Paris*. However, until that

Views of the Gare Maritime at Le Havre

day the *Paris*, together with the *France* and the *Île de France*, was considered as one of the best of the line. It must be said that on this inaugural day, the *Paris* became a point of comparison for the new star. She was not only a delivery service but also a hotel annex, and lodged part of the guests, as certain cabins of *Normandie* still had to be fitted out. That night she sheltered seven hundred people in a royally comfortable style.

And even the onlookers had a treat, if we may call it that, as a strange merry-go-round passed in front of the curious crowd on the dock. A procession of cooks in white hats made their way up the gangways carrying, in groups of four, religious-like litters in a sort of procession. These contained not holy relics, but spectacularly mounted fish, chickens, ducks in gelée garnished with foie gras and truffles, baskets of frangipane, cakes overflowing with fresh cream and other artistically worked gastronomic delights.

A man who seemed to know what he was talking about replied, smiling, to a journalist who seemed astonished by this late delivery: "That's nothing. As the kitchens are working overtime, the cold buffet was prepared on shore. But it has nothing to do with the dinner. This is for afterwards in case those on the *Paris* want a little something to eat before going to bed, after they have returned from the ball."

More than one thousand guests were expected for the gala evening. Some of them were already on board; others continued to arrive on special trains while the President was being shown all the decks on *Normandie*. Quite obviously, Albert Lebrun and his official party were captivated by the space, elegance, and decoration of this ship, which was really a city, with streets, avenues, shops, restaurants, bars, and clubs. And still the President had only visited part of the installation, principally on the upper decks, and had taken the necessary time to thank all those artists, decorators, painters, sculptors, cabinetmakers, weavers, and interior designers who were responsible for the splendor and harmony of this absolutely unique artistic setting.

Yes, *Normandie* was a masterpiece. But the inaugural guests still had many wonders to witness. The management of the French Line accelerated the pace. Dinner would soon be ready, and everybody had to get prepared.

Outside, under a light rain, other guests continued to ar-

The kitchens

rive; those in automobiles drove up the ramp to an especially arranged garage on the terrace of the sea dock. Men were in formal attire or in uniforms covered in medals, the women in evening dresses of organdy, silk, lamé, or velvet. In the cabins, those who had arrived earlier were getting dressed.

This was the first run-through for the servants, undoubtedly victorious but difficult for a whole category of the excellent crew, the cabin stewards and stewardesses who were the best then employed by the French Line.

All these seasoned travelers had persevered through many a storm, had developed an ingenuity to overcome the many deficiencies of working on a liner at sea. On Normandie, of course, they had endless conveniences to help serve the guests. But on inaugural day, a lot of that was still in the hands of the workers.

The water had to be flowing, creased cloths had to be set straight without pressing, everything had to function as if this were not a debut. They succeeded! Some doors which were closed opened up, and into the corridors filled with a golden light from the recessed ceiling illumination flowed dazzling evening gowns and white ties. One thousand guests, dressed to kill and dying of hunger after covering miles of the labyrinthine ship, all looked for the shortest way to the Dining Room.

Extract from _Mémorial de l'inauguration et premier voyage_, by Henry Champly, Éditions de l'Atlantique-CGT

In the Hall, the elevators were continually disgorging passengers who arrived for the opening of the gigantic bronze portals that led to the Dining Room. On the other side of the door, it was not yet 8 o'clock, and the chief maître d'hôtel, or dining-room steward, Naffrechoux, was just finishing the positioning of his men in strategic places, around tables set with linen as pristine as the stewards' boiled shirt fronts or the obligatory napkins draped over the arms of head waiters and their assistants.

Then, the maître d'hôtel took up his post at the mahogany desk, opposite the cloak room, and straightened the great mirror slightly, the better to allow the ladies and gentlemen to adjust their dress before facing the great challenge of descending the grand staircase. At this period, architects still understood that a dinner party was above all a spectacle where the guests were both actors and audience. The grand entrance, therefore, was the true raison d'être of this monumental flight of steps from the vestibule to the actual Dining Room.

Shortly, the ladies would be able to observe one another at their leisure, commenting on gowns and grooming, their bare shoulders and décolletage subject to caresses from the men's admiring eyes.

One last glance at the seating plan established by Chief Purser Villar. This was in order of rank down from the table of the President and Mme Lebrun, government officials, and French Line executives. With a majestic gesture, Naffrechoux gave a signal to the ushers, their necks looped about with silver chains. The doors opened softly, and the crowd stood transfixed, even dumbstruck, by the fabulous sight that spread before them, a perspective stretching nearly 300 feet long, 45 feet wide, and 25 feet high. And then all that gold and crystal, the carved, engraved, and molded glass panels three decks high, refracting on the gilt coffered ceiling the great rush of light projected from Lalique's "fire pot" light towers and wall sconces. The illumination was quite powerful but so beautifully suffused that, instead of blinding, it often seemed to come from candles. In fact, 130,000 candles would have been required to create such a splendid effect. The dinner guests were smoothly ushered toward flower-filled tables where they found — behind tall menus stacked like feudal towers standing guard over the monogrammed silver, crystal, and china — presents and souvenirs of the day: cigarettes labeled Normandie, a commemorative medal, and a rounded flagon, already famous among le Tout-Paris, containing Jean Patou's toilet water called Normandie.

A thousand people sitting down more or less simultaneously is quite impressive and rather noisy, but when suddenly they fall silent it's even more startling.

High above the brouhaha, a strong voice announced emphatically: "Mesdames, Messieurs, the President of the French Republic." Everybody looked toward the staircase, and, preceded by the deafening noise of chairs being pushed

Gaby Morlay (right) at her table during the gala dinner

The table of André de Fouquières (center)

A table in the tourist-class dining room

back, thunderous applause greeted the entrance of Albert Lebrun and his wife, who went to the table of honor dominated by Dejean's statue *Peace*.

The President had hardly sat down when there was a choreography of servants. Champagne flowed, giant platters of hors d'oeuvres were circulated, and a feast for the eyes was followed by a feast for the senses. The menu for this gala dinner, served to one thousand guests, was up to the reputation of Chef Magrin and the gastronomic tradition of the French Line.

Like most of the guests, Odette Pannetier, from the weekly tabloid *Candide*, was delighted with the meal despite a slight misfortune:

The ducks enjoyed the greatest success. They arrived in majesty, carried in the outstretched arms of the waiters who descended the large staircase in a procession.

These butlers, unfortunately, were used to serving on a moving and rolling liner. Only when the ground under them was immobile did they lose the security of their legs. One arrived staggering, just missed my beautiful puce robe, and his platter of ducks, truffles, aspic, and foie gras was dumped on the shoulders of a perfectly inoffensive curly-haired gentleman.

Except for this incident, which took on the aspect of an interlude, the dinner went forward without drama. There were speeches, and it was apparent that Monsieur Lebrun had been quite right to attend the courses at the Conservatoire in Tragedy, which he had been doing for some time.

O. Pannetier, *Candide*, May 30, 1935

Indeed, the President of the Republic did not hold back on grandiose ideas and lyrical phrases. But wasn't that really what his fellow citizens wanted: to justify, in a few well-thought-out words, the sumptuous expenditure of a disturbed and somewhat fragile government.

After the beautiful presidential message, there was a traffic jam to leave the Dining Room as quickly as possible, and the security guard of the President had to come to occasional blows to make a passage for M. Lebrun. Now, professional actors were going to take charge of *Normandie*'s Theatre, the first true theater to float on the Atlantic Ocean. There was great emotion when, after the presentation of a skit by Francis de Croisset entitled *The Lottery Ticket*, with Gaby Morlay and Victor Boucher, the radio MC and entertainer Saint Granier announced the plum of the evening: a cantata dedicated to the liner *Normandie*, with the score by Henri Casadesus and lyrics by René Dorin performed by tenor Georges Thill, star of the Paris Opéra.

May 24

The inaugural festivities, in fact, were far from finished. Few guests had risen when, at exactly 8:00 A.M., the President

Normandie! Normandie!
Don't say "le" or "la."
She's just called *Normandie!*
What a splendid name, tra-la.

Grass lands come to mind,
Apples, fields, and logs.
Pleasant houses, farmers kind,
And flower-covered bogs.
Houses and bogs,
Fields and logs,
A beautiful ship,
A lovely name.
Normandie! Normandie!

The most beautiful ever to be,
The fastest and the grandest,
The fastest and the grandest.
She is the giant of the sea.
Normandie! Normandie!
Don't Say "le" or "la."
She's just called *Normandie*
Normandie! Normandie!
What a splendid name, tra-la.

of the Republic appeared on the Promenade Deck to be introduced to the liner's general staff, along with a delegation of 150 sailors and civilians. Then the former engineer followed Jean Hazard, *Normandie*'s chief engineer, through the entrails of the vessel, past the impressive machinery, questioning and commenting.

At 9:05, President Lebrun went down the gangway leading directly to the seaside Gare Maritime, where his official train was waiting, inspected the 129th Infantry Regiment and returned to Paris, the Élysée Palace, and an impending ministerial crisis.

But on board nobody had time or interest for politics. From now until departure, one party would follow another. Today, May 24, there was a big press lunch; and in the evening the presentation of the boat to the notable citizens of Le Havre with a new dinner and a new theatrical spectacle.

MAY 25

There was a gala evening that night, and all Paris was there for dinner, to have a good time, and to dance in this new capital of fashion. These celebrities were the first paying guests, for this was a charity evening for the benefit of seamen and the unemployed.

Entertainment in the Grand Lounge

MAY 27

Monsignor de la Villerabel, Archbishop of Rouen, in the presence of Cardinal Verdier, Archbishop of Paris, consecrated the Chapel. Abbé Tardi celebrated the first Mass, attentively followed by sailors quite used to fearing the wrath of God on the high seas.

MAY 28

The Chapel was not strictly reserved for the Catholic faith. Today, Protestants took possession, and on May 29 a rabbi brought the Torah, the sacred Jewish book.

MAY 29

Except for the small ceremony mentioned above, this was the great day. Shortly, at the end of the afternoon, *Normandie*, full of passengers for the first time, would make her way across the Atlantic.

Somehow, despite the long series of receptions — the last being a lunch for French and European travel agents — everything was ready for departure. The floating palace was ready to receive, in a dignified fashion, those guests of honor who would be on this first crossing.

There were representatives of the French state: Mme Al-

Dinner on a gala evening

In the Grand Lounge, Mlle Lude, a top model for Vogue

bert Lebrun, wife of the President; her daughter Mme Freysselinard; her daughter-in-law, Mme Jean Lebrun; Rear Admiral Le Bigot, aide-de-camp of the Élysée Palace; M. Dulignier, Chief of Protocol; Minister of the Merchant Marine M. William Bertrand, and his wife; Admiral Vedel; Vice-Admiral Grandclément; deputies; senators; and high-level functionaries. But there were also foreign parliamentarians and politicians and even a Royal Highness, the Maharajah of Kapurthala and his suite, including a personal chef, who would cause Chef Magrin considerable grief. There were businessmen, socialites, the Marquis de Chambrun, Count René de Rougemont, Count and Countess di Chippico, Count Charles de Polignac, Count and Countess de Tocqueville, Mme Achille Fould, and an important American delegation (the main potential clientele of the ship). This included rich widows or heirs of great financiers, Nancy Webb, Frank Jay Gould, the wife of Pierre Cartier, the jeweler, Morgan Belmont, Mrs. Jennings, Benny Davis, and many others.

There were also representatives of the French Line, among them Governor General Olivier and President Henri Cangardel, and, to be fair, a rival, Antonio Cosulich, director of the Italian Line, whose *Rex* then held the mythical Blue Ribbon, plus the directors of the Penhoët shipyards, where *Normandie* had been built, and, of course, the ship's father, the marine architect, Vladimir Yourkevitch. Also on board were such artists as Jean Dunand and Max Ingrand, surrounded by the decorations they had created for the ship.

An important area of French fame abroad was well represented by twelve models who were to present on board the latest fashions of the great Paris couturiers: dresses and ensembles by Patou, Lucien Lelong, Chanel, Lucill Paray, Maggy Rouff, Jenny, Callot, Schiaparelli, Jeanne Lanvin (who was traveling first class), Madeleine Vionnet, and Worth. Furs were by Max and Weil, hats by Maria Guy, Caroline Reboux, Agnès, Rose Valois, and Monnier. Shoes were by Enzel, Padova, Netch and Frater, Greco, Paul Berard; and gloves by Alexandrine.

Elegance? That was with my twelve models, and perhaps Valentine Tessier with her few pals from the boat of Thespis. But the others? I assure you that 300 kids from Paris, prepared by the couturiers and shoemakers to astonish the New World, would have given a better idea of the chic of Paris.

La Vie Parisienne, May 25, 1935

On board were also people from the theater, from music halls, and the world of dance, including Charles Boyer and, of course, Robert Trébor, the director of the Theater who put together the talent to entertain the passengers. And in order to tell the story of this event, the way it should be told, there were academicians and the greatest names in journalism and literature. Among these were Colette, André Chevrillon, Pierre Wolff (*Paris-Soir*), Pierre Brisson (*Le Figaro*), Carl Erickson, *Vogue's* draftsman, Claude Farrère and Blaise Cendrars for *Paris-Soir*, the great daily newspaper which also had on board a rather special correspondent, a fourteen-year-old boy, Roger Echegut, son of a house painter who had picked a lucky number in a group of thirty thousand children gathered in the Buffalo Cyclo-

Consecration of the Chapel

drome on Thursday, May 23. He too cabled his daily impressions of the crossing and was soon to return to France with a New York school child, Peter Dudan.

If you only knew how well he was chosen. His father had been out of work for a long time, and has only been working eight days. Roger is a small boy, charming, gentle, not too rowdy, gay, affectionate. Being small, he was quite seasick, and needs to catch up at school. But if you only knew how everybody congratulated him — the concierge, the fruit seller, the antique dealer, the green grocer, all the people of the street were of the same opinion.

Paris-Soir, May 25, 1935

The ship totaled 1,014 passengers of which 122 were in third class (mostly workers from the Penhoët docks, who were on board to add last-minute finishing touches), 303 in tourist (many engineers and executives of the company as well as models, certain artists, and less well-known journalists), and, most important of all, 589 in first class. Nearly everybody had been invited free by the French Line. This first crossing must have been one of the greatest public relations events ever! But here they all were, arriving in the "boat trains" that had left the Gare Saint-Lazare in Paris. Now came the first impressions, the first wonderment.

. . . The brakes. Tongue rails, many tongue rails and switching points. On the right of the Havreville station. The junction. Bridges. On the left, cranes, sheds, smokestacks, masts set against a fog-colored sky. And straightaway the immense hall of the dockside Gare Maritime. Above all the roofs, three gigantic smokestacks, red and black, black on top, red below. What had been the national colors of the former Péreire company were now those of the French Line for everybody. And very small, in contrast to the giant funnels: *Normandie*.

A precipitous descent. All baggage, human and otherwise, is unloaded from the cars. Already a horde of porters is in movement. Those who don't know what is going on are in a panic.

Four steps more. And there is *Normandie* docked in the immense berth.

The black hull is so high that one can't take in the great finesse of its line. It's like a whaler, an ocean racer, miraculous for its lightness. Yet this yawl wouldn't fit on the Place de l'Étoile and would extend 270 feet beyond it. Her hull would circle the palaces on each side of Avenue Wagram. But the black hull is nothing.

Above the hull of *Normandie*, there are one, two, three, four, five, six stories, all painted in the purest white.

Claude Farrère, Paris-Soir, May 30, 1935

Above all, the interior astonished everybody. But the passengers hardly had time to express their ecstasy. They had to try to find their way, following the pages who took them to their cabins. Shortly, on their own, would they find their way through this gigantic labyrinth?

There is never any question of missing the magic moment when a liner leaves its dock, that astonishing instant when a ship becomes a self-enclosed, moving world. Quickly, everybody made way to the upper decks, pushing the stewards and pages in charge of telegrams, flowers, and chocolates from those who remained on shore to those leaving. Everybody wanted a place with a view of the docks, thronged with curious onlookers.

Suddenly, a great shudder went through those on board. The "typhoon" rang out, that siren on the very top of the forward smokestack. It was the signal of farewell, warning that visitors must leave the ship. Kisses, tears, sad smiles, and the withdrawal of relatives and friends who came to see off those who were leaving. Everywhere the "Exit in this direction" signs led toward the gangway. There a band played a gay march; yet it plucked at people's hearts. Emotion was at its height when everything in the port — from liners to the smallest tug or cargo boats — and even the locomotives of the train played an incredible concert of sirens and whistles, as if the very engines were saying goodbye in a screaming, groaning, and strident language.

Doubtlessly moved but impassive, the sailors and officers were all at their posts. On the bridge, Captain Pugnet was giving his orders. Again, the *Normandie* horn was blown several times. The smoke from the smokestack blackened, the last gangways were withdrawn. "Cast off"; and the tugs *Titan*, *Ursus*, and *Minotaure* began the extraordinary effort necessary to separate the gigantic mass of the liner from *terra firma*.

Next to the Captain was the pilot. His job was to direct *Normandie* into the channel leading towards the open sea. The sky filled with fury: ships' sirens, among them those of *Île de France* and the *Paris*, saluted their younger sister, and there was the noise of planes' motors, full of photographers and cameramen, which flew around the smokestacks and superstructure of *Normandie*, nearly touching the ship as if the planes wanted to replace the seagulls scared away by the racket. The jettys, breakwaters, and even the most distant roofs of Le Havre were black with people. Hands, handkerchiefs, and flags waved, and the human noise reached the highest decks of the ship. In a dignified reply, the bass voice of *Normandie's* siren let out three long blasts. The semaphore flag was lowered three times. *Normandie* advanced majestically into the channel, then slowed to a near halt. There was a whistle, the flag was raised, the pilot left the ship

At 7:28 P.M. the four turbo-propellers were put on full speed, and quickly the shores of France grew faint before being lost in the fog.

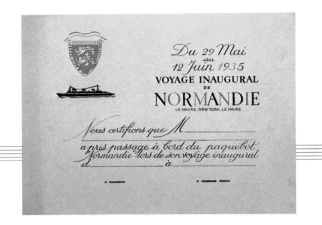

The Voyage

On *Normandie*, life was getting organized. It would soon be the dinner hour. Everyone went back to their suite or cabin to get ready.

The dinner jacket laid on the bed by an adroit and smiling steward, the invitation to cocktails brought by a silent, red-clad page, along with one's place at dinner and the names of one's fellow guests at table, the jazz tune heard through the door just as one is knotting one's black tie — such are the marvels that distract a journalist who is there to cover a sporting event: the race for the Blue Ribbon.

'But it's the Ritz-sur-mer,' he grumbles upon seeing the Dining Room, as broad as the ship, but so high and long that it seems to be a giant corridor. The racket is the same as in the drinking bar at the Palais Bourbon, and you can't get to your seat without saying hello to twenty people on the way. The funny thing is that one finds here all the habitués of the Brasserie Lipp or Chez Weber who have been moved, as if by magic wand, into the décor of a palace hotel — but not even a real palace hotel. It's the grand hotel of one's dreams, as only a Hollywood producer might conceive it. Twelve hundred dinners are being served this evening, and the din of forks knocking against plates mixes with the tinkling glass of light fixtures shaken by vibrations in the stern.

*Tourist-class dining room,
represented in watercolor by André Lagrange*

opposite:
*Paul Iribe's painting
of the Lower Hall*

Normandie by night in Le Havre

For a moment one wishes that the creators of *Normandie* had sent their ship to the United States with only its officers, crew, engineers, and workers on board – all those seamen and engineers who are really capable of appreciating the grandeur of the work they accomplished, all capable of participating in the joy of breaking a world record. Following my fantasy, I would choose to send *Normandie* to New York without its last coat of paint, without the least bit of furniture, for she would be more beautiful if she were more naked. This seems especially apt since one feels in the choice of the artists and decorators a bit of political influence. It is a French effort that built *Normandie*, and it seems to have been decorated by the Republic of Pals.

And, while I'm in a critical mood, I examine the guests who, along with the journalists, will represent France in New York. They all belong to a species which might be described as 'natural sons of a cabinet minister,' who all take such an important place in the Third Republic. They are happy to be on board, are very nice, laugh, drink. Here we are, Washington – but what a change since Lafayette.

I go up one, two, three, four, five stories. Suddenly my mood changes. Wind gallops around smokestacks as large as stables. Reaching out a bit, I find myself thrown with furious force against a steel plate and feel the rivets in my back. At 35 miles per hour, the steel prow plies seas that hardly move and hit the sides of the ship with impotent hostility. The salt spray cuts into my face, demolishes the starch on my shirt front. An officer comes and goes, his sharp profile hidden under a cap. I had just seen him below, bowing in a haughty manner, and smiling at the unjustified complaints of a lady passenger. I hardly recognize him now; his eyes are wide open, his head set back; he opens his coat, bares his neck to the sea breeze, and laughs silently in the shadow. Come on, the ocean is still the ocean, and even on this floating metropolis there are still those who love her with sensuality!

Bertrand de Jouvenel, *Vu*, June 1935

While Bertrand de Jouvenel was prowling the decks, in the Dining Room the guests were enjoying the delicacies prepared by Chef Magrin. There were splendid hors d'oeuvres, five soups, two fishes, a regional speciality, fresh string beans, fresh peas, courgettes à la Maintenon, potatoes puréed, baked, English style, sautéed, or boiled with sprinkled parsley, spaghetti or macaroni au gratin (ten minutes wait, please), or simple or curried rice, English roast beef, Bresse chickens on the spit, five sorts of ham, and an entire cold buffet. This consisted of beef in aspic, shrimp with mayonnaise, on to veal tongues in Spring aspic, chickens mounted in foie gras, roasts of pork, saddles of lamb with mint sauce, sides of beef, brill with Sauce Antiboise, and turkey with cranberry sauce. Six sorts of salad, six cheeses (not only from Normandy), cakes, sweets, ices, compotes, and baskets of fresh fruit. And, of course, as much wine as one wanted – white, red, or rosé.

If you really had hunger pangs, or if you wanted your money's worth, you could take everything as many times as you liked, and none of the waiters would have been allowed the slightest comment. The meals were included in the price of the crossing. But if you were reasonable, you would be quite content with the daily, suggested menu.

Melon (cantaloupe) with sherry
Potage Solférino
Loire pike with clarified butter
Duck à l'orange
Small peas à la française
Mixed salad
Ice Bombe Impériale (with Vienna cream)
Basket of fruit

That's not so bad. The table service was worthy of the menus, and doled it out according to the three classes with special treatment for the luxury apartments, which had their own dining rooms and kitchens.

This evening, however, the diners didn't tarry after coffee, even if, for once, the Theater was closed. As far as spectacles were concerned, the main event of the evening was to be the first stop of the liner.

DINER

Hors-d'Œuvre	Olives Vertes - Olives Noires - Céleri en Branches Œufs Farcis Lucullus Céleri Farci au Roquefort - Sardines aux Tomates
Potages	Consommé Froid en Tasse Consommé Croûte-au-Pot Consommé aux Pâtes d'Italie Potage Choiseul Soupe à l'Oignon
Poissons	Filets de Halibut à l'Angevine Truite Saumonée Pochée Sauce Joinville
Entrée	Ris de Veau Glacé Godart
Spécialité Régionale	LE CANETON A L'ORANGE
Légumes	Haricots Verts Frais au Beurre Fin Petits Pois à la Française Aubergines en Beignets
Pommes de terre	Purée - au Four - à l'Anglaise - en Robe Pommes Nouvelles Persillées
Pâtes	Spaghetti - Nouilles - Macaroni (Gratin 10 minutes) Riz Nature - Riz au Kari
Rôtis	Poularde Rôtie à la Broche Côte de Charolais Rôtie Cresson
Buffet Froid	Jambon de Virginie - Jambon de Prague - Jambon d'York Jambon de Westphalie - Jambon de Bayonne Bœuf Mode en Gelée à la Provençale Longe de Veau à la Gelée Printanière - Poulet Froid Carré de Porc Froid - Selle d'Agneau Sauce Menthe Côte de Bœuf Froide Terrine de Foie Gras Frais de Strasbourg Dindonneau Froid Cranberry Sauce Homard Mayonnaise - Suprême de Barbue Sauce Gribiche
Salades	Chicorée aux Œufs - Salade Mimosa - Combinaison Pissenlit - Salade Soissonnaise - Salade de Choux Rouges
Fromages	Cream Cheese - Bel-Paese - Reblochon Saint-Marcellin - Emmenthal - Munster
Pâtisserie	Gâteau Ananas Langues-de-Chat - Espagnolettes
Entremets	Crème Brûlée - Bavaroises Chocolat Pudding Martiniquais
Glaces	Vanille - Pistache - Noisette - Sorbet Poire Bombe Madeleine
Fruits	Fruit Cocktail Corbeille de Fruits Compote de Fruits Frais
Vins	Bordeaux Rouge Supérieur - Bordeaux Blanc Supérieur Bourgogne Blanc Supérieur
Thés - Cafés, etc.	Thé de Chine - Orange Pekoë Verveine - Tilleul - Menthe - Camomille Café Américain - Café Français - Café Sanka

MENU

DU

Samedi 26 Décembre 1936

Menu Suggestion

◆

Fruit Cocktail

———

Potage Choiseul

———

Filets de Halibut à l'Angevine

———

Le Caneton à l'Orange

———

Petits Pois à la Française

———

Salade de Saison

———

Bombe Madeleine

———

Corbeille de Fruits

S. S. "NORMANDIE"

The Dining Room in first class, watercolor by J. Simont

The Dining Room in first class, detail of a drawing by Pagès

Toward 11:00 P.M. on that 29th of May 1935, *Normandie* put on its most powerful lights and arrived in view of Southampton, all lit up. There was a flotilla of tugs, fishing boats, and other craft arriving to meet a ship which, by one year, preceded England's own masterpiece and future rival of the French Line: the *Queen Mary*.

But on this occasion it was *l'entente cordiale*. From the two ferry boats, bringing the London passengers and visitors, the sounds of *La Marseillaise* suddenly arose, sung — in French — by British voices.

On *Normandie*'s decks, the passengers leaning on the railings instinctively stood up. Patriotism vibrated in this spontaneous homage. Then, in response, the loudspeakers of the liner resonated immediately with "God Save the King," the national anthem of our ally. In the starry night, there was once more a concert of sirens soaring above the waves.

The British authorities came on board, from the Lord Mayor down. The party could have gone on all night, but it was essential to keep the ship's schedule, for soon the true race for the Blue Ribbon would officially start once the liner passed Bishop's Rock lighthouse, the very last piece of Europe. Moreover, Captain Pugnet and his crew had decided to go for the record that was so coveted by every steamship company.

What better publicity could the latest ship of the French Line have than becoming the fastest liner afloat, in addition to all the other generously distributed qualifications for beauty, luxury, comfort, and elegance. So, as the lights of the English coast faded away and the passengers returned to their cabins, Blaise Cendrars, on a special mission for *Paris-Soir*, stole away into the belly of the ship, his Basque beret tight on his head and a cigarette stub stuck to his lips.

Table Service

Grand-luxe Suites

Silver: Puiforcat, plated or gilded, 1,424 pieces, including 120 spoons, 216 forks, 216 knives, 60 fish settings, 60 oyster forks, 60 coffee spoons, 60 ice-cream spoons.
Glass: René Lalique.
Porcelain: Haviland, designed by Suzanne Lalique.

First Class

Silver: Christofle, designed by Luc Lanel.
Glass: Daum.
Porcelain: Haviland, designed by Jean Luce.

Tourist Class

Silver: Ercuis (Christofle).
Glass: Daum.
Porcelain: Haviland GDA.

Third Class:

Silver: Alfenide (Christofle).
Glass: Saint-Antoine.
Porcelain:

Officer's Mess

Silver: Marly (Christofle).
Glass: Saint-Antoine.
Cooking equipment: Wiskeman.

From the very beginning, he had announced to everyone he met: "What interests me are the machines. I don't give a damn about all the fuss and social life." His resolution and tenacity were to pay off, and he spent most of the crossing in the entrails of the ship. From that first night, he was struck with wonder.

A stateroom table

A table in first class

I Saw the Heartbeat from inside the Great Colossus

First night on watch in the boiler room, or the melody of Power.

I saw the shafts of the propellers turning around: each one weighs 30 tons and is regulated to .02 millimeter.

I just spent my first night on watch in the boiler room. I watched the oil flow into thirty boilers, where it takes the form of a torrent of fire. More than 90 feet under the sea, under the Sun Deck, in the pits which are never reached by the noise of jazz bands. I assisted in the mysterious travail of the oilers, standing in front of the red, white, and blue eyes of the boilers.

Then, floor by floor, I climbed up the ladders slipping under the warm tummies of the all-silver condensers, which looked like a herd of kneeling elephants.

Christofle tea service

Finally, pushing a heavy door and nearly being knocked over by a sudden rush of air, I came into the murmuring dynamo room, a-whir and completely alive with a continuous rhythm, the only perceptible evidence of the invisible Power, since nothing was to be seen of a wheel turning or the push-pull of a rod. And the hum, deep yet shrill and eventually quasi-musical, provides the sole evidence of the 160,000 horsepower that animates this 79-ton ship, driving and hurling her mass forward at a speed of almost 35 miles an hour on the way to New York and the race for the Blue Ribbon.

Going out, around 7:00 A.M., I got lost in the corridors, which forced me to go through the kitchens and the bakery, where a delicious odor of chocolate and hot croissants was in the air.

The wind is clean, all is well on board....
Blaise Cendrars, *Paris-Soir*, May 31, 1935

Indeed, all was well on board *Normandie*. Passengers and crew became accustomed to the rhythm of the crossing. In the corridors, stewards in white vests and white gloves were serving breakfast in bed, from coffee and buttered biscuits to T-bone steaks and Bloody Marys. Ask and you shall receive!

Earlier, the pages had slipped the daily on-board paper under the cabin doors, *L'Atlantique*, edited and printed during the night. The latest news was given in both French and English, along with stock quotations and editorials from the

Mealtime in the crew's dining room

leading newspapers on both sides of the Atlantic. And there were also photographs and descriptions of the previous day's happenings — reports on the departure from Le Havre, the stop in Southampton, and some glimpses of the celebrities at the tables of honor during dinner. And then there was the program of the endless activities of the day, mealtimes, the distance run and to be run, average speed, useful telephone numbers, hours of religious service, as well as movie times, etc. In other words, everything to remind the guests of Normandie that they lived in a true town, the capital of floating towns!

Some who have never crossed the ocean on a liner often grumble about the boredom that supposedly reigns at sea. Nothing could be farther from reality. There are always thousands of things to do, and never more so than on the first day out aboard a ship like Normandie.

First of all, there is the exploration of the monster, achieved by running along the decks and through the lounges one by one. In the morning, you could go on the Promenade Deck where Berthelot, the chief deck steward who had been with the CGT for thirty-five years, had installed his innumerable deck chairs at dawn. This was the perfect place to dream, read, or observe others wrapped in large blue woolen blankets waiting for the traditional 11 o'clock bouillon with small salted crackers.

One could choose a chair in the four-thousand-volume library, buy magazines from everywhere in the world at the kiosk of the Messageries Hachette, do one's correspondence in the Writing Room, telephone Paris, New York, or Honolulu from the Post Office, visit one's dog in the kennel or one's children in the nursery.

The sporty types preferred to jog around the smokestacks on the Sun Deck, to play tennis, shuffleboard, ping-pong, or miniature golf. One could poke one's head into the inside swimming pool (it was still a bit cold for the outside one), take a Turkish bath, get massaged, or exercise on the most modern machines supervised by a licensed trainer.

Oh yes, one could also attend religious services every morning, as did Mme Lebrun. On this inaugural trip, Monsignor Queen, a British bishop who resembled Charles Laughton, celebrated Mass. A page served as acolyte while the magician on board played the violin and an officer the organ.

As lunchtime approached, the many bars filled and the tax-free liquor flowed endlessly. Then it was time to get to the Dining Room, or better yet, the Café-Grill, which dominated the first-class Promenade Deck. From one's table, set in an immense rotunda with large, glass bay windows

giving onto the sea, one had only to see the foamy wake below to realize the speed of the ship.

However, there was a certain malaise on board. In fact, the harmony of the voyage was disturbed by vibrations which affected the aft section of the liner. Despite endless efforts by specialists, nothing could be done for the moment, and the vibrations of Normandie provided a good topic of conversation until quickly replaced by interest in the race, and then bets on the arrival time in New York with the blue pennant streaming from the mast.

Meanwhile, it was easy to become lazy on board such a liner. Also, early afternoon was always very calm, a time for siestas in the cabin, or for sunning in deck chairs.

Unless you wanted to go to the movies. A journalist, Jean

Blaise Cendrars

Coupon, was in charge there. The documentaries were *Mont Saint-Michel*, *Vocations*, *The Sahara Oasis*, or *Abbeys of France*. There were great French films — *Crime and Punishment*, *Maria Chapdelaine*, *A Rare Bird*, and Sacha Guitry's *The Pastor*, shown before being premiered elsewhere. And there were American films which had not yet appeared in Paris, projected with French subtitles, *The Bengal Lancers*,

Setting type at high sea for the ship's newspaper

The Winter Garden, by Paul Iribe

The Great Barnum, and even Richard Boleslavsky's *Les Misérables* with Charles Laughton in the role of Javert and Frederick March as Jean Valjean. We must say the French had a guarded welcome for the Hollywood adaptation of one of their great classics.

five manicurists. One detail: in the salon's private reservoirs there were 150 liters of water especially distilled in New York — it seems that this was the very best water for the hair.

Those with doubts about their health could take advantage of the crossing to consult the doctors who were at their

Albert Brenet, The Engine Room on Normandie, gouache

I will quickly pass over the film and theater programs. In the cinema, the American version of *Les Misérables* — that day the French had a great laugh. They laughed less at Sacha Guitry's *The Pastor.* In fact, they didn't laugh at all, and the Americans gradually left the dark room bit by bit. One might have thought they were queasy from the rolling of the ship. Not at all! They were simply bored. And with a film that was to be projected in every French primary school. Let us say no more.

M. Trébor was in charge of theatrical entertainment which was — to be absolutely fair taking into consideration all the limitations imposed by circumstances — absolutely ghastly.

Such was the spiritual fodder offered to the Americans on the 'Flagship of French Quality,' as the CGT would put it.

Madeleine Jacob, *Vu*, June 1935

There was also a Punch and Judy for the children in the playroom which had been installed in a deck house by the forward smokestack.

Those less young could made their way to a clay-pigeon stand where a pupil of Gastinne-Reinette got the rifles ready. The ladies preferred to browse among counters attended by sales girls from the Bon Marché in Paris before visiting the beauty salon, a floating branch of Paris's famous Calou, whose finest hairdresser supervised nine other virtuosi and

service, before going to the bar that remained open from 4:00 P.M. until dinner time, or take tea in the Winter Garden where a head gardener from Vilmorin was studying the resistance of various plants, birds, and fish to life on the high seas.

But the most relished, albeit the oldest, attractions were of a culinary nature. One ate, nearly nonstop, from 9 o'clock in the morning until 10:00 at night. This tradition of transatlantic travel still astonishes us.

Main news. The TSF, radio, telephone, and cinema were all going strong. The whole day we missed nothing of the parliamentary and ministerial agitation that had been rocking Paris for some twenty-four hours. May I say that, seen from a distance, and from above the long, lazy wake which stretches on the ocean from the west to the east, the so-called 'agitations' seemed to all of us — and I mean everybody without exception, as there are about sixty journalists on board — absolutely pitiful. The present and past ministers now on board *Normandie* were little to be seen today. The same applies to deputies and senators. Captain Pugnet, whom we hardly see either, seems a grander figure in our eyes than any of the miserable helmsmen who direct, or appear to direct, our country. At least we feel the presence of our captain on the bridge or in the pump room.

Claude Farrère, *Paris-Soir*, June 1, 1935

Deck games

Celebrating Mass

Hairdressing salon

Punch and Judy

The esplanade on the first-class Promenade Deck

Kennel

Barbershop

Swimming Pool in first class

The Swimming Pool, by Paul Iribe

Central telegraph office (Sun Deck)

Claude Farrère was not alone in the fascination he felt for Captain René Pugnet. Any passenger who came in contact with him never ceased singing his praises. However, as Farrère noted, he was not much to be seen. In fact, several grave family problems rather spoiled his job on the inaugural voyage, and diminished his satisfaction at being the first "master after God" of the most beautiful liner in the world.

The rest of the general staff was up to the exceptional quality of the French Line officers. First of all, there was Pugnet's deputy, Commander Pierre Thoreux. A year later, when Pugnet retired, Thoreux would take charge of *Normandie*, the flagship of the French Line. This was a formidable honor but also the supreme distinction for a commander long in CGT service, a service that in 1935 consisted of 78 different ships, including banana boats, specialized carriers (even sheep carriers), tugs, cargoes, and mixed cargoes, plus 29 passenger vessels plying the North and South Atlantic, the Caribbean, North and South Pacific, and the Mediterranean.

Pugnet and Thoreux were assisted by Hubert Viard, another captain (called "second captain"); Jean Hazard, the full engineer responsible for the machinery, who had been decorated with the Légion d'Honneur a few days before departure; and François Kerdoncuff, Hazard's deputy.

Also to be accounted for was Hervé Le Huédé, the security officer in charge of watching miles of corridors, hundreds of cabins, dozens of public rooms, and, from the main command post, the numerous illuminated dials of the automatic systems for guarding against fire or leaks in water-tight compartments. He was assisted by a team of watchmen and fire fighters, most of them recruited from Paris's Fire Brigade. Along with these, on the bridge or in the engine room, were officers of the watch, radio officers under the command of Jean Kerisit, the head telegraph officer, and even a Captain at Arms, the chief of police on board who, with his men, was responsible for maintaining order in what was a town with a population of more than three thousand souls.

May 31

Since an enormous amount of liquid is consumed on board a liner in the course of an evening, it was essential that the *Normandie* staff understood how on occasion to assert real authority, possibly even backed up with muscle power, but more often with diplomacy and psychology, in confrontations with people who were undeniably drunk but who had also paid for an extremely expensive passage. A drunk was a passenger first of all. There were few noticeable incidents on this inaugural crossing, and yet champagne, wine, and other kinds of alcohol were flowing at all festivities which, every evening until very late, brought guests together in the Grand Lounge with the Chrislers orchestra or in the first-class Grill Room.

The Grill was opened the second evening at midnight and immediately became the favorite rendezvous of the boat. Perhaps the most successful of all nightclubs, it bore the promise of even greater glory. For after an evening of dancing and a late supper, the thrill of seeing the sun rise over the sea through the great bay windows surrounding the room was an unforgettable sensation.

Lee Creelman, *Vogue*, June 1935

The Grand Lounge and the Grill Room were the kingdom of a strange personality, Bouts Durs, a passenger who quickly became known as the clown of the crossing.

One evening while the Grill was languishing in a cacophony of jazz without either gaiety or resonance, a little man stepped on to the dance floor. He danced frenetically with a glass of champagne on his head. He then added another glass, then a bottle, and everybody made a circle around him. Everybody stopped dancing, laughed, and looked at him in astonishment.

'Hey kids, isn't this amusing. Hey you, sweetie, what would you like me to sing?' He then chanted 'I want to see my *Normandie* again' in a lovely boozer's voice. He had more success than any of the attractions on board.

'Do you hear that, boys, and you, Toto?' For him, Toto was any one of his interlocutors. 'Yes, that's what I make of you. Because I, I am the King of the Hard Knocks. I owe nothing to anybody. I have ten factories. Did you get that, Toto, ten factories, and I'm my own banker. As for the Americans, I'm gonna put 'em all in my pocket. I've got the Croix de Feu, *vive la France!* On you go boys, all together. I want to see my *Normandie* again! What, you ain't singing. Eh, waiter, bring me another bottle of champagne. What? It's past the hour? Not for me, and hurry up.'

The waiter rushes away. And as he serves the champagne, Bouts Durs chucks him under the chin.

'Hey, you're a Toto too. And if I was eighteen and had skirts, I'd make you Queen of England.'

Bouts Durs, or Maurice Morel, had been a Paris urchin and was now a millionaire. A street kid who started life at the age of twelve with three francs fifty in his pocket. His brother, one year older, had the same capital. Each worked on his own. Morel worked at a shoemaker's where he learned to hammer soles. He never did tell us what his brother did, but admitted that the kid hadn't turned out well and was now mayor of Pont-de-l'Arche.

'I had images of grandeur, I tell you, Toto. Eh, Toto, are ya listening Toto? International business, I just stick it in my pocket. Just like I tell ya. I got factories in Arpajon, Brussels, Milan, Berlin — got me Toto? You only don't know what *bouts durs* ["hard ends"] are kid? That's the end of ya shoe, got it, Toto? I found a system to harden the felt, nothing smarter than that.'

'Hey, waiter! Your ship's shaking. Why's your ship trembling?'

The maître d'hôtel explained, respectfully, that the boat was

going fast, very fast indeed, and that the engines were slaving away.

Bouts Durs cupped his ear. 'The engines? Captain, send one of your punks with some beer for the engine boys. Got it?'

Around four in the morning, Bouts Durs was drunk, as drunk as you can get, so he had one of those great ideas that only lushes can hatch. Followed by all the dancers in the Grill, musicians, beautiful ladies, he led everybody down to the pool. Since it was empty, he made a great row to have it filled, and since nobody would listen to him, he added a little of his own.

'Hey Kids, I'm gonna get my chocolate fishes that Menier gave me this morning. I'll chuck 'em in the water, and we'll all go fishing tomorrow.'

He returned with a box of chocolate fishes, and everybody tried to stop him from going ahead. He was stubborn.

'Let me tell ya about fishes. You chuck 'em in the water.'

And he did as he said. The hours passed, and he thought it time to go to bed. He had his eye on a somewhat tipsy American lady who giggled at his eccentricities. Having more or less picked his companion out of the crowd, he disappeared with her at dawn, himself swathed in the ermine coat she had let fall from her generous shoulders.

Like the rest of the boat, I saw a very unhappy Bouts Durs the next day. He was wandering through the lounges with a photograph in hand, a present from his lady of the previous night. He asked everybody if they had seen her. He approached us, and addressed me alone.

'Listen Kid, I respect ya, got me? Don't get mad, got me, but I respect ya, that's the way it is. So, I'm gonna tell ya the truth, that's a pain in the ass. You saw the U.S. lady of last night. Well, when I got back to my cabin at eight this morning you know what I found in my pocket? A thousand-franc note and nine hundred-franc notes all wadded up that she stuck there 'cause she was pleased. Look, I can't keep that dough, I gotta find her. Who the hell did she take me for? I gotta give her back her dough, ya got it?'

Madeleine Jacob, _Vu_, June 1935

A luxury liner is a secret place, far from shore and jealous husbands.

Four days on board – a piece of time – a 900-foot boat – a piece of space – no material cares, and a wind to arouse the senses – unity of action – all the conditions for a Racine tragedy are on board. What would have been a passing flirt in Passy took on another dimension here. Lyricism welled up, even for people cut out for rather fickle occupations.

From the first evening onward, little flute sounds began emanating from the more sheltered decks, the ladies with bare shoulders and the gentlemen with starched fronts. Not many went into the full wind to see dawn rise from the gray horizon. For those who did, tragedies started, since the grandeur of the sea lent a far more noble scale to these meetings than the boulevard ever could. Here, the two senses mentioned by Nietzsche – senses which were linked and whose rarity he regretted – developed simultaneously: the sense of tragedy and the sense of sexuality.

Bertrand de Jouvenel, _Vu_, June 1935

However, on a luxury liner, the average age of the passengers (above all in first class) is relatively advanced, except for a few heirs and heiresses, actresses, journalists, and, on this occasion, the gorgeous models representing French fashion.

Beautiful ladies were missing. We had plenty of the sort normally seen at charity balls, ladies with marcelled hair. Oh, really very proper, and twelve models plus a few movie stars. Three of the models were very pretty and one – my friend Nouke – was really something.

She was twenty years old, had the face of a pekinese, Asiatic eyes, golden-blond hair, and with all that she was also charming and nice. Everybody liked her right away. She was first put in tourist class, then third class, but Nouke didn't stay there. She got lots of hospitality in first where she turned more than one head. And one morning, pulling herself up voluptuously, she told me: 'Oh, I'm so unhappy. I'm in love!'

And Nouke kept getting all the looks. She was the great star on board without even trying. Nouke, who was wanted on every movie screen in the world, whom the stars on board regarded as a future partner, who slapped Philippe de Rothschild across the face at the pool, just like that, for fun, asking 'Who is that guy?' Nouke,

Colette with Jean de Rovera and Marcelle Chantal

who could see the great fortunes of Europe and America at her feet, had just murmured to her friend on board: 'Yes, that's that, we'll leave together for somewhere far away, just the two of us. Oh! You can take me. I've got five hundred francs in the bank.'

Adorable Nouke.

Then there is the *femme fatale*, an American friend, very beautiful and troublesome. Once, as we both were taking tea in the

Of course, waking up is sometimes difficult and often cruel.

...Bouts Durs was famous, adored by the musicians, by the staff that he covered in gold, by the night watchmen he drowned in champagne. American journalists wanted to interview him, and he first turned them down cold. Then: 'Ya wanna know, Toto,

Maurice Morel, known as Bouts Durs ("Hard Ends" or "Hard Knocks")

Lounge, we saw the secretary of His Highness, the Maharaja of Kapurthala, come toward us. The secretary said subtly, 'Mademoiselle, I have wagered friends of mine that you would not join me for cocktails.'

'How subtle,' murmured my young friend, 'Well, sir, you've lost your bet.'

And she went off for her drink. A bit later, as we passed on the Promenade Deck, she very rapidly confided to me: 'The Maharaja asked me not to return on *Normandie* but to wait for the next liner. As you can imagine, I wouldn't do that.'

She didn't return on *Normandie*.

Madeleine Jacob, *Vu*, June 1935

what I think of the ship? Well, listen to this kid, and try to get it. You know, I started with nothing, and never believed that one day I would be able to afford a trip like this. Also, when I got on *Normandie* I thought I'd see lots of terrific stuff, and you know what I found, Toto? All I found was the garbage peelings of life.'

And Bouts Durs, with a grand and hopeless gesture, seemed to be chasing away an image as well as everybody around him. But nobody wanted to laugh any more. And we felt a bit ashamed in front of that poor slob, who was really a great man, totally self-made, and who had nothing but scorn for us, for all of us.

Madeleine Jacob, *Vu*, June 1935

BALLADE AU BOIS
II

BALLADE AU BOIS
I

NUIT D'ÉTÉ
III

Three dress designs by Patou

Josette Day wearing "Ballade au Bois"

Fashion show given in New York

A Chanel dress (left) and a Patou dress (right)

Bérard's drawing for the program accompanying a fashion show on board

Patou's "Nuit d'Été" (left) and a dress by Worth (right)

A Maggy Rouff "number" (left) and "Contrastes" by Patou (right)

Josette Day in "Belle Aventure"

Happily, on a liner one rapidly loses all notion of time. Once night finishes here, doesn't it start somewhere else at the same time? And despite the miles run on the ocean, the time differences pass unnoticed.

Each day, we stop the clocks for sixty minutes. Soon, we will forget to restart them. Don't look at your friends' watches. Some passengers are on Paris time, others go by New York. I met one who was holding to Shanghai time.... Never mind, the nights are too beautiful, and it's useless to get up in moments of affluence. Let's get served in the cabin.... Your head turns, the day is deprived of its temporal structure. To sleep, to taste that delicious air spicier than a Mexican dish, to touch the sea visually and feel it soft and heavy like a salty syrup.

Bertrand de Jouvenel, June 1935

Beyond and behind, however, on those immobile continents, life went on. In France, for example, Flandin's government fell, and William Bertrand, who walked on board as a minister, was suddenly a simple citizen. But Paris assured him, by cable, that he was still the official representative alongside Mme Lebrun, who, preparing for arrival in New York, addressed American women live via radiotelephone.

Mme Lebrun was very discreet, and was hardly seen except in church and at dinner.

And Colette, the scandalous Colette, showed herself capable of exemplary behavior when in the company of her husband, Maurice Goudeket. Every day, in her casual wear, she tramped along the Promenade Deck followed by an army of photographers and curiosity seekers.

Normandie's Maiden Voyage

I wanted *Normandie* all to myself. Until now, I must confess, this has not been easy, even when getting up and leaving the cabin at dawn. During these long days, dawn holds no mystery. That deep, austere red which proclaims the sun's approach — the sanguinary and excruciating color of almost every birth — changes quickly into gold, and, once warmed, the still, thin mists hovering over the sea lighten and lift away.

I hoped the ambiguous hour would give me *Normandie* while everyone else aboard lay sleeping, but a ship never sleeps. The cleaning watch — thirty-nine silent men — commence their work at two in the morning, and the liner's interior lights never go out, day or night.

No matter! At half-past five, the ring of black-satin chairs in the Hall on the Main Deck draws an assembly of nothing more than a council of shadows, presided over by the enamel paladin, and the Grand Lounge is radically empty.

In the Winter Garden, a strange silence still reigns over the birds, albeit not all of them are quiet. But it seems a precarious fate to be a bengali on board a ship and so near the bow, yet submissive to the impetuous wind generated by our speed.

No one in the blue swimming pool and no one in his favorite bar. In the gymnasium, ready for a troupe of phantom athletes, the horse saddle, the exercise bicycle, the camel back, the rowing machine — everything that moves, oscillates, or springs remains stock still, betraying the silence of seduced muscles. Ablaze with light, *Normandie* throws a party for the invisible.

An empty corridor makes quite a spectacle, especially when it runs long enough for the parallel lines of floor and ceiling to appear, by virtue of distance, to converge and meld together. Not a passenger in sight. Occasionally, the blue back of one of those watchmen evaporates as soon as seen. If I lost my way, would I be able, even running, to reach the man in blue and ask directions? No doubt he is a figure in a dream, and such men never reply.

Up the stairs, down the stairs. Nothing stands in my way. Doors obey me with hallucinating docility.

Squirrels, cats, and dogs, painted over the walls of a playroom and well behaved since the night before, sleep standing up to await the children's morning arrival.

Here I am, quite out of breath, under the low, hospitable ceiling in tourist class. But then I lose my way. I cry out 'Help!... Please!' to a blue man whom I catch sight of, or at least his shadow, probably his shadow, which there in front of me stumbles through the half-open theater curtains and steals away. I now slip in behind him, only to come back alone — fast! This was no place for me, a world of darkness relieved by a single fixed star of weak light burning over stage center. The odor of hospital beds greeting the end of night gives one a turn, and if I run into a blue man, a real one, and not a fallacious silhouette, or a reflection gliding over the walls of polished metal, I shall ask him where the nearest gangway is. But there is no semblance of a blue man, only an immense stream of cold air to guide and deliver me.

The gaiety of a morning still fresh and hardly tasted. Beyond the broad rear decks, the ample skirt of foaming wake spreads and marks our path on the sea. But *Normandie* is no longer mine alone. I share her with several men from the cleaning watch, silent and furtive as ever. Real this time, the four of them seem to dance their way through the ship's toilette, doing it with love and infinite care, and also in step. On the lowest deck, soft under bare feet, a bending carpenter uses a broad axe to scrape the floor clean of some imperceptible wart. After each light stroke of the tool, he fingers, feels, scratches, and examines the hardened tissue like a surgeon. And there he will stay until certain the spot has been healed.

The morning's sun and wind give one an appetite. Moreover, it is time to return to hosts and guests alike a domain lent to me by the dawn. In the Dining Room with the translucent walls, a batallion of impeccable stewards has come back to life, under a basilican ceiling, in the sunlight filtering through a grove of columns. As far as the eye can see, frosty, giant icebergs, organs of crystal. ...I am alone, and I hesitate to order what, by contrast, strikes me as the tiniest *café au lait* in the world.

Colette, *Notebooks*, 1935

The arrival in New York

Pier 88 as Normandie came alongside for the first time

June 1 – Gala Dinner

Between a sketch by Louis Verneuil and a one-act comedy, *Daily Bread* by Jules Renard, Colette gave a lecture in the Theater on the evening of June 1. The occasion was a benefit for the good works of the CGT. It continued in the Grand Lounge with a variety show, a tombola, and a collection for French and American charities. This was followed by dancing in the Grill to the music of the French Tango Orchestra.

June 2

Finally, the last night on board had come. The farewell dinner was followed by a symphony concert performed by the Bonnety orchestra in the Grand Lounge. In the Theater, Claude Farrère mixed humor and *belles-lettres*, after which Pills and Tabet, two stars of the day, gave a recital. It was a farewell evening, but who wanted to break up? Particularly since everybody had sworn to stay awake until the first American lights had been sighted on the ocean. This meant the Nantucket lightship.

June 3

But at 5:00 A.M. in the early morning fog, few were around to recognize this anchored ship, painted red as a sort of lighthouse tossed about by the waves.

On the other hand, not one passenger missed the magic of the moment when *Normandie* passed Ambrose light, the lighthouse marking the entrance to the Port of New York and, of course, the finish line of the race for the Blue Ribbon. It was precisely 11:03, which everybody confirmed.

There was a great burst of joy on board when, in keeping with tradition, the ship was dressed all over, while a pennant of blue bunting 30 meters long (1 per knot of average speed) streamed from the truck of the tall mizzenmast.

At that very moment, a plane flew over the ship, pulling behind it a great banner with large letters emblazoned against the sky: NEW YORK WELCOMES NORMANDIE.

Even in normal times, having nothing to do with maiden voyages or Blue Ribbons, an arrival in New York by ship is a stunning experience, an unforgettable moment in anybody's life, yet one that becomes no less unforgettable with each repetition.

First of all, there is the land – bluish, violet, green – the silhouettes of distant skyscrapers that come closer and seem to run toward the ship until she reaches Quarantine, where a brief pause allows the police, customs, and health officials, as well as the pilot, to come aboard.

And then, more slowly, the vessel and her passengers pass

150

Mme Lebrun receiving the Key to the City of New York from Mrs. Fiorello La Guardia

Normandie's bow nosed up to the quay in New York

Staten Island to port and Brooklyn to starboard. On the way, the *Statue of Liberty* holds out her flame to the new arrivals just before the ship gets to Ellis Island, where immigrants were previously sorted into various categories. Finally, there is the tip of Manhattan after a turn of the helm to the left, and on up the Hudson to the home pier as the whole city glides by on the right.

Normally, that by itself is overwhelming. But on June 3, 1935, New York offered the new arrivals an even more fabulous spectacle.

The docks along the river, the roofs of shops and warehouses, the cranes to which men clung like grapes — everything was black with people, and it was all in motion, arms waving, handkerchiefs by the dozen, by the hundreds and thousands. Myriad bits of white and colored paper fell from the top of the skyscrapers. The fireboats of the port's fire brigade put their hoses into action, and water played as in Versailles's great fountains. And despite the presence of aircraft, of a huge Mickey Mouse balloon, a rubber sea serpent, and other modern publicity gadgets, despite the din and cacophony, this trip up river had the allure of a triumphal, even royal procession.

Blaise Cendrars, *Paris-Soir*, **June 5, 1935**

There was an equally impressive moment when *Normandie* stopped, turned against the current, and steamed straight ahead, her stern veering toward the west side of town. "...The boat slowly came alongside the pier, where her stern, standing tall among the skyscrapers, seemed right in scale with New York."

Arrival in New York

We passengers furtively look at each other. Many don't want to show that they have tears in their eyes. I am frank about my sense of wonderment.... I'm bowled over. We want to kiss each other, to say that France is a grand country which knows how to accomplish a great *tour de force*, and that the Americans are good guys to recognize this with such enthusiasm.

And then, in reality, we can't move, overwhelmed by the greeting. All the small jokes and little stories I have told to date don't count any more. *Normandie*, the most beautiful and the fastest ship in the world, is in New York!

Odette Pannetier, *Candide*, **June 6, 1935**

There was delirium in the streets of Manhattan. Nothing counted but *Normandie*, and the liner now berthed at the center of town was being celebrated in shop windows, in newspapers, and on the radio.

As soon as the boat docked, Mme Lebrun, who while still on board had already received a floral key to the city, was allowed to disembark with her suite and bypass the normal formalities. A police motorcycle escort led a procession of limousines to the Waldorf-Astoria Hotel on Park Avenue. It

Mayor La Guardia receiving Mme Lebrun, accompanied by the French Ambassador, M. de Laboulaye

Gala dinner on board while in New York, June 5, 1935

Gala dinner at the Waldorf-Astoria, June 3, 1935

was there that Mayor La Guardia was to give a dinner that evening in honor of the wife of the President of the French Republic and the official delegation from *Normandie*.

A few minutes before 8:00 P.M., dinner jackets and long dresses invaded the public rooms of the great hotel. All New York had come to toast *Normandie*.

In the Waldorf's grand ballroom, all done up in red, white, and blue (the colors of both France and the United States), there were flags on the walls, flowers on the tables, and, shortly to come, 115 dressed platters. At the table of honor, near Mme Lebrun and Mayor La Guardia and his wife, were the French Ambassador to the United States, André de Laboulaye, Count Charles de Ferry de Fontnouvelle, the Consul General of France in New York, the now-former Minister of the French Merchant Marine, William Bertrand, the Lieutenant Governor from the State of New York, William Bray, and Governor General Olivier, chairman of the French Line, his President, Henri Cangardel, and the general manager of the French Line in the United States and Canada, Henri Morin de Linclays, who barely arrived for dessert owing to business on board the ship. There were also admirals and government officials from both countries.

At the other tables dined the cream of Franco-American society, plus many of the richest men and women in the world: Guggenheims, Morgans, and Vanderbilts.

The dinner was a gastronomic tour of the United States: New Orleans creole-style gumbo, soft-shell crabs from Maryland with warm cucumbers, breast of Long Island duck with Carolina succotash, a salad of Florida avocados, California asparagus, and blueberry ice cream with fresh raspberries and strawberries, doused in New England applejack.

The wines were French: Château Latour Blanche 1928, and Côtes de Beaune 1923, as were the liqueurs: Courvoisier VO, Benedictine DOM, or Crème de Menthe.

The cigars were Cuban as was Xavier Cugat's orchestra, which had been hired to liven up the evening.

Robert Echegut, "the *Paris-Soir* brat," met up with his New York counterpart, Peter Dudan, to the popping of flashbulbs. The French journalists covered the streets and avenues of New York, astonished and fascinated.

Over the next four days parties and receptions came in cascades.

Then, on June 7, following a last reception at New York's City Hall and after Mayor La Guardia personally accompanied Mme Lebrun to the gangway, *Normandie* weighs anchor around 1:00 P.M.

Again, crowds thronged the docks to see the ship depart. It was a fine, hot day. Men were already in shirt-sleeves, women in light dresses. On board, 1,500 passengers leaned on the railings, fascinated by the streamers and confetti, while orchestras played both on deck and on Pier 88.

This moment was less solemn than the departure from Le Havre, closer to a holiday. In New York, a departing liner is a great occasion for the traveler to give one of those farewell parties so dear to the American heart. It brought 10,000 letters and telegrams, along with 3,000 bouquets of flowers and 2,500 bottles of champagne, the latter consumed by *Normandie*'s new guests practically until the ship pulled away. And there was no counting the telephone calls received. But now the last visitors disembarked, the gangways were lowered, and the lines untied.

Normandie blew her powerful horn, the sound resonating over skyscrapers whose terraces, roofs, and windows seemed filled with swarms of ants waving their arms. The ship slipped slowly backward, stopped an instant in the middle of the Hudson, made a quarter turn, and headed for the bay and open sea, passing along Manhattan Island. On the way, she was saluted by the sirens of all the liners docked in the port of New York, whether German, Italian, English, as well as French vessels still at Pier 57, the old French Line berth. From the nearby streets and avenues rose a great din of automobile horns, fire engines, and police cars, plus the sirens of the same flotilla that had escorted *Normandie* on her arrival. And, of course, the immense *petit nouveau* hastened to acknowledge the new tribute.

After the Narrows, that strait between Brooklyn and Staten Island, the ship was increasingly left on her own as she approached Quarantine. A last farewell concert: planes dipping their wings toward *Normandie* before regaining altitude. Then the ship would soon pick up full speed for the return trip to Europe.

The east-bound voyage was to be even more perfect than the west-bound. The first crossing had been like a dress rehearsal, and now the crew would fully carry out their roles without any of the isolated problems and hesitations already cited on the voyage. But just imagine the effort and sacrifice this took on the part of *Normandie*'s anonymous staff, who had endured not only the infernal rhythm of a crossing but also the official ceremonies in Le Havre, mad nights on board until the wee hours, more of the same in New York, and then on to the next arrival.

In fact, the waiters in the restaurant worked that month an average of eighteen hours every day. Eighteen hours to run tens of miles from the kitchen to the Dining Room, arms loaded with heavy platters, sometimes on an unsteady surface, yet performing without evident fatigue or any loss of humor.

However, sometimes they just could not heed the call, and

Dali and Gala upon their arrival in New York in 1936

A. Sebille, *Normandie, at Midnight on the Atlantic,* gouache

the section of the hospital reserved for the crew was always full. Overwork, nervous depression, psychological problems – all took their toll. A dozen beds were always occupied, but the doctors, nurses, and other involved parties remained very discreet, and most of the passengers knew nothing of these problems. A similar subtlety prevailed in other cabin arrangements of a more particular nature:

Of course there are other idylls. The most striking is that of the models. The poor girls who were quite bored on the trip out are even more to be pitied on the trip back. They had been lodged in cabins that vibrated, which meant that they couldn't even sleep to kill time. But what some worked out on their own proved to be quite clever. On the first day, men traveling alone in first-class cabins with twin beds noticed that their charm had a strong effect on one of these beautiful passengers. By the second day, she could finally get the kind of good rest her friends envied.

Odette Pannetier, *Candide,* **June 20, 1935**

While the parties went on, *Normandie* added a new record: 4 days, 3 hours, 28 minutes at an average speed of 30.31 knots.

June 12

At 7:20 P.M. *Normandie* came alongside at Le Havre. Again flags, *La Marseillaise,* and on the Sun Deck the West Point Orchestra in full dress uniform playing American and French military marches.

What a triumphant arrival for the American passengers. But for those celebrities and journalist veterans of two crossings, the moment was sad. Nostalgia, and even regret, on leaving the ephemeral world of the transatlantic liner shown through even the cynicism of this privileged group.

The dock at Le Havre. How small Le Havre is, how thin the crowd, albeit immense by European standards. It's over.

At the Gare Saint-Lazare, we hug our pals of yesterday – minister, deputy, senator, movie star, great writer, or beautiful actress. We were on intimate terms, or nearly, with practically all of them. We were together, became friends, friends for life until death. We told each other everything, we drank coffee with Charles Boyer, danced with admirals, slept on a deck chair between Claude Farrère and Henri de Rothschild. But it's over; in Paris we no longer know one another. We ran the Blue Ribbon together, but now we go our separate ways. We lived under the same roof as the President of the Republic, said hello as if we were real pals, and the Chief of Protocol confided in us. In Paris, all that is gone, forgotten forever.

Madeleine Jacob, *Vu,* **June 1935**

The Secret Life of *Normandie*

Reading a few of the surviving volumes of *Normandie's* "Night Service" (the on-board register in which the officer of the watch noted all incidents that occurred between 10:00 P.M. and 7:00 A.M.) immediately disclosed that there were two *Normandies,* one going west and the other east. The first was as well behaved as the second was dissipated. At a time when the United States was openly prudish and straitlaced, *Normandie's* essentially American clientele sought release in Europe, the cradle of every forbidden pleasure. The passage out, with its intoxicating sense of remove, became a moment of mad, untrammeled liberation.

The crew lost count of the American passengers (and certainly their names, which were always kept secret!) who got themselves, as it was euphemistically put, "under the influence," made scenes, or fell down staircases. There were loud parties in the cabins, adventures about which the staff kept their peace, and vamps who caused havoc in the Grill Room.

Once their European jaunt was over, the Americans seemed to want to use the voyage home as a time to calm down before arriving in New York.

One "sport" common to all crossings was getting from one class to another. Their careful separation seemed to encourage transgression. Gentlemen in first, sure of their charms with the young ladies, would venture into tourist, there to slum a bit or simply have a good time. To tell the truth, the atmosphere in first class was a bit staid, even if the evening's program was full and often lasted until dawn.

As for the tourist passengers, they were ready to try anything – however unauthorized – in order to taste forbidden fruit, even if this meant taking down communicating doors. Guards had to stand watch against this intrepid crowd, who could be readily spotted by their way of dressing.

One could never fully imagine all that went on in the course of 139 Atlantic crossings. But the few "authentic" stories given below, little fragments of life on board, can help fill out the full picture of *Normandie,* like the final pieces fitted into a puzzle.

Marlene Dietrich in the Rouen Suite, November 19, 1938

Madeleine Carroll and Henry Morgenthau, U.S. Secretary of the Treasury, August 2, 1939

Cary Grant, November 19, 1938

James Stewart, August 28, 1939

Tristan Bernard, May 26, 1936

Thomas Mann in 1937

Ernest Schelling, La Argentina, and José Iturbi in the late 1930s

Antoine de Saint-Exupéry with two Paris-Soir reporters, July 26, 1939

Lucien Lelong, August 25, 1937

M. and Mme. Pierre Cartier,
September 25, 1937

Jules Romains, May 20, 1936

Othon Friesz (left) and Jean Patou (right),
November 12, 1938

157

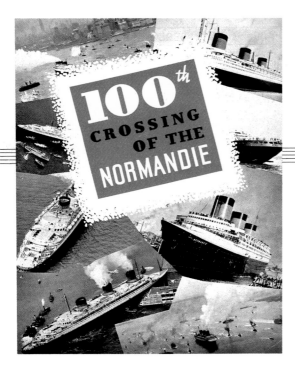

A Night on Board *Normandie*

(From "Night Service") July 4–15, 1936

22:00 Start service. Everybody present. Sub-Chief Contant remains on call in tourist until 1:00 A.M. on A Deck portside to handle tourist passengers allowed to go to first.

23:20 End of concert in first-class theater.

24:00 Lights turned down. Left at the desk a black, tulle handbag found in the theater.

1:10 Tour of the rooms. All OK.

1:15 Miss Kate Davin O'Neill, cabin 808, due to ship's rolling, fell from the staircase of A Deck to B Deck to the level of tourist-class B Deck landing. Rather serious injuries to the back of the head. Dr. Dupuy and the nurse did the necessary.

2:30 General tour OK. Following roll of ship, door of telegraph office on Promenade Deck portside opened, and its glass found broken. Inform carpenter in the morning, please.

2:45 Orchestra stops in Grand Lounge.

3:05 Grand Lounge is empty; many passengers still in Smoking Room and Grill, where Chrysler orchestra continues playing. Left in the office, a black fur cape found in Grand Lounge.

3:10 Informed engineer of slight leak in ceiling cab. 479 (M. Hustis); when engineer arrived, passenger was asleep. See in morning, please. Orchestra stops in Grill Room.

3:30 About a dozen passengers still in small portside lounge (including Sir and Lady Fraser). Depart at 5:30.

4:20 Led Mr. B. to his cabin (227) since he was in an inebriated state.

4:25 General rounds. All OK.

5:15 Closing of first-class bar.

1936

May 28–29

4:15 Grand Lounge empty. Request silence in the cabin of Mrs. L. Kayser (l50), who had four visitors, and forbade phonograph playing.

4:30 Again urged silence upon the occupants of cabin 150.

5:00 Departure of Mrs. Kayser's party.

May 31–June 1

1:15 The lady passengers from cabin 346, Mr. R.W. accompanied by Mrs. B.S. (lady passengers evidently in a state of inebriation) fell on the lateral staircase leading down from the Embarkation Deck to the Promenade Deck. Lady complaining of pains in the left shoulder, I informed the doctor, who visited her.

3:45 Delivered two urgent telegrams to Mme Josephine Baker (cab 350).

June 20–21

2:35 General rounds. Everybody at his post. Despite closing numerous communicating doors, many tourist passengers still coming to first, probably by way of the Embarkation Deck.

2:45 Returned to tourist class several tourist-class passengers found wandering about in first.

July 18–19

23:10 Asked Head Nurse to go to cabin 413 to see Mrs. Rothschild whose dog was sick.

1:30 Opened the winter garden to two passengers who took a photograph of Miss Marlene Dietrich there.

July 30–31

1:45 Watchman Ruault informed 3rd-class passengers playing cards for money that such games were forbidden on board. They stopped playing immediately. Sub-Chief Contant came to the scene (Smoking Room 3rd class).

August 15–16

3:25 General rounds. All shipshape. Met on A Deck aft two ladies from tourist class who were attempting to open communicating door with a key. Asked to see key, passengers refused. Opened the door so that they could return to tourist class, but could not find out their cabin number.

August 19–20

Sub-Chief Contant and watchman Ruault met a young American about 20 years old, in the 3rd-class Smoking Room, who had no ticket of passage. They brought him to the office in first class, where I interrogated him. He claims to be called Salvatore de Maria and to be an American citizen. I inform the officer on watch, who has him taken away by the Captain at Arms.

December 26–27

23:45 Mr. F. (cabin 1105), in a state of inebriation and extremely violent, was making noises in the corridor and threatening the watchman. I intervened and took the passenger back to his cabin. Sub-Chief Rouff also had to come between this passenger and another occupant of the same cabin. It would be a good idea to lodge this passenger in another cabin, to prevent repetition of such an incident and to keep things under better control.

December 27–28

0:15 Sir James Dunn (cabin 162) is extremely unhappy that we have neither yogurt nor buttermilk on board.

1938

February 8–9

2:00 General rounds. Miss G.S., from cabin 61, in a state of inebriation and overwrought, screaming in the corridor. After a quarter-hour of effort, I persuade her to return to her cabin.

2:30 The passenger becomes violent once more and makes a great deal of noise in the corridor.

May 20–21

4:00 The Grill Room is empty. Last passengers, Mlle Danielle Darrieux, Mr. M. Decoin, and friends.

June 16–17

4:30 On my rounds, I met several tourist passengers who were in first class and some 3rd-class passengers in tourist, all without passes. Requested Chief of Central Security to instruct fire-watchmen not to allow passengers through and to inform me of any incidents.

June 17–18

0:30 From Purser Henry, delivered to Mrs. Woods Plankington (cabin 141) a letter and a flower vase.
3:40 General rounds. All bars are shut and public rooms empty. Asked numerous passengers in tourist class (students) to make less noise in returning to their cabins.

June 30–July 1

22:30 Mrs. B.R. (cabin 605) in a state of intoxication and gesticulating in front of information office. Took her back to her cabin, and, at her request, called in the doctor. It would be a good idea to limit Mrs. R's alcohol intake.

July 1–2

3:30 Rounds of tourist and third class. Sent away from the tourist-class writing room two couples who were not properly dressed.

July 9–10

23:00 Returned Mr. T.T. to his cabin (369) in a state of drunkenness.
3:00 Returned Mr. T.T. to his cabin (369) in a state of drunkenness. The passenger had returned to the Grill Room.

3:30 The communication door from first to tourist class on deck near cabin 227 has been partly taken down, doubtlessly by passengers who wanted to return to or from tourist class.

July 14–15

1:00 Sub-Chief Micoin, on his rounds, met about 50 third-class passengers, on the crew deck. Impossible to remove them. Sub-Chief Micoin informed Purser de Villeneuve, who alerted officer on watch.

July 16–17

4:30 Mr. B. Toland of cabin 818 injures his left index finger in an attempt to pass the barrier separating tourist class and first class on the Embarkation Deck at the entrance of the Grill Room. Maître d'hôtel Bugeaud is informed. The tourist-class doctor makes a bandage for the passenger.

July 17–18

3:00 The Grill Room is empty, last passengers the Marquis de Cuevas and his friends. Bar closed.
4:30 Two gray felt hats found in smoking room. Turned in at office.

June 3–8

On July 4, Harold Nicholson, the British diplomat and writer, traveling with his younger son, Ben, began a long letter to his wife, Vita Sackville-West, which he finished only as the ship was docking on the 8th in New York, whence he posted what was really a travel journal. It would be reproduced much later in John Maxtone-Graham's marvelous book *The Only Way to Cross* (1972). Here is a short excerpt:

... We went straight to our cabins. Mine is Maritime with satin-wood cupboards and every form of gadget conceivable, including a telephone.... Now that we are in full Atlantic, I can see what is

Fred Snite, "the man in the iron lung," traveling in the Fécamp Suite, June 21, 1939

The Maharajah Manikya of Tripura, August 16, 1939

Comte and Comtesse Adalbert de Chambrun, November 3, 1937

William C. Bullitt, U.S. Ambassador to France, in the Trouville Suite, September 25, 1937

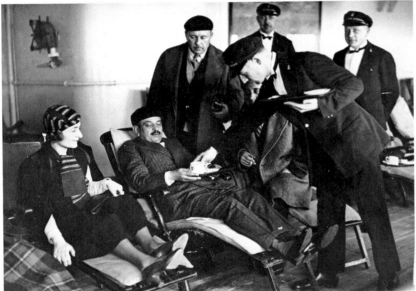

Pierre Laval, undated

Captain Pugnet with some of his American passengers

Paul Reynaud, September 16, 1936

Rio de Janeiro Bay

Sunbathing on the Promenade Deck

The Cruise to Rio in 1938

The Swimming Pool bar

Ceremonial baptism to mark Normandie's crossing of the equator

Luncheon buffet

A cocktail party in the tourist lounge

Cocktail party given for the Rotary Club, June 23, 1937

A magician's act in the Theater, June 17, 1939

meant by the vibration. At the stern, where the Le Corbusier circular grill room is — the nicest part of the ship — the flowers on the little tables wobble something dreadful and it would be difficult to read for long.... It must be even worse in the tourist class and I can well imagine that in some cabins it is really intolerable.

But where we are, one does not notice the vibration in the least and I have never known such luxury as that in which Ben and I live. The food is really delicious and although I am still careful, Ben eats a lot. Caviar and pâté for dinner yesterday....

As he observes, the whole place is like the setting for a ballet. Choruses of stewards, sailors, firemen, stewardesses, engineers and passengers. There are also some fifty liftiers in bright scarlet who look like the petals of salvias flying about these golden corridors. That is the essential effect — gold, Lalique glass and scarlet. It is very gay, but would drive me mad after a week....

The Harvard rowing team on their way to England to compete in the Henley Regata, June 28, 1939

Ludwig Bemelmans, an habitué of the CGT, was traveling with his daughter Barbara when he fell in love with *Normandie* and particularly with one of the ship's more astonishing passengers:

...The other outstanding figure on that trip was a young widow. She was dressed in long, glamor-girl blonde hair and black satin. I think she rubbed herself with a lotion every morning, and then pasted her clothes on her body; there wasn't a wrinkle on them. A doctor could have examined her as she was. Her arms were weighed down with bracelets, all of them genuine, and of course she had a silver fox jacket. An icebox full of orchids helped her bear up throughout the voyage. She appeared with fresh flowers at every meal, and she had with her a sad pale little girl, who was not allowed to play with other children. She wore a little mink coat on deck — the only junior mink I have ever seen.

The way the young widow managed her entrances into the dining-room reminded me of Easter at the Music Hall. She waited until the orchestra played Ravel's *Bolero* and then she came, surrounded by expensive vapors, heavy-lidded, the play of every muscle visible as a python's. At the first landing of the long stairs, she bent down, while everyone held their breath, until she succeeded in picking up the train of her dress.

Then a faultless ten inches of calf and ankle came into view and, with industrious little steps, she climbed down the rest of the stairs to the restaurant. Once seated, she smeared caviar on pieces

of toast and garnished them with whites of eggs until they looked like cards one sends to the bereaved; with this she drank champagne and looked out over the ocean. The sad little girl said nothing the whole day long.

The last night on board, the widow fell out of her role. A beautiful, an exquisitely modeled, long, slim, gartered leg came dangling from a high-held knee, out of black satin and lingerie. She danced like Jane Avril and let out a wild cowboy yodel, "Whoopee," and blew kisses to everyone....

(*The Only Way to Cross*)

Souvenirs of Purser Jean Henry

Most of the artists we asked to participate in the benefit concert, given on every crossing for the Seamen's Fund, did so very gladly and also helped out with the other shows which filled our crossings. Charles Boyer always agreed to be the master of ceremonies who presented the artists participating in the concert, and he used his deep voice with unusual skill. Henry Fonda had become the specialist in refereeing boxing matches. We had formed a sports club of which I was president, and the boxing section was run by Gaston Paumelle, France's former middle-weight champion, who was in charge of the health club. Paumelle chose and trained the boxers among the young and dynamic crew of pages and elevator operators, and the fights were slightly fixed as we couldn't afford to have disfigured boxers at the end of the day. Still, we needed a referee for these bouts, and Henry Fonda did this quite professionally on all his crossings. The day's ticket always ended in a pillow fight between six blindfolded pages, much to the delight of the spectators, who cheered on their favorites.

Horse races were organized by the energetic Head of Reception, but we often had the help of an important passenger who gave the competition a particular attraction. The low voice of Charles Boyer was most useful for us in this connection.

My great friend, Antoine de Saint-Exupéry was a faithful *Normandie* traveler, and I owe a special debt of gratitude to him, in that I never met, during my professional career, a man with so much knowledge, quality, and talent. One evening, on the New York—Le Havre crossing, he came into my office with an enormous packet of paper covered in his writing, which he put under my nose.

Exhibition ping-pong, September 15, 1937

The Captain's table, with Germaine Aussey on the right, October 1, 1937

Dinner honoring the premier of The Prisoner of Zenda, attended by Mr. and Mrs. Douglas Fairbanks, September 2, 1937

'Could you please spend two or three nights reading this file,' he said to me. 'I know it's a lot to ask for in view of everything you already have to do, but you can't refuse me this favor. Read all this, make corrections, erase anything you like, and we will talk about it before the end of the trip.'

I couldn't refuse, and with the help of Bohec, the head doctor on board who gave me some pills, I went to work, sleeping only two hours each night. When I gave the manuscript back to Saint-Ex, I was exhausted, and it was only later that I realized I had devoted three nights to reading *Terre des hommes* [in English known as *Wind, Sand, and Stars*], one of Saint-Exupéry's most famous books. That man could do anything, and one evening, around eleven o'clock, he sat in a corner of the Smoking Room with a few friends, and we were present at one of the most exciting card games I have ever witnessed.

I remember a crossing with the tall and beautiful Madeleine Carroll, Désiré Defrère, the baritone from the Chicago Civic Opera, Formichi, a tenor from the same company, and several other artists loyal to our beautiful ship. Saint-Ex was there and brilliant, as usual. During lunch the next day, Madeleine Carroll told me that she had never been so excited as when she talked to the great author – and in what a marvelous setting, under Jean Dunand's magnificent lacquer panels. I met Saint-Exupéry again in Algeria, where I was held up in the Allied invasion of November 8, 1942. I was running the French Line's hotel chain there, and when he had the time Saint-Ex would accompany me to Constantine, Biskra, Touggourt, and Ghardaïa. We dined together a few days before his death. Commander Billotte, who became a General after the Liberation, was in our party along with the nephew of General Catroux. In the course of dinner, he told me of the missions he was about to undertake. It was during one of these that he was shot down over the Italian coast by a German 'ace.' His book *Terre des hommes* has a place of honor in my library.

During the only crossing she made with us, Mistinguett, who was obviously no longer the great artist I had applauded in 1922 on the old liner *France*, along with Maurice Chevalier and Earl Leslie, agreed to sing *Mon homme* and show her still beautiful legs.

But certain artists refused to participate in our galas, and the great opera singer Lily Pons explained, on the *Lafayette* in 1931, that her vocal chords suffered from the salt air.

The famous Russian violinist Jascha Heifetz promised Chief Purser Villar of the *Île de France* that he would play once, but only once, and chose an ideal crossing when the Atlantic was particularly calm to keep his word. At 5:00 P.M. one day, he informed the Chief Purser that he would play that evening at 10 o'clock in the Grand Lounge, and at that time the Captain reduced speed. Heifetz played for one hour using a microphone because of the poor acoustics of the Grand Lounge.

On *Normandie* we once had a show of trained seals, but I think this was the only such occasion in the annals of the French Line. A pair of seals had been brought on board in a tank, and the butcher, who was in charge of the kennel, placed them on the Sun Deck with a group of canine friends. We naturally got the idea of organizing a show for the two splendid animals, which could only stay out of water for a good half-hour. The day of the concert, an extra tank was installed near the entrance door of the lounge, and at exactly 10:00 P.M. the passengers saw the dance floor invaded by two fellow travelers whom they had not realized were on board. The performance was a great success, and we felt that the seals had been delighted to show us their stuff.

Raymond Barbar, president of Jean Patou, often represented high fashion on board, and his childhood friend, Jean Borotra, the tennis champion, tried to make his trips to New York coincide with those of Barbar. 'The Leaping Basque' was always present at the auction that followed the charity concert, and put his racket up for sale in an event that was always very popular among the passengers. I remember his racket once going for $1,500, which permitted one of his American admirers to have a souvenir of one of the four musketeers of French tennis.

But we also had passengers who were quite special and had to be watched with great discretion. These were the 'professional gamblers,' which our transatlantic experience enabled us to detect, despite our rather limited means. Blending in with five or six hundred passengers, these types pretended not to know each other and discretely arranged a bridge game. When three of the crooks found a gullible passenger, they would fleece him.

Dinner given by Fred Snite, "the man in the iron lung," June 21, 1939

One evening around 10 o'clock, when Villar and I were in the central hall, we were stopped by an American passenger who insisted on seeing the Captain immediately. 'Impossible, he is kept on the bridge by impenetrable fog,' was our response, and upon our insistence the passenger admitted that he had just given a check for $32,000 to a team of professionals that he had invited to his cabin. Called into our office, the players admitted – under threat of being reported to the Scotland Yard inspector who was coming aboard in Southampton – that they had won fairly doubling thirty-two times, which is extremely rare, and that they had already posted the check in the ship's Post Office. The Captain asked the postal agent, whom of course we knew quite well, to open the most recent mailbags, and since the players had given us the address on the envelope, it was found in ten minutes and the check returned to the victim. We expected a generous reaction from the passenger in the form of a small check for the Seamen's Fund, but to our great astonishment he didn't make the slightest gesture, merely saying: 'My wife will be with you on the next trip from New York. I beg you not to say anything to her as the reaction will be terrible.'

Dogs got particular care. In principle, they were not allowed in the cabins, and they were always given over to the butcher, who took excellent care of them in the Sun Deck kennels, where their barking was drowned out by the wind! One day a charming American lady came to my office holding in her arms a lovely little poodle that she wanted us to take special care of. But when I replied affirmatively, saying that the butcher would take good care of it, she blanched and ran out of my office to stop the butcher from cutting her dog into tiny pieces. And that's a true story!

Jean Henry, February 21, 1985

One place had already taken on its definitive characteristics. That was *the* bar of the Grill, the smartest of the seven bars on *Normandie*, the one where the stools are surely higher, the bar that took on that Anglo-Saxon cachet before the ship was even launched. The English and especially the Americans went there straight from the gangway, having consigned their coats and baggage to that double row of scarlet consisting of liveried pages standing attendance in the Embarkation Hall. Ignoring their cabins, they went directly to the Grill-Bar, guided by an infallible memory or drawn by the terrible craving that a bar stool evokes for those with parched throats.

The barman, Yves, looking a bit like a father confessor, had been pouring libations for the French Line for years, knew all his old clients, and greeted new ones like long-lost friends.

'Still rum, gin, and orange juice, sir?'

'No more orange juice, Yves. It's terrible for my liver.'

The *Normandie* bar was quite American in the sense that serious business and faithful friendships – or romance – needed the benediction of a barman.

'My daughter, Yves, gives me lots of trouble.'

The coast was not yet out of view before the white-jacketed father confessor had heard the latest family news from the Kentucky Colonel or the financial troubles of the Chicago broker. In

Mr. Mac Gray (far left) and Bob Hope at a reception in the Winter Garden , August 4, 1939

addition to his discretion, he mixed great cocktails. This model barman honored me with a souvenir, serving me his drink, 'Normandie,' an invention that was the crowning achievement of his career.

Merry Bromberger, *Le Matin*, May 15, 1938

August 30 On *Normandie*, the purser took us to "Mont Saint-Michel," a gorgeous suite; a luxurious, pretty, dining room; bedroom in pale lemon wood with beds covered in pink satin; bathroom; shower room; large entrance with a wardrobe. At 1:30 they put up a lovely table for lunch. It was short, but a true fairy tale.

Liane de Pougy, *Mes Cahiers bleus*, 1936

I know, every year fifteen million francs are paid out in tips on *Normandie*; that's more than the budget of a major prefecture. There is more than one cabin boy who, at the end of the month, would gladly exchange his white vest against a ten-gallon hat. And the pages, with their scarlet caps, who take the hotel-management course on board in order to be head waiters, are already dreaming about the pretty villa they will own by the sea, where, in a few years, they can spend the forty hours between crossings.

Merry Bromberger, *Le Matin*, May 18, 1938

But a visitor is already at the door. A husband has lost his wife at the stroke of midnight and wants the sea searched or the cabins checked out so that he can find his spouse, dead or alive.

All the diplomacy of the purser is needed to point out three scenarios which might calm the man down. First, it has happened that a perfectly healthy woman simply got lost at night in the corridors. Then, Madame's sudden disappearance certainly must have taken place for the most worthy of reasons and under the most honorable of circumstances. Finally, it is in nobody's interest to give exaggerated importance to this incident.

And while the pacified husband returns to his cabin, the purser, for whom walls have ears, finds the lost lady by telephone, provides her with a satisfactory explanation, and sends her back to her husband. The next day, he will be rewarded with two grateful visits, both of which he could have done without.

Merry Bromberger, *Le Matin*, May 19, 1938

The Lady Who Watches Herself Dine

Here the star of the crossing – there is always one to eclipse the others – makes her entrance. Most of the time, she is a charming woman tête à tête, and even in the company of two or three people. But having become the focal point of the whole ship, she never dines. Her companions just get distracted answers out of her; she laughs to show her teeth and to shake her pale locks. She sprinkles sugar on her steak to show off her naked arm. If she lights a cigarette, it is to demonstrate the grace of her attitude.

With her, said a wag, you don't have lunch or dinner. You simply get fed up.

Merry Bromberger, *Le Matin*, May 21, 1938

Josephine Baker on *Normandie*

It was inevitable that *Normandie*, on occasion, would become the theatrical setting of veritable psychodramas.

The voyage that Josephine Baker made to New York in 1935, following an eleven-year absence from the American scene, brought such a bundle of sorrows that, understandably, she all but skipped over it in her memoirs.

With a mixture of joy and anxiety, the lustrous black entertainer had accepted to appear in a new edition of *The Ziegfeld Follies*, the production scheduled two years after the death of Florenz Ziegfeld.

The arrangements made for her embarkation on *Normandie* in October 1935 were altogether worthy of the star status La Baker enjoyed in France. She had been allowed to drive her Bugatti onto the quay, where Captain Pugnet presented flowers and accompanied her to a deluxe suite, trailed by a personal maid, dogs, a cat, and sixty pieces of luggage.

Hardly had *Normandie* weighed anchor when the Queen of the Folies-Bergère came down with seasickness, which continued unabated all the way to New York. Nonetheless, having learned that Billie Burke, a star in her own right and the widow of the great Ziegfeld, was on board, Miss Baker expressed a desire to have dinner with her.

And so, sumptuously attired in a svelte pale-yellow Erté gown, the famously lithe performer made a sensational entrance into the Dining Room, causing the whole assembled company to honor her with a standing ovation. A few minutes later Billie Burke made her entrance, headed for the Baker table, gave its mistress a contemptuous look, turned her back, and left the room. In glacial silence, Miss Baker sat down again and dined alone. When finished, she made her way to the top of the stairs, then turned back to her audience and flashed that renowned smile, which produced a new wave of applause. "I assume she belongs to the black-hating race," is supposed to have been the wounded star's comment.

Unfortunately, the problems that plagued her did not end there. Poorly received or simply ignored in New York, she hired three taxis and, elegantly attired in a Balenciaga, arrived at the Waldorf-Astoria, where she thought she had a reservation. Refused admission, she finally found shelter at the Hotel Saint-Moritz, which, however, required that she use the servants' entrance.

Next, this remarkable woman discovered that she had been given third-rank billing under Fanny Brice and Bob Hope. And when the show opened, it was a disaster first in Boston and again in New York, with the press especially savage in its treatment of Miss Baker.

Finally, after a number of terrible scenes, she broke off her ten-year relationship with Pepito, whose death, which she learned about only upon her arrival in Paris, came as a crowning blow on top of a long series of griefs.

Miss Baker's return voyage on *Normandie* was, under the circumstances, a more discreet affair than the outward-bound crossing. This time the star traveled simply in cabin no. 350.

Josephine Baker and her first husband, Pepito Abatino

EPILOGUE

CHARLES OFFREY

The Last Crossings

Against a background of gathering clouds, which since the Munich crisis had been growing ever darker, and under threat of a storm that seemed ready to break at any moment, *Normandie* continued along her peaceful, majestic, sovereign way, back and forth across the North Atlantic.

In contrast to the climate of extreme tension that reigned on the outside, sorely taxing the nerves and morale of France, the atmosphere on board the liner had never appeared more gracious or assuring. The passengers savored it like a precious possession they knew to be menaced. The luxury and comfort of the fittings, the refinement of the cuisine, the attentiveness of the staff and crew wrapped *Normandie*'s charges in a downy, protective cocoon, at the center of which they tasted the full pleasure of living well and free of care.

At the beginning of summer in 1939, *Normandie* still had a great many passengers, drawn across the Atlantic mainly by the New York World's Fair, then in full swing and burning brightly. But how many of those who left New York on August 16 could have imagined that this would be the last time the great ship would set sail for Europe?

It is worth noting that among the passengers were the general staff of the French Line, President Jean Marie, Henri Cangardel, and Edmond Lanier, returning from an inspection tour along the West Coast of the United States. The crossing was perfect in every way; only news picked up by the ship's radio brought back the tough reality of events that were leading inexorably to war. The passengers were busily occupied with the traditional shipboard parties, the usual games, theatricals, and festivities. Rarely had they been more brilliant than for the Seaman's Fund gala on August 19, which offered a fabulous array of stars. Simone Berriau, Gisèle Préville, Rosine Deréan, Lise Courbet, Jacques Baumer, Michel Simon, Erich von Stroheim, André Lefaur, Claude Dauphin, and René Fleur joined together in a little skit by Yves Mirande entitled *I Want to See My Normandie Again*.

Normandie left Le Havre as scheduled on August 23, 1939. She would never return. Over a thousand passengers – 1,147 to be exact — were aboard, among them many Americans desperate to get back home before the international situation became worse. That evening, cables received at sea led everybody to believe that the beginning of hostilities was imminent. The Captain ordered the reserve boilers brought on line and made ready for any eventuality. Bridge lights were reduced to a minimum and portholes in the engine room painted black. For the next two days, the radio officers noted that their communications were being scrambled by German ships at sea. *Normandie* ceased all transmissions.

She docked on the north side of Pier 88 in New York City at 10:15 A.M. on Monday the 28th of August. That very day, Germany invaded Poland. Twelve hours later, the *Bremen* tied up at the adjoining Pier 86, refueled, and requested permission to depart immediately without taking on passengers. The American authorities were strongly opposed to this and sent customs inspectors aboard to make a complete, if fruitless, search of the ship. The *Bremen* was therefore allowed to leave on August 30 at 6:35 P.M. As tugs towed her into the Hudson, her crew stood at attenion, made the Nazi salute, and sang *Deutschland über Alles*. Later it would be learned that she headed for Murmansk via the Gulf of Mexico in order to evade the British cruisers waiting for her on the high seas.

Normandie was supposed to sail for Le Havre on Wednesday, August 30. The departure was canceled that morning and the booked passengers transfered to Cunard–White Star's *Aquitania* due to leave the same evening. Early the day before in Paris, Henri Cangardel had acted, in view of events, to halt the departure, doing so with the permission of the CGT President and by way of the French Navy, which telegraphed France's Naval Attaché in Washington to relay the instructions to Captain Étienne Payen de la Garanderie, *Normandie*'s commander. It was feared that hostilities would commence within hours, and on September 3 Britain and France did indeed declare war on Germany.

Laid-up in New York

In his letter of September 22, 1939, to the Minister of the Merchant Marine, President Jean Marie justified the CGT's decision: "The order to depart was, in the end, not given to *Normandie* since the Navy and ourselves felt that she could be torpedoed. In fact, it is impossible for a ship of this tonnage not to be noticed from far away, whatever route she might take. In addition, the only port which could have handled her upon arrival in France would have been Le Havre, where *Normandie* would have been an easy target for air raids."

It was therefore decided that *Normandie* would remain in New York, at least for the time being. On Monday, September 4, the *Queen Mary* arrived at 8:00 A.M., packed with passengers. For the first – and last time — the two largest liners in the world were docked side by side. On Wednesday, September 6, an order was received on board to lay up the ship and repatriate the crew. Upon their arrival in New York, the crew consisted of 1,227 men, among them 136 deck hands, 278 engineers, and 913 passenger-service personnel. The first contingent of 650 men got off *Normandie* on Friday, September 8, to board the *De Grasse*,

Captain Payen de la Garanderie

which had been ordered to proceed to Halifax. A second group of 165 left on the 11th aboard the *Champlain*. During the following month, the remaining crew put *Normandie* into mothballs. A third, and final, group left the ship on October 21 and returned to France on the *De Grasse*, which had been dispatched to take them on in New York.

From this date forward, *Normandie* was interned with a skeleton crew of 113, including 5 officer engineers, 5 assistant engineers, and 35 oilers and stokers. The fate of *Normandie* was discussed again in 1940, this time with the idea of sheltering her temporarily at Fort-de-France in the Antilles or in Halifax. There was also the possibility of transforming her into a troop carrier. Henri Cangardel was opposed to this plan, as he explained to the Minister of the Merchant Marine, in a letter dated May 2, 1940:

We must not only think about the war, but also about the postwar years. Once *Normandie* has been refitted as a troop ship, she won't get back into service for at least six months to a year. In view of the delicacy of her fittings, I would not dare to estimate how much it would cost to repair the damage done. In addition, the liner might be sunk. She cost 600 million francs, and after the war a similar vessel will cost at least 2 billion francs. Finally, the Compagnie Générale Transatlantique has presently lost nearly all its share of the U.S. traffic to the competition, Americans among others. The company could immediately reactivate its passenger service if it had the possibility of refloating, right after the armistice, a magnificent ship like *Normandie*, provided she is in a sufficient state of readiness to attract a large clientele. I fully realize that *Normandie* in New York is not a risk-free proposition, and the danger in laying her up aroused some criticism. But have you thought how much it would cost to transport troops on *Normandie*, and have you considered the price of carrying a soldier on a ship of this sort? Putting *Normandie* back into service is a last-ditch solution, which I ask you to delay until every other possibility has been exhausted.

The French government concurred, and *Normandie* remained in New York. Now, the men in charge of the ship entered an extremely difficult period, morally and psychologically, if not financially, which lasted until the Coast Guard occupied the vessel in May 1941. Cut off from the home office, separated from their families, confused, traumatized by the news from France (until June 1940 they received mail by way of the hydroplane service between New York and Lisbon via the Azores), the invasion and fall of France, the armistice and occupation, and the June 18 call-up, while also besieged by divergent propaganda, each member of the small *Normandie* staff reacted according to his own sensibility, convictions, or interests.

One common task, however, kept them together and united: the defense of "their" ship and her maintenance in

top running condition, against the possibility of an eventual resumption of postwar service. In a letter dated November 17, 1939, to Henri Cangardel, Captain Payen de la Garanderie described the situation perfectly:

After nearly two months of being laid up in the port of New York, after a thousand difficulties of all sorts, we have prepared the ship for a very long stay without her being damaged in terms of either security or maintenance. I have found among my staff and crew the best of will for this very heavy and, I might add, painful task. Their effort has been totally unselfish despite what are, I'm sure you understand, totally legitimate worries of a personal and family nature. In this, I have discovered the sailor's innate discipline and devotion. I also have witnessed the sailor's attachment to his ship.

Another letter, dated March 12, 1940, reveals equally well the feelings of self-respect and pride on the part of the crew toward *Normandie* and her flag, the spit and polish they expended to make certain that, in war as in peace, their great ship might still outshine every competitor:

I think that you will be interested in the photo taken from the air that was in yesterday's *New York Times* and that I am enclosing with this letter. I take pleasure in noting that, despite her age, *Normandie* looks more modern than the ships that came after her. The stern of the ship in the left corner belongs to the *Mauretania*. The three British ships, the *Queen Elizabeth*, the *Queen Mary*, and the *Mauretania* are all covered with the gray paint prescribed by the British navy, which leaves them at a disadvantage.

I have often been asked the names of these dirty and apparently delapidated 'old tubs' that are berthed next to us. In the future, thousands of people will find it difficult to forget the impression of filth and decay they have witnessed in these ships. That is why I have recommended that our ship keep her normal appearance at all cost. Our place on the docks gives us the very best publicity.

Apart from their morale, *Normandie*'s crew had not suffered such a terrible fate, particularly in relation to that of their compatriots in France. Still, early winter was a difficult time. Having been caught by surprise when the ship came to a halt in full summer, they were quite unprepared for the rigors of a New York winter. But in early October 1939, such caring individuals as the director of the French Hospital in New York came to their aid. And so they wrote:

People everywhere say they are running into these poor boys all over town, alone or in small groups, walking about in their summer clothes. Just think of it! What an edifying spectacle for Americans to see the sailors of *Normandie*, the world's most luxurious liner, shivering in the street!

Given these circumstances, we have decided, following a discussion with *Normandie*'s Chief Purser, M. Henri Villar, to purchase a sweater and two pairs of woolen socks for each crew

Captain Le Huédé

member. In addition, American Tobacco has kindly sent 1,000 packs of cigarettes.

An allowance of $75 a month for officers and $30 for the crew was scarcely conducive to a high style of living. But the balance of their wages was being paid by the CGT to the men's families in France, a system that continued throughout the war, thanks to Henri Cangardel. At least Normandie's marooned crew could eat well and be warm and comfortable on board. To such a degree was this true that Captain Hervé Le Huédé (who relieved Captain Le Bez who in turn had replaced Captain Payen de la Garanderie) felt prompted to say upon his arrival from France: "I found people's life aboard far too easy for the present times. Thanks to American generosity, they are terribly spoiled. Everything they hear about France and its misery is taken in as if it were a movie plot."

As far as security was concerned, orders of the strictest sort were rigorously maintained and with the tightest discipline. Regular security watches were mounted by the deck crew. The engine crew were responsible for protecting the steam and propulsion machinery, along with its auxiliary equipment. A constant watch was kept by a squad of guards. Outside, further extraordinary security measures were taken by the local authorities.

Captain Payen de la Garanderie explained all this in a letter of November 17, 1939, to Henri Cangardel:

At different times, the city authorities, in the person of Mayor La Guardia, have shown great concern for us, wanting especially to protect us against acts of sabotage. That is why a police sentry is permanently posted at the entrance to the pier. At night, a second sentry takes up a position at the bow, touching the dock. The Navy itself contributes to our protection by placing a Coast Guard cutter at the other end of the pier. In addition, the police watch the rest of the pier and the gangway. Meanwhile, our people have established a system for watching the exterior.

All these measures were taken following some sabotage threats discovered by the American Navy's counter-espionage service.

As for risk of sabotatge inside the liner, this has been eliminated by preventing anybody except the crew from coming aboard.

In the event of fire, you know that, according to the rules of the port of New York, the Fire Department is required to take charge of all operations on board ships in port. In this connection, the responsible authorities have already inspected Normandie, and have put us in touch with the officers who would come aboard in case of an alarm. They have already made special couplings for their hoses to fit our Pugnet valves.

I might add that they were most complimentary about our fire precautions.

In short, given all the measures taken so far, we may consider the ship to be safe from surprise.

Sabotage — this dreaded word keeps coming back like a leitmotif every time Normandie is discussed, but always with a different sense, depending on who is speaking. For some, sabotage meant the possibility of acts by Nazi agents, or by members of the Fifth Column in the United States, or an eventual raid by a pocket submarine, provided it had succeeded in slipping past the Coast Guard and penetrating the Hudson. For others, the threat came from within, from the French on board who might be acting on behalf of the Vichy government in order to keep the liner from benefiting the Allies. Circumstances, alas, made the latter theory seem the most plausible.

In April 1941, the press made a public issue of the suspicion that Normandie's crew might be preparing to sabotage their ship. Under the headline "Free French Set to Place Crews on Ships in U.S.," we read the following in the New York Herald Tribune for April 2, 1941:

Followers of Gen. Charles de Gaulle, the 'free French' leader, are prepared to place trained crews, loyal to the Allied cause, aboard any French ships seized by the United States . . . and pointed out that the danger of sabotage of the French ships by their present crews was considerable, because of the artificial anti-British sentiment being drummed up by the Vichy government. 'If the Germans put pressure on Vichy to give orders to the crews of French ships now in neutral ports for destruction of the engines and other equipment, some of the seamen probably would do it.'

An indignant Captain Le Huédé replied violently to these insinuations: "The article that has appeared in the New York Herald Tribune of April 2 contains threats and accusations that cannot remain unanswered." Citing his impressive World War I record (the Verdun and Somme campaigns as a corporal in the Zouaves, wounded three times, a disabled right arm, military medal, and the Croix de Guerre), he goes on to say:

The very reduced general staff and crew of Normandie have had a perfect understanding of their role, and we are proud to be able to show our ship in a condition that astonishes connoisseurs, seamen, and artists.

The order and cleanliness are the result of well-organized work. All the equipment and all the engines are in working order. The security crew is on watch day and night, performing with such care that there has not been a single incident.

Yet you dare suggest in regard to this general staff and these crewmen that the danger of sabotage of French ships by their present crews is considerable!

The officers and crew of Normandie have a very deep sense of their duty and are well aware of the great value of their ship. It has been my great joy to find here officers and men who came aboard in October 1934 and have never left the ship, which they love as only a sailor can love his ship.

Don't look for sabotage from these men, nor should you look to me. They are deeply grateful for the generous hospitality extended to them in New York, thanks to which they have found the courage to bear their long days of exile.

They hope that one day they will be able to express their appreciation to joyful passengers on a dazzling, radiant *Normandie* sailing her way to France.

Nevertheless, the Americans continued to believe in the possibility of sabotage. The example of Italian ships sabotaged in American waters by cutting the main shaft with an acetylene torch only accentuated their fears. The local port authorities became even more worried about *Normandie* when the United States government learned, through informers in France, of the accord reached on May 6 by Admiral Darlan with the German High Command, an accord that served as a prelude to the Paris protocols of May 28, 1941, in regard to Syria and Iraq, North Africa, and both French Occidental and French Equatorial Africa, establishing the basis of a true common Franco-German defense of the Middle East and Africa.

Occupation by the Coast Guard

On May 15, 1941, radio station WCBX announced in French that the American government was ready to take strong measures. Indeed, that very day without warning, the Americans boarded the ship by the right of angary — that is, of a belligerent power. At 7:00 P.M. Captain John Baylis, Captain of the Port and a Coast Guard commander, went on board accompanied by two officers and announced that he had been assigned to protect the ship against sabotage, whether from without or from within. He made clear that this was by no means a seizure and requested the cooperation of *Normandie*'s officers and crew in carrying out his mission.

The Coast Guard was responsible for securing the American coast and ports and for guaranteeing the security of ships. In New York, the service's commandant was Rear Admiral Adolphus Andrews of the Third Naval District, while Captain Baylis was his assistant. Baylis, therefore, was well known to the officers of *Normandie*'s general staff, who had long maintained a professional relationship with him. In fact, truly warm ties bound the American to several of the French officers.

From the time the ship was laid up, the possibility that the United States would abandon its neutrality and enter the conflict became more real every day as President Roosevelt prepared public opinion. The problem of how, in such an event, to use *Normandie* had already come up, and it had been examined with Captain Baylis himself. In their memoirs, this is confirmed by both Captain Agnieray, the assistant

skipper, and Chief Electrician Yves Guillou. One of the solutions considered was the conversion of the liner into a troop transport, with room for 15,000 men — more than a division! Another idea was to take her to Brooklyn or Newport News to serve as an electric power plant capable of generating 150,000 kilowatts, enough for the whole city of New York in the event existing facilities should be sabotaged. Another plan would have had her used as a barracks for troops or a hospital for the crews of ships in dry dock or under repair.

The closeness of the cooperation in all these studies — which the American authorities, at least at the local level, could not but know — bears witness to the true feelings of *Normandie*'s general staff and gives the lie to all the fears of sabotage from within. Captain Le Huédé knew very well to whom he spoke when he gave his word of honor that there could be no possible danger from those on board. In his report describing the turn of events, he reproduced the exchange that took place between him and Captain Baylis:

B   You are taking a great responsibility.
L   I know my crew, and I know what responsibilities I can assume. I trust them to guarantee the safety of the ship.
B   How many men are presently standing watch on the ship?
L   At this moment, only two.
B   I can give you between two hundred and five hundred Coast Guardsmen.
L   I understand, but I feel more comfortable with my two watchmen who know the ship inside and out than with your five hundred Coast Guardsmen who don't know her at all. And then, do you have as much trust in your men as I have in mine?

Baylis replied only with a smile.

L   We will never sabotage *Normandie*. On that you have my word of honor. But if we wanted to do that, nothing could be easier for us. All we would have to do is totally abandon the ship and leave her in your hands!

In the end, Captain Le Huédé was able to retain control of security inside the ship, while the Coast Guard took over outside. But this had to be approved in Washington.

At 11:00 P.M. the orders were modified, and, without warning *Normandie*'s captain, a detail of eleven Coast Guardsmen went on board and spread out: one at the central security station, one on the gangway, four on the outside decks, and five in the engine and boiler rooms. The next day, on May 16, Baylis explained to Le Huédé that he was acting on orders from Washington, and that the ship, with her 8 officers and 105 crewmen, was henceforth under protective custody. The Americans, despite the objections of the liner's general staff, organized a watch, and the French sailors were replaced in their posts by armed Coast Guardsmen. Considering themselves humiliated, the French accepted the change with bad grace.

Gradually, however, the tensions subsided. Guns were replaced by bludgeons, which in turn were left at the gangway. Living together reduced the friction, and finally relations became quite correct. "There have been no incidents, no desertions," noted Captain Le Huédé. "We have made an effort on both sides to get along."

But if the orders were clear and the security theoretically reinforced by the Coast Guardsmen, the latter, all new recruits, were in fact useless — when they were not an actual liability. "Even the least or most normal handling of the engines, as in a change of generating set or boiler," noted Yves Guillou, the officer electrician responsible for the central electric plant, "created total panic in [the Coast Guardsmen]."

On June 18, 1941, at 4:45 A.M., Guillou noted in his report, "the in-service turbo-dynamo, which generated electricity for power and light, shut down. With the help of my colleague Fontaine, we restored power after three hours of steady work. An investigation established that one of the Coast Guardsmen had pressed a button to see what would happen! He got 15 days in jail."

Until November 4, the Coast Guardsmen were quartered on board but not messed. As of that date, the kitchen was shared, with provisions bought by the French, and part of Normandie's electric oven was used by American cooks.

None of this, however, could prevent the mounting tensions outside, in the political sphere. The American press became increasingly shrill in demanding that Normandie be seized and made into a carrier for either troops or airplanes. Those critical of the French presence on board grew ever more vociferous. On September 1, the New York Daily News published an NBC report broadcast two days before, stating that, whether the Coast Guard realized it or not, French officers on board had received orders to sabotage their ship.

During the autumn of 1941, the Compagnie Générale Transatlantique managed to send a fresh team to relieve part of Normandie's crew in New York. The Americans disapproved of this change and thus reinforced the Coast Guard contingent, bringing it up to 160 men. And on November 2, 1941, the Coast Guardsmen, who had been under the Treasury Department, were suddenly reassigned to the United States Navy. Henceforth, the pace of events would accelerate.

On December 7, 1941, at 8:00 A.M., the radio announced the Japanese attack on Pearl Harbor. The United States was now at war with Japan. The next day, Captain Le Huédé was asked to prepare to quarter and mess 944 additional

men. This decision meant that all equipment had to be brought back into service: light, energy, and water. The boilers were refired and a second turbo-dynamo reactivated.

On December 9, New York had its first alert. Mayor La Guardia decreed a blackout, following an announcement on the radio that German U-boats had been sighted off Long Island! On December 11, 1941, the United States declared war on Germany and Italy.

The Seizure of Normandie

On December 12, 1941, all French ships in American ports were seized, and the crews removed and replaced by Americans. The order of seizure had been sent directly from Washington by the FBI and was received around 1:00 P.M. by Lieutenant Commander Earl G. Brooks, adjutant to Captain Baylis, in the presence of M. Morin de Linclays, the general representative of the CGT. The order for the French officers to assemble in their quarters and the crew in the passenger-service mess hall was carried out post haste. Armed officers and Coast Guardsmen blocked access to and from the ship. Sentries appeared everywhere, as communication with the outside world ceased. The Coast Guard contingent was brought up to 275 men, with some 40 of them assigned to special security.

In the engine and boiler rooms, the officers and men of the watch were immediately replaced by Coast Guardsmen who were henceforth in charge of maintaining steam and guarding against fire. While still with his machines, Yves Guillou met a junior Coast Guard officer leading a small armed detachment and asked him: "Should I assume that as of now [3:20 P.M.] I no longer have any responsibility?" The reply was categorical: "We have taken charge of the ship. Follow this sailor [armed] and ask your men to go to the mess hall."

Guillou joined the other officers, who that day had two guests to lunch. They were Mrs. Alexia Ortis Dupont de Nemours and Pierre Ortis, her first cousin, an ex-Foreign Legionnaire who had been imprisoned on the eastern front and released due to severe illness.

Meanwhile, Captain Le Huédé had been attempting to negotiate with Captain Baylis since the order of attachment called for an immediate disembarkation of the French and their transfer for detention on Ellis Island. Quite conscious of the difficulties posed by the situation, Baylis asked Le Huédé to indicate the officers and crew whom he felt were absolutely indispensable for the safety of the ship. After several telephone exchanges with Washington and the French Ambassador, firm and categorical orders were finally issued: disembarkation was to be effective as of 4:00 P.M.

Thereafter 16 men were authorized to reboard in order to assist with security. These were Captain Le Huédé, Second Captain Agnieray, Lieutenant Le Berre, six officer engineers: Cusset, the chief engineer; his deputy, Le Borgne; Guillou; Fontaine; Faity; and Carriou.

The French, therefore, had two hours in which to pack up the accumulation of more than two years on board. Without Captain Baylis's understanding, the removal, as on certain ships, might have had to take place in two minutes!

At 4:00 P.M. the ship was evacuated. Everybody, led off by Captain Le Huédé, descended onto the pier. Two cutters came alongside Normandie's stern and took the men on for their trip to Ellis Island. As they departed a Coast Guardsmen lowered the French flag which had flown from the bow. Le Huédé lodged an immediate protest with Baylis, who gave the order to raise the flag once more. In a spontaneous gesture of courtesy, which touched the French to their very core, Baylis had a spotlight trained on the tricolore as night fell.

Under a sad and lowering sky, streaked with flakes of snow, the two cutters pulled away silently, with the French huddled on the after deck, bare-headed, immobile, transfixed with emotion. Suddenly, in one voice, they burst out singing La Marseillaise, joined by those who remained on the dock. It was a poignant and moving scene.

From that day on, the fate of Normandie was out of French hands, hands that had taken such care to keep their ship in mint condition for over two years. Now, powerless and choking with rage, they were forced to aid and abet the disorder, incoherence, and incompetence that reigned on board, and always subject to the constant and suspicious surveillance of the new occupants.

The latter, ignorant of how anything worked, began their apprenticeship on the liner. But at what price in problems and accidents! Every day brought some new disaster. Stuck elevators, stopped electrical clocks, general shutdown of electricity, trouble with the fresh-water pumps, water drained from the fire-prevention system, jammed watertight doors, etc., etc. And, always, it was the Normandie men who were called in to set things straight.

Theft increased as well. The Captain's personal wine cellar was visited and emptied early on; mattresses disappeared by the dozen; safety lamps used by the fire watch were sneaked away. The beautifully decorated public rooms came in for hard use, with 200 Coast Guardsmen, weapons and all, camped out in the magnificent first-class Dining Room.

On December 13, a mechanical engineer from the Navy asked Yves Guillou to show him plans and diagrams of Normandie's complicated machinery. There were some 4,500 of them, all clearly classified and labeled. Within a few days, they would be distributed to the Coast Guardsmen, Navy officers, and representatives of the naval shipyards, to use as they wished. In the engine room Guillou proceeded to translate and devise labels necessary for operating the ship's electrical propulsion and for supplying electric current on board. He also took care to do a dry run and demonstrate how the equipment and its auxiliaries worked. Moreover — in a detail that would assume capital importance in events to come — he took special steps to point out for the American engineer a circuit breaker attached to the control panel on the portside bulkhead of the high-voltage fuse box; it governed the whole system of ventilation for the engine and boiler rooms.

Meanwhile, the French security officers in charge of the decks and machines were asked and did all they could to help the newcomers gain a knowledge that they themselves had taken months to acquire and transmit to their crewmen.

For the sake of drill, a fire alarm was set off, only for the Coast Guardsman stationed on the gangway to look on phlegmatically, without doing a thing or taking into the slightest consideration that this could really have been the signal of disaster on board. The patrol, even with a list of check points in hand, got lost while making the rounds and had to call central security and be rescued.

On December 16, 1941, at 2:00 P.M., the official notice that Normandie had been requisitioned was posted on the gangway. The Maritime Commission took legal possession of the ship, which had now become American property. The French flag, still flying from the bow, was removed and never put back. This time, the disembarkation order was final, and so at 4:00 P.M. Captain Le Huédé left the ship, the last to do so. He, his officers, and crewmen departed with their heads high and their consciences clear, knowing that they had done everything possible to accomplish their mission. Still, their hearts were heavy — and full of apprehension!

The officers were taken to the Bristol Hotel, where they would henceforth live on an allowance of $6 a day, while the crewmen joined their friends already lodged at the 23rd Street YMCA, with the exception of the black Antillais, who had been put up in Harlem.

On December 18 the inventories began. They were taken, contradictorily, by representatives of the Maritime Commission working with officers and personnel from Normandie, assisted by agents of the CGT in New York who had been authorized to come on board for this purpose. It was an enormous job and an extremely important one for the company. A lot was at stake, and the task assumed particular delicacy when decorations and art works had to be appraised and decisions taken as to what should come down and what could remain on board.

On December 24, the Maritime Commission transferred custody of the ship to the Navy Department, retroactive to December 16.

On December 27, 1941, a decision made in Washington to convert the liner into a troop carrier was passed on by the Chief of Naval Operations to Rear Admiral Adolphus Andrews, commandant of the Third Naval District. The conversion was to be effected in the shortest possible time with the minimum of modification to the ship's structure and internal arrangements. The deadline was set for January 31, 1942, and a schedule of operations projected therefrom. On January 1, 1942, the liner received her new name, Lafayette, a symbol of Franco-American friendship. The next day, the letters making up NORMANDIE on the bow were taken down in the presence of newsreel cameramen, whose film would be shown that very evening in several New York cinemas.

The inventories were finished on January 7, but the American authorities made an official request through the CGT and the French Embassy that Normandie's officers continue to be available for consultation. A commission was therefore established, consisting of Morin de Linclays, the French Line's general representative in New York, Captain Le Huédé, Second Captain Agnieray, Deputy Chief Engineer Le Borgne, Chief Electrician (propulsion) Guillou, and Chief Electrician (hull) Fontaine. The group would meet eight times in January and answer countless requests for information and clarification concerning the operations of the ship.

At a meeting on January 15, Captain F.M. Adams, chosen as the future Second Captain of the Lafayette, questioned Le Huédé about the condition of the safety equipment. An officer of the Navy, Lieutenant Commander Lester G. Scott, stated that there was no reason for worry since all the French equipment would be replaced with American material.

On January 23, the officers of Normandie were informed that they would be contacted in the event of further need. At 10:20 A.M., Captain Le Huédé and Chief Engineer Le Borgne left Normandie for the last time. They were never to see her again "alive"!

Situation on Board, February 9, 1942

What was the situation on board the Lafayette the morning of February 9, 1942?* Almost total confusion! There was feverish activity all over the ship. In addition to the 281 Coast Guardsmen under Commander Brooks, there were about 500 men brought in, only on February 3, to make up the new crew. The commander designate, Captain Robert C. Coman, was to take control only after the ship had been "delivered" to him on February 11. Also on board were 1,750 workers from the Robins Dry Dock & Repair Co. and 675 workers from about 60 subcontractors. Robins, a subsidiary of Todd Shipyards, had won the contract to convert the ship for a flat fee of $3,890,000.

Commander Scott had been designated Naval Inspector with full responsibility for supervising the work, but he had no jurisdiction over the men of either the Navy or the Coast Guard. On January 9, the Navy offered the ship to the Army as a troop carrier. Five days later the Army accepted on condition that the conversion be supervised by the Navy. Even so, the Army put its own technicians on board, who requested changes in the initial plans. On January 24, there was yet another change of policy, and now the ship was to be returned by the Army to the Navy.

And the debate went on about what future use to make of the ship — aircraft carrier or transport ship, troop carrier with Navy or Coast Guard crews, troop carrier for the Army, then the Navy!

All this indecision caused those responsible for the work to recommend a delay in the departure of the ship until February 28. But the Bureau of Ships in Washington would brook no delay. The Lafayette had to be delivered on February 11, and she had to set sail for Boston on the 14th, where the conversion would be completed. This meant making up for a two- or three-week delay. To accelerate the work, Robins brought still more workers on board.

On February 6, Captain Coman and the Naval Inspector, realizing the virtual impossibility of making these dates,

* The archival documents now available, from both official and private sources, which complete and confirm one another, make it possible to reconstruct, with reasonable certainty, the circumstances of the disaster. The official documents, of necessity American, consist mainly of two reports: one issued by the Committee on Naval Affairs, House of Representatives, on the fire and capsizing of the USS Lafayette, formerly the TEL Normandie, dated April 20, 1942; and the other by the Committee on Naval Affairs, United States Senate, "to investigate all the facts and circumstances with respect to the fire which severely damaged the USS Lafayette and resulted in her being capsized," dated May 11, 1942.

The most interesting of the private documents come from the files of Henri Cangardel, above all the following: a general, and confidential, report from Captain Le Huédé covering the entire period from August 1939 through March 1942 and dated September 15, 1942; various reports from Chief Engineers Cusset and Le Borgne; correspondence (letters and telegrams) exchanged with Morin de Linclays, French Ambassador Henry-Haye, the Admiralty in Vichy, etc.; and the written testimony of the last eye-witnesses present on that day, most importantly those of Commander Agnieray and Chief Electrician Guillou.

sought an interview with the Chief of Naval Operations in Washington. Now they learned that the superstructure was to be removed for the purpose of increasing the ship's stability, a job that would take between sixty and ninety days, which would provide all the time necessary to finish the work in progress. Given this information, Robins decided to dismiss a number of workers they had just hired.

On February 7 came yet another about-face from Washington, which canceled the order for the additional modifications. The old date of February 14 was reinstated for the ship's departure. This change of orders, quickly relayed to Robins, made it necessary for the contractors to revise their schedule once again and to call back the new workers, which only added to the general chaos.

Realizing the danger of the situation, Captain Comon and Captain Clayton Simmers, the District Materiel Officer of the Third Naval District, decided to make a joint and final effort, in Washington and New York, to obtain a delay and to do it at the highest level of authority. A general meeting was set for February 9 at 3:00 P.M. to discuss the problem. This meeting would never take place. That very day, at 2:35 P.M., fire broke out on the *Lafayette* in the first-class Grand Lounge.

The Fire

In the Grand Lounge stood four tall metal lighting stanchions or towers, one at each corner of the dance floor and all now stripped of their fluted Lalique glass. The room was to be a recreation space for the troops on board. The 15-foot structures were to be cut down to a height of 20 inches, and the bases left for use as tables. Between February 1 and 3 the space had been stacked with 1,140 bales of life jackets filled with kapok and wrapped in waterproof tarpaper. They were piled on the port side in a semicircle around two of the lamps scheduled to be cut down.

The Coast Guard Commander in charge of security had not been told of the cutting work. The job was taken on by Alphonsus Gateley, Robins's welding supervisor, who assembled a team of seven men, including a welder named Clement Derrick, a foreman, and several unskilled laborers. In lieu of a fire watchman, Charles Collins, an ironworker, was assigned.

The job consisted of using an acetylene torch to cut through the base of each metal stanchion weighing some 500 pounds. To protect the work area against flying sparks, one man was to place a semicircular metal shield around the base of the shaft, while another workman held an asbestos board above the shield. When two of the three "clips" supporting the tower had been cut, the metal shield was removed and the

vertical member brought down to a 90-degree angle, its descent controled by guide ropes. The welder then cut the remaining bit of metal, with protection provided only by the asbestos board.

The morning the cutting took place, three of the stanchions came down without incident, except that the third one fell and crushed the screen or shield, rendering it useless. After a lunch break, when work resumed, the fourth and last lamp was brought down to the 90-degree angle, whereupon one member of the team, considering his job finished, left. Collins now abandoned his asbestos board to help the other men hold the stanchion; thus, Derrick proceeded to cut the last bit without the protection of either the metal screen or the asbestos board. A spark hit one of the nearest kapok bales and ignited the tarpaper wrapping.

As the cry "Fire!" went up, the men tried to put out the flames with their hands. The other workers, in order to prevent the fire from reaching other bales, starting throwing the packs toward the center of the Grand Lounge, only to spread the blaze. There was no fire extinguisher nearby, and the bucket of water the cutting team had filled was accidentally overturned. Ten minutes went by before an alerted Coast Guardsman telephoned to the central security station on board.

The Coast Guardsman on duty tried in vain to reach his supervisor. He then telephoned to the electrical control center to turn off the ventilator blowers, then to the Coast Guardsman on bridge watch to sound a general fire alarm. But the latter could not find the switch; moreover, the switches had been disconnected a few days earlier by a subcontractor, who forgot to tell anyone.

The automatic alarm on the bridge linking the ship to the New York Fire Department had been removed on January 13. As a result, the nearest alarm box was on shore at Pier 88.

Once the security crew finally pulled themselves together, they distributed fire extinguishers to the workmen. Somebody shouted from the gangway to a policeman on the dock to call the Fire Department. In the Grand Lounge, now full of flames, nobody knew how to operate the fire door, which would have sealed off access to the Smoking Room. None of the fire hoses could be activated owing to the fact that they had been capped with American fittings, which did not match the French outlets! Thick smoke threw a pall over everything. The men, unable to find the safety lamps, because they had all been stolen, could not fight the fire at its source. In the engine room, the electrician at the control panel had no idea where to find the circuit breaker that would have switched off the ventilation. Consequently, smoke

February 9, 1942, fire on board

coming from the Grand Lounge was drawn in and recirculated throughout the heating system and into the engine room. There, the lack of air quickly made the atmosphere unbearable. The engineers on duty shut down the boilers and abandoned their post. Around 3:15 P.M., the dynamos stopped. As the generators ran out of steam, the ship lost power for lights, water pressure for fire pumps, and the air compression needed to drain excess water.

An order was given over loudspeakers for the Robins workers to evacuate the ship. In the confusion, this was taken as a general order to abandon ship. Coast Guardsmen, Navy men, and crew all clambered onto the gangway just as the New York City firemen arrived. The latter had only received the alarm at 2:49 P.M., fifteen minutes after the fire had broken out.

Gradually this equipment went into service. By 4:15 P.M. there were 36 fire trucks, 3 fireboats, and several tugs with their hoses all trained on the ship, pouring water both on the burning decks and through the portholes. Torrents of water flooded onto and into the *Lafayette*, particularly on her port side, her starboard being against the pier – more than 3,000 tons of water in 4 hours, not counting what the tugs put out. About 6,000 tons of water collected in the upper part of the ship, forming a heavy, topsided, liquid mass that could not be flushed away since the machines for doing this had lost air pressure. The top-heavy imbalance soon caused the ship to list disturbingly, some 5 degrees by 4:00 P.M. The ropes attached to the mooring started to fray. By 4:45 P.M. the list to port had increased 10 to 15 degrees.

Normandie's French officers, having rushed to the pier, followed all these operations with the greatest anguish. Le Huédé, Agnieray, Le Borgne, and Guillou in turn offered their services to the U.S. Navy on the pier. They were fully aware of the danger of a capsize if something were not

February 10, 1942, Normandie capsized

The scale model of Normandie made and studied in preparation for the ship's refloating left to right: U.S. Navy Captain C.F. Chandler, the officer in charge of salvage operations in New York; Commodore William A. Sullivan of the U.S. Navy, the inspector of the salvage operation; and Captain John I. Tokker, a commercial expert in salvage work

done immediately to diminish the supply of water from the fire hoses, which were still going full blast. They proposed refilling the ballast tanks in order to ground the ship on the slip bottom, remembering as they did the *Paris*, which had burned and capsized at Le Havre under the same circumstances. These remarks went largely unattended. However, holes were finally drilled through the hull into four ballast chambers, and fire hoses began filling them, but only much later, around 10:00 P.M.

At approximately 6:00 P.M. the fireman announced that they had the fire under control. Two hours later, the fire was practically extinguished, but everything had burned from the Promenade Deck upwards. Below, a Navy officer was pleased to note that all was "dry as a bone," failing to realize that herein lay the greatest danger. At 9:30 P.M., Admiral Andrews held a press conference. The Mayor of New York City called President Roosevelt to assure him that the situation was fully in hand.

At 9:55 P.M. an announcer on radio station WMC accused *Normandie*'s "Vichy-minded" officers of having planted an incendiary bomb on board. Captain Le Huédé lodged an immediate protest with Admiral Andrews, who officially denied the report and insisted that not the least trace of sabotage had been found on board.

Le Huédé renewed his offer of assistance and that of his officers and crew. He was thanked politely, but when he asked whether the ballast tanks had been filled, he was told, "That's our business." As Chief Electrician Guillou left the pier around 10:30 P.M., he warned the officers selected for the *Lafayette* to make certain that all openings in the lower hull — cargo ports and portholes — were securely closed; otherwise, the vessel would ship water and capsize at high tide. And, indeed, by midnight, on February 10, the list gradually increased as water flowed through portholes and other openings. At 12:30 A.M. Admiral Andrews gave the order to abandon ship. The last ropes snapped and the gangways crashed. At 2:45 A.M. the boat capszied at 80 degrees to port. She lay on the muddy bottom, her two starboard propellers in the air and her three funnels half submerged in the frozen Hudson. A desolating spectacle for the tens of thousands of New Yorkers who could come to see it!

The costs of the disaster were not only material. Some 94 men of the Coast Guard and Navy, 38 firemen, and 153 workmen had suffered burns, smoke inhalation, and various other injuries. One of Robins's men was killed when he fell from the Sun Deck.

With the passage of time, and in the light of all the reports, interrogations, and investigations concerning the loss of *Normandie*, it has been established beyond every doubt — and beyond all need to consider some hypothetical sabotage or Machiavellian machinations on the part of the Mafia — that the catastrophe had multiple causes. And they arose from two areas of failure: first, personnel and command; and second, material, equipment, and their use.

In regard to the first area, one cannot fail to be struck:

—by the gross negligence in the work done on the ship, in the way personnel were hired and used, and in the training given the security services;
—by the total lack of coordination between the shipyards and the other authorities involved in the conversion;
—by the division of responsibility and authority, and by the total absence of a single, unified supreme command;
—by the indecision of government authorities at the highest level concerning the conversion, by the ill-considered and unrealistic nature of their instructions as to the deadline set for completing the work and for beginning operations.

In regard to the second area:

—by the indifference to danger and the imprudence evinced in the accumulation of flammable materials such as kapok in a place where cutting by acetylene torch was to be done;
—by the indifference to fundamental procedures governing security and by the grave deficiencies in the state of the equipment, as in the fire door; the ventilation circuit breakers; the disconnected telephones, fire bells, and alarms; the absence of fire extinguishers; the incompatibility of fire hoses and water outlets; the disappearance or nonuse of such specialized items as safety lamps;
—by the failure to consider the weight accumulated on the upper part of the ship during the conversion work and its effect on the ship's stability.

Probably the best conclusion to be drawn for this chapter is that pronounced by District Attorney Frank Hogan when he closed the first, on-the-spot investigation shortly after the disaster: "There is no evidence of sabotage," he said. "Carelessness has served the enemy with equal effectiveness." One can still hear the words of Captain Le Huédé when he said: "We will never sabotage Normandie.... But if we wanted to do that, nothing could be easier for us. All we would have to do is totally abandon the ship and leave her in your hands!"

Refloating and Demolition

Very quickly, the Americans had to resolve the problem of removing the wreck that was immobilizing two of the main

The pumping operations carried out
from August to October 1943

Berthed in the Port of New York, Normandie waits for the U.S. Maritime Commission to decide her fate

Normandie *being towed away for dismantling into scrap metal by Lipsett, Inc., a junk firm*

piers of the Port of New York. A commission set up to study the project made its recommendation on May 1, 1942.

On June 11 an order to start work, work made extremely difficult by the position of the water-logged ship, two-thirds of which had settled onto the slip's mud or silt bottom, while the forward section leaned on a rocky knob projecting up from the bottom. All this made the vessel subject to the pressures of the rising and falling tides, and thus to the risk of damage to the great steel hull.

Every possible effort was made to recover the ship. Vladimir Yourkevitch, the engineer who had collaborated on the ship's design and construction, was consulted. He estimated that it would take four to five months to divide the hull into several watertight compartments that could then be pumped dry. In fact, the job was still in progress one year later.

In the end, however, the pumping process worked. In August 1943, the ship, once pumped free of interior water, began to resume her natural buoyancy. On September 3, the hull was upright, and on October 27 she was afloat once more. It had taken eighteen months and $19.2 million to bring this about. On November 3, 1943, Normandie was tugged down the Hudson for dry-dock inspection in Brooklyn. That day, Captain Agnieray was in New York between voyages and happened to be at the CGT's office at 17 State Street in lower Manhattan. Here is how he describes the scene:

When I heard that Normandie was coming down the river to be taken to the Brooklyn Navy Yard, I went up to the building's roof and watched my unfortunate ship go by, cut down to a hulk, without masts or smokestacks, surrounded by tugs pulling and pushing her like a prisoner. Still, she was imposing, majestic, full of nobility, inspiring a certain respect, and giving the impression of a champion overcome by fate and human stupidity but not yet beaten.

But her martyrdom was not yet finished, inasmuch as the inspection in Brooklyn made the idea of repairing the ship seem futile, given the immense work that would be required

to get her back in shape. And so the wreck was dragged to Bayonne, on the New Jersey side of the Hudson, for demolition. Put up for sale as scrap, Normandie was awarded on October 3 to Julius Lipsett, a New York junk dealer, whose winning bid had been $161,680.

"Every time I passed the river," Captain Agnieray sadly remembered, "I could see her being dismembered and miserably disappearing piece by piece, bit by bit, just as I had seen her grow bigger at Saint-Nazaire during her birth."

Compensation

At the beginning of 1941, well before the American government's requisition of the ship, the problem of Normandie had come up. There were active negotiations between the Admiralty in Vichy and the United States Ambassador to the government of Marshal Pétain. A sale of Normandie to the United States had been proposed, with the right of repurchase or restitution at the end of hostilities, or, failing that, a transfer to the CGT of an equivalent tonnage.

The telegrams sent by the French Ambassador in Washington, Gaston Henri-Haye, bear witness to the fact that the form as well as the guarantees of the transfer were discussed at length. They prove that the French government, at that time, was not opposed to a takeover of Normandie by the Allies. This negotiation was linked to the use in North Africa, for supplying metropolitan France, of certain merchant vessels then immobilized in the United States. But the turn of events after April 1941 made it impossible for these negotiations to be concluded.

At the end of the war, the CGT had a credit with the United States government corresponding to the estimated value of the liner the day she had been impounded — $63 million. A symbolic down payment of $400,000 had even been entered and set aside in the Treasury Department's bookkeeping.

After 1945, however, the French government assumed responsibility for the totality of private French claims against the United States arising from the war and included them in

Normandie, *reduced to scrap metal, leaves for the smelter*

the general Franco-American, or the so-called Blum-Byrnes, accords. The French government thus replaced the American government in making compensation to the CGT for the loss of Normandie, with compensation in tonnage left to be hammered out with the French Merchant Marine.

In February 1942, an exchange of notes — between the Admiralty, the Ministry of Foreign Affairs in Vichy, and the French Embassy in Washington — had taken up the issue of compensation, making clear it that a ton-per-ton replacement was out of the question since a ton of liner like Normandie was worth three tons of a cargo boat. Normandie weighed 83,422 tons and was five years old when seized. At a 20 percent rate of depreciation, she would have been equal to 66,738 new tons, or about 200,000 tons of new, ordinary cargo weight. In case of replacement by new liners or fast mixed-cargoes, a different system of evaluation would have been used. And this was what actually happened.

When the time came to evaluate the hull of Normandie, the Americans suggested using the price of the hull built for their America. But it was pointed out that such a comparison was unworkable, since the hull of Normandie had been made by an assemblage of very different plates, none of them straight, whereas the America was a ship of classic construction. A coefficient of correction was therefore allowed in favor of Normandie for the purpose of arriving at a fair valuation. With this made part of the accounting, France ultimately obtained a more important tonnage in Liberty ships.

In the final settlement the CGT received in compensatior for Normandie:

—the former German passenger ship Europa, a vessel weighing 51,839 gross registered tons that would become the Liberté and serve on the Le Havre—New York route;
—a new liner to be built, at a weight of 20,000 gross registered tons, and called the Flandre, also for service to and from New York:
—two other liners, also to be built, weighing 9,500 gross registered tons each. These were to be the Ville de Marseilles and the Ville de Tunis, both serving North Africa.

Hence, we come to the end of the very beautiful, very sad, and, alas, all-too-short story of Normandie. With her disappearance, the CGT lost a priceless asset and its most valuable money turner. And so, this may be the time to bring out the dazzling financial results produced by Normandie during the four and a half years of her commercial life.

Financial Results

From May 1935 to September 1939 Normandie made 139 crossings — or 69.5 voyages, since the last one did not have its return leg. She transported 45,765 tons of freight and 132,508 passengers, or an average of nearly 1,000 passengers per crossing, and realized gross receipts of just over 713 million francs. The gross profit was almost 288.5 million francs, and after deductions for maintenance, insurance, recasting the propellers, and major repairs, the remainder came to 168.5 million francs — the net profit to the CGT. Moreover, she was unburdened by amortization and interest charges, thanks to the special status accorded the liner by the postal convention signed with the French government.

Since the total, all-in cost of the ship had been 863 million francs,** it becomes clear that — given the CGT rule of depreciating passenger ships at a rate of 5 percent over 20 years, which would come to 194 million for four and a half years of use — more than four-fifths of this charge had been recovered by the net profit.

These figures prove that, contrary to all the criticism and all the reservations at the time the decision was taken to build her, as well as contrary to everything said or written since, Normandie was not the white elephant she has often been made out to be. In fact, the ship proved to be a great financial asset to her owners, the Compagnie Générale Transatlantique.

And if things had turned out differently, the contribution made by Normandie would have been that much greater. An analysis of the accounts shows that her gross profit increased from year to year, quadrupling between 1935 and 1939. This suggests how cruelly Normandie would be missed when transatlantic travel resumed after the war. Her luckier competition, Cunard mainly, with its Queen Mary, the rival that survived Normandie, would benefit enormously.

But if the French Line lost its strongest trump card for the future, France herself lost her most famous ambassador, an essential element of French renown and prestige, the value of which lies beyond all estimate.

Fifty years later, for those who had the privilege of knowing her, Normandie evokes an unforgettably great moment — a stirring time of national pride shared by an entire society. For those less fortunate, like myself, she seems a wonderful dream of grandeur, power, and beauty, something mythical, a lost paradise!

** The figure of 700 million francs cited at the time the ship was ordered had increased meanwhile by reason of revised costs, accumulated interest, the cost of fitting out, and the alterations made in 1936.

NORMANDIMANIA

FRANÇOIS ROBICHON

Poster created by A.M. Cassandre (1901–68) in 1935, a work that survives in several versions, each with a different text

Original flagon for Patou's "Normandie" perfume

Patou's "Normandie" reissued in 1984

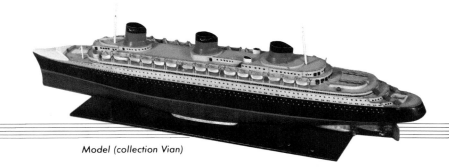

Model (collection Vian)

Normandimania

1935–85: It was fifty years ago that *Normandie* first pulled away from her berth in Le Havre and set sail for New York. And in this instance the benchmark anniversary means more than a simple fatality of the calendar, but rather a moment ripe with a desire to commemorate – and to inquire. Will *Normandie* become a key moment in the history of France?

The present volume provides a kind of chalk outline of the posthumous history of a famous and distinguished ocean liner. And any new look at the "Giant of the Seas" cannot but fuel the myth of a gilded ark absurdly lost in the frozen waters of New York one awful day in February 1942. It brings to mind those untimely and tragic ends suffered by certain Hollywood stars!

But however grand and sensational the life led by the 1930s "Queen of the Atlantic," the portrait would not be complete without some mention of the cult that came into being with the ship's triumphant maiden voyage. *Normandie* contributed generously to her own legend, and, like all stars, she gave rise to a fashion, an elitism, a fetishism that so overheated as to become a veritable mania.

According to the *Grande Encyclopédie*, "mania" designates cases of mental disturbance in which, to quote Esquirol's definition, "the delirium extends to all sorts of objects and is accompanied by excitation." The symptoms of so-called "Normandimania" developed early and generated their first epidemic in 1935–39. The ship was virtually pillaged by souvenir-hungry passengers, at the same time that her image came in for outrageous exploitation, thanks to a publicity campaign of fantastic dimensions. After the ship was destroyed, the happy, harmless mania assumed a touch of nostalgia. While some were content simply to dream about bygone and irretrievable grandeur, other, more industrious souls busied themselves collecting whatever remnants survived from the boat and her career. This new worship of relics soon became a veritable voodoo that is nothing less than the magic face or mask of Normandimania.

The dazzling performance put on by *Normandie*, that luminous body glittering in the firmament of a dark Depression decade, was accompanied by a genuine "cult of personality," the foundation of which was a vast proliferation of posters, displays, and promotional events, all orchestrated by the CGT. The public was simply inundated and overwhelmed by the "Leviathan" of the seas.

Well before the inauguration of the ship, the French Line began its campaign by giving away small scale models of *Normandie*, which, oddly enough, seemed to take a place somewhere between a stage coach and an airplane. Did *Normandie* – within her new streamlined silhouette – harbor a mortal archaism? Never mind, those who loved miniature boats were delighted with the CGT's gifts.

But when the inauguration came in May 1935, the French Line decided to attempt a great coup. And the press, always avid for news, cooperated by giving *Normandie* front-page coverage. *Le*

A tank model of Normandie operating under remote control in 1935

opposite: Yvan Magnien, manager of a ready-to-wear shop in Les Halles, with his collection of Normandie memorabilia: biscuit tins, brier pipe, Patou perfume bottle, ashtrays, plates, etc.

A display in New York

The obverse and reverse sides of the medallion distributed at the time of the maiden voyage (collection Schall)

Figaro even organized a contest for the best estimate of the time the maiden voyage would take, the first prize in which was to be – paradoxically – a Mediterranean cruise! The winner, it turned out, had refined his estimate to 4 days, 3 hours, 13 minutes, and 38 seconds, thereby missing the actual count by 3 seconds!

For those lucky enough to be on board and in first class during that initial time across the Atlantic, the CGT offered a medallion, another small model of the ship, and a travel clock designed by Hatot.

Simple tourists and curiosity-seekers who came in tremendous numbers to share in that grand premier cast-off were also given ample means to indulge their fetishism. Madeleine Jacob, a reporter for *Vu*, wrote: "A whole iconography sprang up within a matter of days. *Normandie* everywhere, in the bazaars as paperweights, miniatures made of wood, lead, copper, under glass, with or without waves, in the stalls of itinerant merchants, in brooches and fetish-like charms, in chocolate bars, in 'artistic' bonbon boxes, all the way to the pastry

shops with their *Normandies* confectioned of frangipane, glazed fruit, butter cream, and nougatine." All that lacked was "Saint Normandie" in the multiple forms of miraculous, holy relics.

Meanwhile, the French Line had the bright idea of stuffing the luggage of Roger Echegut, the shrewd little Parisian urchin who won the *Paris-Soir* contest, with packages containing large as well as small models of *Normandie*, and such gifts as writing tablets, medals, puzzles, etc., all meant for the Boys Club of New York and its youthful members.

However, the mania to collect souvenirs drove many passengers to commit rather unfortunate acts. They carried away ashtrays, whole packages of letter-head stationery, linen, silver salt cellars, and even table silver – anything to help recall *Normandie*'s maiden voyage. Under the title "Souvenir, Souvenir!" Odette Pannetier, in the June 20, 1935, issue of *Candide*, told of the soirées in New York during *Normandie*'s maiden-voyage layover:

The Arts Menagers, or "Ideal Home," exhibition in 1936

Not an ashtray, not a vermeil dessert spoon, fork, or knife remains. The Americans are forever 'souvenir' hunters. And nothing wrong in combining this pious custom with good taste and utilitarianism, for the flatware is ravishing. So irresistibly ravishing that even four policemen were caught discreetly slipping into their pockets a little something to show their families. A lady trying to purloin a pretty silver plate did not quite get away with it. Unfortunately, it is difficult to guard against art lovers who go so far as to cut 4-inch squares from the Aubusson tapestry covering the chairs.

Upon their return to France, the chic passengers who made the first round trip were feted like conquering heroes and the founders of a new aristocracy: the Knights of the Blue Ribbon won since the inaugural sailing. And in honor of the Americans who came back on *Normandie*, a banquet was staged at the Ritz Hotel. *Le Figaro* gave a full report of the occasion in its society column for June 15, 1935:

The hotel had been decorated in a special manner. Outside, a red and white canopy, guarded by sailors, was floodlit by klieg light so that the elegant guests could be filmed as they stepped out of their limousines. The gardens, ornamented with white and blue balloons, formed a sort of quay, as the world's most beautiful ship displayed her illuminated hull, moored in a geranium bed. The guests received *Normandie* paperweights, yachting caps, sailors' berets, and balloons colored like clouds and ocean.

Thus it had to be, for a boat christened "Ritz-sur-mer" by Bertrand de Jouvenel. And the fashionable ladies could wax ecstatic over a new perfume, "Normandie," launched by Patou in a flagon evoking the bold forms of the ship's innovatory hull. But, according to *Votre Beauté* in June 1935, the relationship between scent and seamanship went still further:

[Patou's "*Normandie*" offers] the phantomatic charms of sea and sailing magnified by a wildly luxurious ambience conjured in the mind by the name of the largest ship 'in the world.' Her namesake is a warm, stubborn, obstinate perfume that evokes all manner of elegant symbols. Its freshness, like moist seaweed, or Mediterranean bark and moss – the product of its Cypriote base – evokes the aromatic welcome of calls made during a cruise. A touch of Oriental wood, finally, adds to the sense of being borne away, eyes closed, into those chests of polished cedar, mahogany, and macassar that often are the great transatlantic liners' most beautiful staterooms.

Normandimaniacs can still make their olfactory voyage, since the House of Patou has recently reissued the perfume in its original formula.

Once the initial venture across the Atlantic had been achieved, when *Normandie* made her entrance into history, the great ship began her commercial adventure. With her immense store of prestige and her sacred image, *Normandie* defies the passage of time. The star of sand-castle contests, the ornament of countless shop windows, the liner became the "keystone" of the Paris World's Fair of 1937. In 1935, Edmond Labbé, head commissioner of the Fair, announced that *Normandie* represented the very synthesis that "we hope to offer the

The Salon Nautique, or "Sailing Show," in 1935

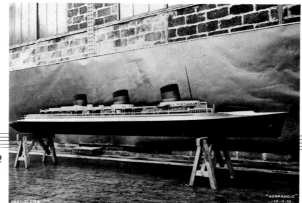

Saint-Nazaire December 13, 1932

Scale model at the Le Havre Chamber of Commerce

A cinema window on the Champs-Elyseés in 1937

A window display in the Gare Saint-Lazare during the summer of 1937

A reproduction of Normandie's four-bladed propeller at the Paris World's Fair in 1937

below: The cover of the June 1, 1935, issue of L'Illustration, by R. Lefébure

Cover by Sandy Hook for a special issue of L'Atlantique

opposite page: Cover, by Wilquir, of the brochure reproducing Sébille's longitudinal section

international public two years hence on the banks of the Seine: the synthesis of the art and technology of our time." Thus, the designer of the fair park conceived the notion of building a replica of *Normandie* large enough to be visited inside and out. But the president of the French Line took serious objection, believing that his company was "the trustee of a national patrimony that it could not allow to be disfigured by any means whatever." From *Normandie* herself, only one of the new four-bladed propellers would go on display.

If the Fair's overscaled toy, meant to entertain the masses, never saw the light of day, the "little boats" for children cropped up everywhere. One toy merchant even named his shop "Au Paquebot Normandie."

All such avatars, however feverishly pursued by collectors, lack a certain nobility. It was, obviously, with only variable success that *Normandie* played an immortal role in the art of her time. Artists, whether painters or theater directors, were not always inspired. Of

MARIN-MARIE

1

2

6

5

7

8

9

10

1 Albert Brenet, View of Normandie's Port Side (CGT sale,
item no. 17, July 18, 1983)
2 A Sébille, Normandie Crossing the Path of a Small
Cargo Ship (no. 100)
3 A. Sébille, Normandie Crossing the Path of a Small
Cargo Ship (no. 87)
4 A. Sébille, An imaginary view of Normandie, c. 1932–33
5 A. Sébille, Normandie (no. 95)
6 A. Brenet, Normandie, five studies (no. 24)
7 G. Dufresse, Normandie (private collection)
8 Worden Wood, Normandie, 1935 (no. 112)
9 B. Latham Kidder, The Liner Normandie (no. 47)
10 A. Brenet, Normandie at Le Havre, published in
L'Illustration, June 1935

overleaf double page: Marin Marie, Normandie Coming
down the Hudson, 1936

opposite page: Jules Lefranc, Normandie's Launch, 1932
(Musée du Château, Laval)

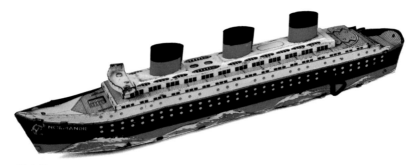

"Sand castle" contest in 1937

Metal toy

The Normandie and Queen Mary crews before their soccer match on January 21, 1939

The toy shop "Au Paquebot Normandie" on the Rue de Tolbiac in Paris

course, there are the beautiful paintings by Brenet and Sébille's superb *Normandie, at Midnight on the Atlantic*, all true classics. An important work that flaunts every convention is the *Normandie's Launch* by Jules Lefranc, a follower of the primitive master Henri Rousseau. Before Cassandre, Lefranc used an aggressive red to emphasize the plastic drama of *Normandie*'s hull.

The Seventh Art also appropriated *Normandie*. As early as 1931, the CGT management arranged for Atlantic Film to train its cameras on the ship's construction and keep a full record of the progress. Other films would follow, such as *On Board Normandie, Cruise to Rio de Janeiro*, and *Normandie: The Floating City*, all made primarily for publicity purposes. Then, with *Les Perles de la Couronne* ("The Pearls of the Crown") in 1937, starring Sacha Guitry, *Normandie* began a real career in the cinema. The multi-episode story of seven pearls would reach its climax and conclusion on *Normandie*.

In March 1937, *Normandie*, then in dry dock at Le Havre, was transformed into a movie studio. Sacha Guitry invited some fifty friends and Parisian personalities to perform as extras in a scene representing a splendid dinner party in the first-class Dining Room. This was the moment when the Raimu-Jacqueline Delubac romance would come to an end. Raimu returns to his stateroom, there welcomed by Pauline Carton, and then disappears – leaving the audience to wonder where, since the final image is of *Normandie* plying her way across the high seas!

With *Les Cinq sous de Lavarède* ("The Five Sous of Lavarède"), *Normandie* continued her film career in another genre, this time high adventure comedy. Lavarède, played by Fernandel, is to inherit the fortune of an eccentric relation only if he succeeds in traveling around the world on 25 centimes. The resourceful and plucky hero secretly embarks on *Normandie* for New York. During the voyage, Lavarède makes an appearance in the Grand Lounge. The scene was shot during an actual crossing in 1938.

The following year Yves Mirande made *Paris-New York* while on board for the August 9–14 voyage in 1939. Here, on the very eve of World War II, a dazzling parade of stars made a series of cameo appearances in the course of a police investigation. Thus, Erich von Stroheim paddled about in the tourist-class swimming pool under the close scrutiny of the camera, Michel Simon, and Jacques Baumer. *Normandie*'s sailors lent a technical hand as the ship, unbeknownst to anyone, was making her last round trip. Her final Paris-New York crossing would immediately follow.

Burnt and capsized in the waters of the Port of New York, *Normandie* made a brief appearance in Alfred Hitchcock's 1942 film entitled *The Fifth Column*. The director included the image because the opportunity presented itself while the picture was being made, but the U.S. Navy felt it had been made the target of an implicit accusation, to the effect that its own negligence had allowed the ship to be sabotaged! As a result, the passage was cut from several prints of the film.

3

5

6

Filming the movie Paris-New York: 1. Mock-up of the Grand Lounge; 2. Michel Simon; 3. Erich von Stroheim; 4. A scene from the film, with Michel Simon and Jacques Baumer flanking the camera while Erich von Stroheim stays afloat in the tourist-class swimming pool; 5,6. Doing a scene with Jacques Baumer and Simone Berriau

4

FERNANDEL ....
LES CINQ SOUS DE LAVARÈDE

A scene in the Grand Lounge from the film Les Cinq sous de Lavarède

Raimu and Jacqueline Delubac in a scene on the Smoking Room staircase for the film Les Perles de la Couronne

JEAN DUPAS
dessins pour le grand salon du «Normandie»

October - November 1980

Galerie Alain Blondel
du mardi au samedi - 4, rue Aubry-le-Boucher - téléphone 278 66 67 - parking Beaubourg

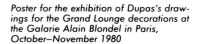
above: A Revillon ad in 1984

Poster for the exhibition of Dupas's drawings for the Grand Lounge decorations at the Galarie Alain Blondel in Paris, October–November 1980

Exhibition prior to an auction in 1979

With this, *Normandie* ended her film career. And as with show-business luminaries, her fans began vying with one another for her jewels and other finery. Even at the time of her inauguration, Henri Cangardel had prophesied a posthumous life for *Normandie*:

Unlike an exhibition that lasts a matter of weeks, or a few months, we will go on for a number of years. Our art works, now launched upon the sea, will end up being acquired by private collectors and museums. Lessons will have been given and ideas disseminated. Across the ocean the best of France will have been carried to the four corners of the earth.

Reality proved more prosaic. At the time of the conversion in 1941, *Normandie*, as we have seen, was stripped of all her decorations. Many of the stateroom furnishings and wall decorations were sold on the spot, with the rest packed up and shipped back to Le Havre after the war. Certain pieces would be reused in the fitting out of such ships as the *Île de France* and the *Liberté*. Then, owing to the critical state of its affairs, the CGT liquidated everything, either to private collectors or at auction.

After the Le Havre sales in 1962, when Dunand's *Aurora* went, and in 1974, which took care of the chairs and carpet from the Grand Lounge, the sales organized by Ader, Picard, and Tojan in 1979 at Monte Carlo, Geneva, Biarritz, Honfleur, and Paris brought the dispersal to a climax. The CGT got rid of all that remained of silver, china, utensils, and clothing. Many of the pieces had never been used and were simply part of the supply left stored on the docks in Le Havre. Nostalgia could have its fill at every price level, from that of a simple flower vase to a sumptuous tea service from Puiforcat.

Normandie was a "floating city," which meant that the number of objects and art works carried on board was considerable. And if some people failed to realize that they owned a precious relic coveted by collectors, others have often been presumptuous about the authenticity of certain items, especially since the revival of Normandimania.

Finally, the CGT would part with its horde of art in July 1983. Now collectors could acquire a few pictures that once hung on *Normandie*, but, for the most part, they were offered numerous works by marine painters who had taken *Normandie* as their principal subject.

As the fiftieth anniversary approached, heated up by the new "retro" taste, *Normandie* has become a prime hallmark of the 1930s. At the same time that Patou is relaunching its "Normandie" perfume, Revillon has brought out "French Line," a scent "for the men of the great crossings."

Normandie has lost nothing of her aura. A phantom vessel of French prestige and grandeur, she fascinates and increases her devotees of every kind. Her cult appears to have a promising future, a possibility confirmed by the 1985 commemoration, for which the present work could serve as a breviary.

And so, it is you – Normandimaniacs – that this book is dedicated!

Poster for a sale in Geneva, June 22–23, 1979

Normandie plying the waves toward her centennial in 2035.
Photomontage by Fancine Digard (1985)

The steamer Normandie at Le Havre in 1886.

Passengers in first class for the maiden voyage

Madame Albert Lebrun

Monsieur William Bertrand
Minister of the Merchant Marine

Governor General Marcel Olivier
President of the Compagnie Générale Transatlantique

Monsieur Henri Cangardel
General Director

Acton, Mrs Vera
d'Anthonay, Mr René
Antoine, Mr Jean
Ara, Mlle Silvia
Areizaga, Mr Adolfo de
Armstrong, Mr C. Dudley
Arnaudas, Mr Emile L.
d'Artois, Mme
Aswell, Mr James

Barrière, Mr Émile
Bauer, Mr Gérard
Bauer, Mme G.
Beaumaine, Mr B.
Beaumaine, Mr Raoul B.
Beck, Mr Martin
Beck, Mme M.
Beecher, Mr Mathew
Behar, Mr V.
Behar, Miss Denise
Belfils, Mr Georges
Belmont, Mrs Morgan
Bendick, Mrs Marquis
Bennett, Mr W. Cooke
Bennet, Mrs W. Cooke
Benoit du Rey, Mr
Bergeron, Mr Michel
Bernard, Mr B.
Bertrand, Mr William
Bertrand, Mme William
Bigot, Mr Maurice
Binois, Mlle Simone
Block, Mr Monroe
Block, Mrs Monroe
Blodgett Jr, Mr John W.
Blodgett Jr., Mrs John W.
Blum, Mr Harry
Blum, Mr Robert E.
Blum, Mrs Robert E.
Bocquet, Mr A.
Bocquet, Mr René
Bonnet, Mlle Louise
Boomer, Mr Lucius
Boomer, Mrs J.,
Borius, Mlle Jeanne
Bottin de la Boulaye, Mme
Bowman, Mr E.
Bowman, Mr Lester
Brady, Mr A. S. A.
Branic, Miss J.
Bremont, Mlle L. H. de
Bright, Mr Philip V.
Brisson, Mr Pierre
Brooks, Mrs Alexander
Brooksbank, Mr C. B.
Brooksbank, Mr C. P.
Brousse, Mr Charles E.
Brousse, Mme C. E.
Bruce, Miss Grace
Brunswick, Mrs Frederic
Byron, Mr Percy C.

Cabrières, Mr Henri E.
Cady, Miss Celeste
Cahen d'Anvers, Comte
Caldagues, Mr
Caldagues, Mme
Campbell, Mrs John J.
Cangardel, Mr Henri

Cangardel, Mme Henri
Cangardel, Mr Edouard
Carcouet, Mr Clément de
Carle, Mr Louis
Carles, Mr J. R.
Cartier, Mme Pierre
Carron, Capt. P. J.
Caussade, Marquis de
Cavelier, Mr Marcel
Cavelier, Mme Marcel
Champly, Mr Henry
Chantal, Mme Marcelle
Chapat, Mr L.
Charabot, Sénateur Eugène
Charlemaine, Mr Alexandre
Charpentier, Mr J. C.
Charpentier, Mme J. C.
Chase, Mr Ernest Dudley
Chevrillon, Mr André
Cippico, Comte G.
Cippico, Comtesse G.
Claeys, Mr Charles M.
Clark, Mr W. J.
Clark, Mrs W. J.
Clerget, Mr Louis
Colcombet, Mr John
Cole, Mrs J. J.
Colette, Mme
Colin, Mr Louis
Colombier, Mme Florence Walton
Conolly, Mr Jack S.
Conolly, Mrs Jack S.
Coppens, Mr Robert
Coqueret, Mr
Coqueret, Mme
Coquillat, Mr André
Cordonnier, Mr
Corniglion-Olinier, Mme R.
Cosulich, Mr Antonio
Cosulich, Mme Maria
Couvreur, Mr Jacques
Cros, Mr Jean
Currier, Mr J. A.
Curtis, Miss Caral

Damour, Mr Maurice
Damour, Capitaine de Corvette
Dass, Mr Sirdar Mathra
Davis, Mrs Benny
Debucourt, Mr
Debucourt, Mme
Decros, Mr Albert
Delage, Mr Edmond
Delehanty, Mr Thornton
Demangeat, Mr Marcel A.
Demierre, Mr J.
Dennis, Miss Gene
Depassé, Mr Henri
Despres, Mme Jean
Desalles, Mr Roger
Dollfus, Mr Maurice
Donon, Mlle Andrée
Dorman, Mr R. P.
Dreyfus, Mr Louis
Dreyfus, Mrs Louis
Dreyfus, Miss V.
Dreyfus, Mr François L.
Driscoll, Mr R. A.
Drouilly, Mme Charley J.

Duffy, Mr James Edmund
Duffy, Mrs James Edmund
Dulignier, Mr Henri
Dumas, Mr Pierre
Dumesnil, Mr R.
Dunand, Mr Jean
Du Pasquier, Mr Herman Louis
Du Pasquier, Mme H. L.
Dupuy, Mr Louis
Duval, Mme Isabelle André
De Vries, Mr Herman E.
De Vries, Mrs Herman E.
Dougherty, Miss Mary

Ebbs, Mr W. G.
Ebbs, Mrs W. G.
Ebrard, Mr Hippolyte
Echegut, Mr
Edmond, Mr Yvan
Edmond, Mme Yvan
Emery, Mr R. G.
Erickson, Mr Carl
Erickson, Miss Lee
Erickson, Miss Charlotte
Enstrom, Mr Wm N.
Eppstein, Mr Louis B.
Ettinger, Mr A.

Farr, Mrs Ida Maria
Farrère, Mr Claude
Fenoux, Mr
Fenoux, Mme
Fesneau, Mr Frédéric
Fisher, Mr C. L.
Fischer-Pignier, Mme Agneta
Flondrois, Mr Auguste
Fonteney, Mlle Catherine
Fould, Mme Aichlle and maid
Franzoni, Mrs Mary Kelley
Fraser, Mr Léon
Fraser, Mrs Léon
Fraser, Master Jimmie
Frew, Miss Peggy
Freysselinard, Mme Jean
Frost, Mrs E. W.

Gallon, Mr W. J.
Ganz, Mr Paul H.
Ganz, Mr Rudolph
Ganz, Mrs Rudolph
Cavin, Mr Basil
Gavin, Mrs Basil
Gavin, Mrs Signe
Geffroy, Mr
Gilles, Mr Albert
Girardin, Mr Joseph
Goetz, Mr Wm
Goetz, Mrs Wm and maid
Goldsborough, Mr Laird Shiel
Goldsborough, Mrs Laird Shiel
Gourdeket, Mr Maurice
Goudier, Mr
Gordon, Mrs Midred
Goujon, Mme Pierre
Goulard de Lacam, Mr André
Gould, Mme Frank Jay
Grandelement, Vice-Amiral
Grandelement, Mme
Gras, Mr Henri
Grasle, Mr Walter
Grefne, Mr Louis A.
Greenwald, Mr Harold D.
Greenwald, Mrs Harold D.
Grennwald, Mr Frank
Greenwald, Mrs Frank
Greenwald, Mrs Hattie
Greuze, Miss Lilian
Groucy, Mr de
Groucy, Mme de
Guillomet, Mme Line
Gurry, Mr Thomas F.
Gurry, Mrs Thomas F.
Gurry, Master John V.

Haire, Mr J. Russell
Haire, Mrs J. Russell
Hanousek, Mrs Anna
Harloe, Mr W. V.
Harloe, Mrs W. V.
Harrison, Mr Paul
Hawley, Mr Hudson
Hazard, Miss M. L. and maid
Herisson, Mr William
Herisson, Mme C. W.
Herrell, Miss Ethel
Hicks, Mr George
Holmes, Mr Burton
Holmes, Mrs Burton
Homo, Mlle Magdeleine
Honnorat, Sénateur André
Honoré, Mr Pierre
Horne, Mr George F.
Hoxard, Miss Almeda
Hoxard, Mr Frank
Howe, M. Walter Bruce
Howe, Mme Walter Bruce
Hsieh, Mr Hsueh Lian
Hubbell, Mrs Vincent
Hubert, Mr Raymond

Illges, Mr A.
Illges, Mrs A.
Ingrand, Mr Jean-Pierre
Ingrand, Mme J.-P.
Iribe, Mr Paul

Jackon, Mr Alfred
Jacob, Mlle Madeline
Jaeckel, Mr Richard
Jackson, Mr A. E.
Jahrling, Mr Robert G.
Jahrling, Mrs Robert
Jennings, Mrs R. G.
Johnson, Mr Merle
Johnson, Mrs Merle
Jordy, Mr Jacques Lucien
Josefowitz, Mr G.
Josefowitz, Mme G.
Jouvenel, Mr Bertrand de

Kapurthala, S. A. le Maharaja de
Kapurthala, Prince Amarjit de
Kassapian, Mr Antonio
Kassapian, Mme Antonio
Kelly, Mr John E.
Kelly, Mrs John E.
Kirby, Mr Earl G.
Kipps, Mr W. T.
Koch, Mr Robert
Kramer, Mr Howard W.
Kulp, Mr Jacques
Kulp, Mrs Pontalba

Labusquière, Mr
Lacaze, Mlle Isabelle
Lafont, Mr Jacques
Lait, Mr George
Lance, Mr A. H.
Lance, Mrs A. H.
Lanvin, Mme Jeanne Melet
La Rochefoucauld,
    Comte Armand de
Larrouquère, Mr Louis
Larsh, Mr E. P.
Larsh, Mrs E. P.
Lasnier, Mr Edmond
Lebrun, Mme Albert
    and maid and valet
Lebrun, Mme Jean
Le Bigot, Contre-Amiral
Leclercq, Mrs Marie
Legier, Mr Louis
Le Maire, Mr Rufus
Lemaitre, Mr Georges F.

Le Maire, Mr R.
Le Prat, Mr Guy
Le Provost de Launay, Mr
Leslie, Mr Fred D.
Le Troadec, Mr
Levi, Mr Harris
Levy, Mr André
Levy, Mr André
Levy, Mme André
Lillis, Mr James M.
Lindsley, Mr Halstead
Lit, Mr David
Lit, Mrs David
Lizars, Mr Rawson
Lizars, Mrs Rawson
Loewenstein, Mr Julius
Lord, Mrs Harry D.
Lord, Miss Nancy
Lugue-Poe, Mr Aurelien
Luyties, Mr Frederic A.
Luyties, Jr Mr Frederic A.

Magid, Mr Maurice
Maleville, Mr
Mallin, Mr Milton
Manigler, Mlle Madeleine
Margolis, Mrs Olga
Marie, Mr Jean
Markheim, Mr Harry
Markle Jr, Mr Alvan
Markle, Mrs Gladys F.
Marks, Mr Lionel
Marks, Mrs Lionel
Maroteau, Mr
Martel, Mr Charles
Martin-Binachon, Mr
Martin-Binachon, Mme
Mata, Mr Jose M.
Mathis, Mr E.
Mathis, Mme E.
Meillassoux, Mr
Meillassoux, Mr Lucien
Meillassoux, Mme Lucien
Mellerio, Lieutenant de Vaisseau
Mellerio, Mme
Melville, Mrs Frank
Melville, Master Frank III
Mendelssohn, Mr Pierre
Merot du Barre, Mr
Meyer, Lieutenant de Vaisseau H.
Mintz, Mr Abraham
Mohring, Mr Léon
Mohring, Mlle Marcelle
Molan, Mrs M. L.
Montemuzo, Marquis de
Montemuzo, Marquise de
Moodie, Mr John
Morain, Mr Alfred
Morain, Mme Alfred
Moral, Mr Jean
Moran, Mr Edmond
Moran, Mrs Edmond
Morgan, Mr Thomas
Moreau, Mr Jacques
Morel, Mr M.
Morgan, Mr Clayland Tilden
Morgan, Mrs Clayland Tilden
Morisset, Mr Ernest
Morpain, Mr Jean
Moser, Mme Elisabeth Luyties
Mozer, Mr R.
Muto, Mr Frank P.
Mc Carty, Mr Barclay Verplan
Mc Carty, Mrs Barclay Verplan
Mc Clain, Mr John
Mac Coll, Mr René
Mac Fadden, Miss B.
Mac Innis, Mrs C. Ogilvie
Mc Lennan, Mr Donald D.
Mc Lernon, Mr J. R. S.
Mac Neil, Mr Neil
Mac Neil, Mrs Neil

Newcomb, Mr A. G.
Newhall, Mrs Norman
Norman, Mr Reginald
Norman, Mrs Reginald and maid
Noyes, Miss Nancy

Olivier,
   Gouverneur Général Marcel
O'Sullivan, Miss Adrienne
Owen, Dr Jess, W.

Pages, Mr. Jean-Michel
Palmer, Mr Thomas Russell
Palmer, Mrs Thomas Russell
Pannetier, Mlle Odette
Papasian, Mr Aram
Pays, Mr Denis
Pearsall, Mr Charles H. C.
Pearsall, Mrs Charles H. C.
Painter, Mr John
Pernod, Mr André
Pernod, Mme André
Pesson-Didion, Mr M.
Pesson-Didion, Mrs M.
Philipps, Sir Percival
Peytral, Mr V.
Pierce, Mr Arthur J.
Pierce, Mrs Arthur J.
Pilaski, Comte Max de
Pills, Mr Jacques
Pinot, Mme
Platier, Mr
Platier, Mme
Popper, Mr Frank
Porée, Dr Prudent Léon
Porter Jr, Mr Nathan T.
Porter Jr, Mrs Nathan T.
Powers, Miss Alice
Prax, Mr Maurice
Prince, Mr André
Prince, Mme André

Quesnel, Mr Jean
Quinn, Monseigneur William

Reagan, Mr Richard
Reagan, Mrs Richard
Reardon, Mr William A.
Resor, Mr
Resor, Mrs
Resor, Miss Ann
Reek, Mr E.
Rothner, Mrs Leah M.
Richard, Mr Albert J.
Righino, Miss Lena
Riley, Mr Lawson H.
Ripley, Mr Robert
Ross, Miss Ruth
Riss, Mr Lucien
Rivers, Mr Fernand
Rivers, Mme Fernand
Rivère, Mr Pierre
Rogers, Mr William B.
Rohrheimer, Mr Maurice
Romano, Mr
Romano, Mme
Ronan, Mrs W. P.
Rosenberg, Mr John A.
Rossignol, Mr Abel
Rougemont, Comte René de
Roumefort, Vicomte Roger de
Roure, Mr Georges
Revera, Mr Jean de
Rovera, Mme Jean de
Rozelet, Mr René
Rubinstein, Mr Abraham
Rubinstein, Mrs Esther
Rudell, Miss Mildred
Rundall, Mr Chas. O.
Rundall, Mrs Chass. O.

Saacke, Mr Chas. W.
Sacks, Mr Joe
Salmon, Mlle Yvonne
Sampson, Mr John
Sanz, Mr Alphonse
Sauvestre, Mr Eugène
Sauvestre, Mmme Eugène
Schupbach, Mr Peter R.
Sciandra, Mr Marcel
Schwarz, Mr Arthur
Schwarz, Miss Peggy
Schweisguth, Mr Charles
See, Mr André
Seguin, Mr Amédée
Sell, Mr Henry
Sickles, Captain Daniel
Silvela, Mr Angel
Kapurthala,
   Prince Amarjit Singh de
Snevily, Mr Henry M.
Snevily, Mrs Henry M.
Snevily, Miss Marjorie
Solomon, Mr Herbert
Solomon, Mrs Herbert
Sommier, Mr E.
Soupault, Mr Philippe
Spencer, Mr A. B.
Spencer, Mrs A. B.
Spencer, Miss Joséphine
Steele, Mr Harry
Steele, Mme W. S.
Stein, Mr Jules
Stein, Mrs Doris J.
Stephan, Mr Alfred
Stephan, Mme Alfred
Stevens, Mr Arthur Wesley
Stevens, Mr Joseph E.
Stockman, Dr Frank J.
Studin, Mrs R. Michael
Stuyvesant, Mr Alan Rutherfurd
Susini, Miss Louise
Sutor, Mr Hermann
Swainston, Mr H Imrie

Tabet, Mr George
Tarcher, Mr J. D.
Tarcher, Mrs J. D.
Tauber, Mr L.
Tauber, Mme L.
Taylor, Mr Davidson
Terrail, Mr André
Tessan, Mr François de
Tessan, Mme François de
Tessier, Mlle Valentine
Thibaud, M. Roger Jacques
Thomain, Mr
Thomain, Mme
Thomasson, Mr Robert de
Thompson, Mr R. M.
Thornewill, Mr Miles
Tilly de Langen, Mme
Tocqueville, Comte de
Tocqueville, Comtesse de
Trilnick, Mr Percy

Fully aware that some of the names are
misspelled, we have preferred not to correct
them, but rather to offer the list as it was
originally issued.

Uhl, Mr
Uhlmann, Mr Richard
Uhlmann, Mrs Richard
Ulrich, Mr Alfred
Undewood, Miss Henrietta

Vallée, Mr
Vallée, Mme
Vallejo, Mr Jean
Vallejo, Mme Juan
Van Leer, Mr Bernard
Van Leer, Mme Polly
Vaughn, Mr M. W.
Veaudelle, Mr Jacques
Vedel, Amiral
Vedel, Mme
Vernier, Mr L. Charles
Veyet, Mr Marcel
Viner, Mr Emile
Virot, Mr Alex
Viner, Mrs Emile
Violette, Mr Georges
Von Herberg, Mr John Grey

Waldvogel, Miss Anna Marie
Warburg, Mr James P.
Warburgh, Mrs James P.
Webb, Mr E. A.
Webb, Miss Nancy
Weicher, Mr Lewell P.
Weicker, Mme Lowell P.
Weinstock, Mr Murray
Weiss, Miss Rose A.
Westover, Miss Edith
White, Mr Paul W.
Whiting, Mr Oliver K.
Wiess, Mr H. C.
Wiess, Mrs H. C.
Wiess, Miss Elisabeth
Wiess, Miss Margaret
Wignall, Mr Trevor
Wiley, Mr Samuel Hamilton
Wiley, Mr A.
Williams, Mr John C.
Williams, Mrs Anna
Wilson, Mr R.
Wilson, Mrs M.
Winner, Mr Howard
Wolf, Mr Gustave
Wolf, Mr Pierre
Winlinger, Mr Jean
Wyle, Mrs J. J.

Young, Mr James W.
Yourkevitch, Mr Vladimir
Yourkevitch, Mme V.
Yungmann, Mme
Yvan, Mr
Yvan, Mme

SUMMARY

First class	**589**
Tourist class	**303**
Third class	**122**
	1,014

Bibliography

Relative to the size of the literature on the subject of *Normandie*, the listing given here is far from exhaustive. It consists primarily of articles and books contemporary with the life and death of *Normandie* and are of particular interest or served as sources for the various authors. The articles and books dating from subsequent years are works providing evidence of the ship's history or information about her decoration.

1932–44

Art et industrie, November 1932, July 1935
L'Atlantique, daily newspaper published by the CGT, special issues for 1935
Bourcier, Émmanuel, *Le Plus Beau Navire du monde: à bord du colosse "Normandie,"* 1935
Bromberger, Merry, "Petite Chronique de Normandie," *Le Matin*, May 15, 16, 17, 18, 19, 21, 23, and 25, 1938
Brousson, Jean-Jacques, "Normandiana," *Je suis partout*, June 1, 1935
Cangardel, Henri, "Normandie," pavillon de la qualité française, lecture delivered on February 16, 1935, at the Michodière Theater in Paris. Imprimerie de l'Atlantique, n.d.
Champly, Henry, *Inauguration et premier voyage de "Normandie," 23 mai–12 juin 1935*. Éditions de l'Atlantique, n.d.
Cheronnet, Louis, "Normandie," *Art et décoration*, July 1935.
La Cinématographie française, March 5, 1937, January 13, 1939
Clouzot, Henri, "Le Paquebot Île de France," *La Renaissance de l'art*, March 1928
Colette, *Mes Cahiers*, 1935
Comoedia, May and June 1935
Creelman, Lee, "Normandie," *Vogue*, August 1935 (drawings by Carl Erickson, known as "Éric")
Dayot, Magdeleine A., "L'Art à bord de Normandie," *L'Art et les artistes*, June 1935
Dieudonné, Robert, "Propos parisiens," *La Vie parisienne*, May 25, 1935
L'Espoir français, May 25, 1935, special issue by Louis Merlin
L'Excelsior, May 13, 1935, special issue
Le Figaro, June issues, 1935
Garrigues, Rémy, "Normandie à l'ecran," *Ciné-Miroir*, May 31, 1935
L'Illustration, June 1, 1935
Mallet-Stevens, Robert, "L'Architecture des paquebots," *Paris-Soir*, January 16, 1935
Mallet-Stevens, Robert, statement made on the occasion of the Salon d'Automne in 1934 and published in the catalogue entitled "Cabines en

acier de paquebots," Office Technique pour l'Utilisation de l'Acier, 1935
Mallet-Stevens, Robert, "Normandie, 1935," *L'Architecture d'aujourd'hui*, 1935, No. 8
Marie, Jean, *La Naissance du géant des mers, "Normandie,"* three lectures delivered at the Sorbonne on March 12, 19, and 25, 1935. Éditions de l'Atlantique, 1935.
Marie, Jean. "L'Oeuvre maîtresse de notre génération: Normandie," *Je sais tout*, May 1935
Normandie, brochure published by the CGT, with drawings and layouts by Paul Iribe. Éditions de l'Atlantique, n.d.
Normandie, brochure published by the CGT, with a preface by Claude Roger-Marx. Éditions de l'Atlantique, n.d.
Pannetier, Odette, "Choses vues," *Candide*, May 30, June 6 and 20, 1935
Paris-Soir, May 24, 25, 30, and 31, June 1, 2, 3, 4, 5, and 13, 1935; reportages by Blaise Cendrars and Claude Farrère
Philippar, Georges, "La Décoration des navires," lecture delivered on December 11, 1926, at the Institut Océanographique, *Journal de la marine marchande*, 1927
Plaisir de France, June 1, 1935
Plaisir de France, July 1939, special issue on the New York World's Fair
Quéant, Olivier, "Paquebots et tourisme: nouvelles tendances dans la décoration des paquebots," *Art et industrie*, April 1933
Rambosson, Yvanhoé, "Le Paquebot Normandie héraut de France," *Mobilier et décoration*, 1935
Report of the Salvage of USS Lafayette, ex SS Normandie, submitted by supervisor of salvage, US Navy, New York Navy Department. Bureau of Ships, n.d.
Richard, René, "Mon Carnet," *Adam*, June 15, 1935
The Shipbuilder and Marine Engine-Builder, June 1935, special issue
Soupault, Philippe, "L'Épopée de Normandie," *La Revue de Paris*, July 1, 1935
Trogoff, Jules, *La Course au Ruban Bleu*, Paris, 1935
Votre Beauté, June 1935

Vu, special issues in May and June 1935, with reportage by Madeleine Jacob and Bertrand de Jouvenel

1945–85

Barbance, Marthe, *Histoire de la Compagnie Générale Transatlantique*, 1955
Baschet, Jacques, *Sculpteurs de ce temps*, Paris, 1946
Cangardel, Henri, *De Colbert à Normandie: études et souvenirs maritimes*, Nouvelles Éditions Latines, 1957
Connoisseur, October 1984
Coquin, Maurice, "Quatre Ans sur Normandie," *Notre Temps*, February 1975
Cusset, Georges, "L'Épopée de Normandie, la dernière traversée," *Bulletin de liaison des officiers mécaniciens de Ire classe de la marine marchande*, June 1965
Foucart, Bruno, "Paquebots Art Déco, des machines à rêver," *Beaux-Arts Magazine*, May 1983
Hazard, Jean, "L'Épopée de Normandie, 1935–37," *Bulletin de liaison des officiers mécaniciens de Ire classe de la marine marchande*, March 1965
Hazard, Jean, and Maurice Coquin, *Atlantique Nord: Dix mètres sous la ligne de flottaison*. Éditions Louis Soulanges, 1969
Jean Dupas, les dessins pour le grand salon du "Normandie," exhibition catalogue. Galerie Alain Blondel, Paris, 1980
Kjellberg, Pierre, "Normandie," *Gazette de l'Hôtel Drouot*, January 14, February 18, March 18, April 15, 1983
Lanier, Edmond, *De La Pêche à la morue au paquebot "France."* Paris, 1962
The Metropolitan Museum of Art Bulletin, Vol. XXXVII, No. 3, 1979/1980
Miller, William H., Jr., *The Great Luxury Liners, 1927–1954*. New York, 1981
Mogui, Jean-Pierre. *Le Normandie, seigneur de l'Atlantique*. Denoël, 1985
Mohrt, Michel, "Les Très Riches Heures de 'Normandie,'" *Maison et jardin*, September 1983
Offrey, Charles, *Henri Cangardel: armateur*. Éditions de l'Atlantique, 1973
Reif, Rita, "New Treasures from the Normandie," *The New York Times*, December 23, 1984
Roger-Henri Expert, 1882–1955, exhibition catalogue. Institut Français d'Architecture, Paris, 1983
Thoreux, Captain Pierre, *J'ai commandé Normandie*. Paris, 1963
Wall, Robert, *L'Age d'or des grands paquebots*. Brussels, 1978

Photographic Credits

Illustrations reproduced in the book and not cited here derive from the archives of the French Line (the CGT), by gracious permission of the directors whose invaluable contribution the publishers acknowledge with grateful thanks.

Associated Press: p. 35
Bettmann Archive: p. 154
Bibliothèque Nationale, Teuffert collection: pp. 28, 29, 32, 108; Seeberger collection: pp. 125, 146, 147
Boucher, Pierre: pp. 27, 208
Bulloz: pp. 78, 79
Charmet, Jean-Loup: pp. 190, 191, 194
Cinémathèque Française: pp. 202, 203
Delleuse, Henri: pp. 134, 135, 186
Guignard, Philippe: p. 146
IFA: pp. 52, 62, 81
Keystone: pp. 22, 34, 46, 47, 49, 160, 166, 181, 182, 183, 196, 197, 202, 203
Landin, Raymond: p. 85
Marie Claire: p. 187
Metropolitan Museum of Art, N.Y.: p. 67
Morain, André: p. 63
Perzel: pp. 63, 74, 87, 94, 95, 97
PPP/IPS: pp. 176, 177, 179, 180
Roger-Viollet: pp. 37, 165
Schall: pp. 6, 28, 29, 33, 42, 43, 120, 122, 123, 125, 127, 128, 136, 137, 138, 140, 141, 144, 145, 150, 187
Sotheby-Parke-Bernet: p. 87
South Street Seaport Museum, N.Y.: p. 41
Sully-Jaulmes, Laurent: pp. 70, 71, 72, 73, 79, 82
Sygma: pp. 62, 102, 104, 130, 134, 194
UCAD: p. 70

Illustration Rights

Alavoine: p. 85, rights reserved
Auvigne, Jan: p. 115, rights reserved
Bérard, Christian: p. 147, © SPADEM
Bouchard, Henry: p. 64, © SPADEM
Brenet, Albert: pp. 138, 194, rights reserved
Cassandre: Jacket and p. 185, © ADAGP
Delamarre, Raymond: p. 94, rights reserved
Ducos de la Haille, Pierre-Henri: p. 64, rights reserved
Dufet, Michel: p. 110, © ADAGP
Dunand, Jean: pp. 76, 77, 78, 79, © SPADEM
Dupas, Jean: pp. 67, 72, 73, © SPADEM
Espagnat, Georges d': p. 95, © ADAGP
Gernez, Paul-Élie: pp. 82, 83, © ADAGP
Iribe, Paul: pp. 92, 93, 118, 131, 139, 142, rights reserved by Mmes Maybelle and Anita Iribe
Janniot, Alfred: p. 94, rights reserved
Jouve, Paul: p. 63, © ADAGP
Le Bourgeois, Gaston: pp. 88, 89, rights reserved
Lefranc, Jules: p. 195, rights reserved
Marin-Marie: pp. 192, 193, rights reserved
Martel, Jan and Joel: pp. 88, 89, © SPADEM
Pagès, Jean: pp. 68, 69, 135, 159, rights reserved by Pierre Pagès
Sarrabezolles, Charles: p. 82, © SPADEM
Saupique, Georges: p. 60, rights reserved
Schmied, François: p. 87, rights reserved
Sébille, Albert, pp. 155, 194, © SPADEM
Subes, Raymond: p. 91, © SPADEM
Valière, Claire: p. 100, rights reserved

207